THE NATURE OF TEACHING

Schools and the Work of Teachers

THE NATURE

OF

TEACHING

SCHOOLS AND THE WORK OF TEACHERS

ROBERT DREEBEN

University of Chicago

KEYSTONES OF EDUCATION SERIES

ACADEMIC EDITORS

MERLE L. BORROWMAN, *University of California at Riverside*

ROBERT J. SCHAEFER, *Teachers College, Columbia University*

ISRAEL SCHEFFLER, *Harvard University*

SCOTT, FORESMAN AND COMPANY

Library of Congress Catalog Card No. 79-111932

Copyright © 1970 by Scott, Foresman and Company,
Glenview, Illinois 60025. Philippines Copyright 1970 by
Scott, Foresman and Company. All Rights Reserved. Printed in
the United States of America. Regional offices of Scott, Foresman
and Company are located in Atlanta, Dallas, Glenview, Palo Alto,
Oakland, N.J., and London, England.

For William and Mary Dreeben

FOREWORD

The study of education is today in a state of ferment. With the expansion of educational horizons in American society, specialists of various sorts—historians, philosophers, psychologists, sociologists, political scientists—are to an ever greater extent joining with professional educators in inquiries into the nature of our educational ideas and institutions. Together, these scholars are enhancing the vitality, authority, and inspiration required of educational concepts in a revolutionary era of social change and scientific discovery.

In some measure, the Keystones of Education Series is intended to reflect and, hopefully, to advance this educational development. It brings to instructors and students, indeed to all those concerned with education, a unique group of relatively brief but authoritative books, selective in content so as to develop in considerable depth key areas of knowledge. Each book is an original treatment of its special topic. The series may be profitably used in both introductory and advanced courses, for the instructor is free to construct a course with the content, emphasis, and sequence he desires, by selecting a combination of books to serve as text material. Because of the distinguished academic consultants and authorship, instructors can confidently take full advantage of the flexibility of the series without fear of uneven quality, superficiality, or duplication.

The Keystones of Education Series for the first time makes available a variety of superior materials, in convenient and inexpensive format, for the entire pre-service education program at colleges and universities.

The Publishers

TABLE OF CONTENTS

PREFACE

The great bulk of writing about teaching is invitational rather than analytical. Its purpose is to convey alluring, "come-hither" messages to the tens of thousands of wide-eyed innocents who must be seduced each year into service in the nation's classrooms. Or to be more accurate, since the imagery of teaching emphasizes altruism and the nurturing instincts rather than clandestine thrills, such writing seeks to arouse visions of a socially critical, intellectually fulfilling, and yet not too demanding "profession."

Robert Dreeben's book may indeed attract able young recruits into teaching, but not by easy, romantic promises nor by sentimental appeals to the presumed joys of serving others. The real seductiveness of *The Nature of Teaching: Schools and the Work of Teachers* is in its logic and its persuasiveness in describing teaching as it is and as it may become. It employs a primarily sociological mode of inquiry, in the tradition of studies in the sociology of work, but it never permits disciplinary strictures to limit its view of the realities of the teaching experience. When appropriate, it uses data and ideas derived from other social sciences.

Professor Dreeben's intent is to increase our understanding of the teacher's work-a-day world and, patently, not to offer nostrums for the improvement of education. Yet, no proposal for reform, whether it involves curriculum revision, extending pedagogical skills, or increasing the financial support for schools, can hope for success unless it takes into account the occupational influences upon the teachers. It is no accident, therefore, that *The Nature of Teaching: Schools and the Work of Teachers* is published in the Keystones of Education series. The insights it provides are crucial in supporting our understanding of all aspects of the educational system.

Robert J. Schaefer

ACKNOWLEDGMENTS

In retrospect, this book began in 1953 when Robert Schaefer, then a member of the Harvard Graduate School of Education faculty, interested me in teaching. The sense of excitement he communicated about it, its importance, and the importance of being curious about it, became abundantly clear to me later as a teacher. As editor for the Keystones of Education Series of which this book is a part and for this book in particular, his comments and suggestions have helped me considerably. My intellectual debt to him is large and of long standing.

Once the design and planning of the book were underway, several people gave me the benefit of their thought and labor by reviewing literature—much of it dreary—and commenting on it: Gordon McIntosh, Roger Riffer, and Glenn Watts. Their help is gratefully acknowledged. In addition, I spent much time picking the fine mind of Larry Weiss whose intimate knowledge of teaching and acute observations and comments made my task easier and more interesting. John Beasley and Anna Lei, editors at Scott, Foresman, have provided me with welcome and patient encouragement.

As everyone knows—or should if they don't—it is an author's secretary who produces a book. My thanks, then, to Charlene Worth (now Mrs. Charlene Ramirez Vital) at Harvard University, and to Mrs. Alison Lauriat at the University of Chicago. Jane, Jill, and Tom Dreeben checked the proofs, and I greatly appreciate their help. I also wish to thank Richard Falcone for his help and support and Ruth Grossman for preparing the index.

Finally, I wish to express my gratitude to the Harvard Center for Research and Development in Educational Differences, directed by Dean Theodore Sizer and John Herzog of the Harvard Graduate School of Education, whose award of a generous grant enabled me to carry out the research for this book. The grant was supported by funds provided through a contract (OE 5-10-239) with the United States Department of Health, Education, and Welfare, Office of Education (under provisions of the Cooperative Research Program), which financed the Center.

R. D.

•

CHAPTER ONE

Introduction

•

Teaching as an occupation, rather than teachers as people, is the central concern of this book. The distinction may sound at most like a difference in emphasis and at least like a quibble, but neither is the case. Inquiring about an occupation (rather than the people employed in it) requires us to address different questions to different phenomena. Although we do not know a great deal about teachers, we know much more about their characteristics as people than about the character of their work, the settings in which they carry it out, the institutions in which they are trained, or the nature of their careers. Hence my interest in the occupational question.

As a matter of strategy, to discover what one occupation is like, it is useful to compare it with others; in this way one can identify which of its characteristics are peculiar to it, and which of them it shares. But some comparisons are more germane than others, and so their selection is a matter of some importance. Without doubt, teaching is one of several service occupations whose mission is to effect changes in people. Its central activities are carried out in organizational settings, and members of the occupation undergo both academic and on-the-job training to learn the skills entailed by the work. One need look no further to find important differences and similarities between teaching, on the one hand, and social work, medicine, librarianship, nursing, law, and the clergy, on the other. These are all occupations that serve clients; and, if we view them both from the clients' perspective and from that of society at large, competent performance becomes a key issue. When people pay for a service and put their hopes and often their fate in the hands of a practitioner, they can hardly be expected to be indifferent to the quality and efficacy of the service tendered. At the same time, there are many other vantage points from which to view the nature of the service. I consider some of them here simply to provide a context for this volume, to consider the option I have taken in light of those open to me.

One such viewpoint is formulated in George Counts' tract of 1932, *Dare the Schools Build a New Social Order.* Having recounted the depredations of capitalism during the early years of the Depression and argued how the workings of that system had negated the founding principles of the nation, he calls, for some opaque reason, on the teachers to:

> deliberately reach for power and then make the most of their conquest. . . . To the extent that they are permitted to fashion the curriculum and the procedures of the school they will definitely and positively influence the social attitudes, ideals, and behavior of the coming generation.[1]

Assume power to what end? To create some form of democratic collectivism at the expense of conservatism, reaction, and the *laissez faire* exploitation of natural and human resources. The specific content of Counts' program has no particular relevance to the occupational problems of teachers today (as in most tracts, program is subordinated to rhetoric), but it does contain a conception of teaching that transcends the events of that historical period. Implicit in his work is the notion that teachers can exercise leverage to effect broad social, political, and economic changes primarily through their impact on the younger generation and through their persuasive influences on the powers that be.

This position, I believe, is at best a will-o'-the-wisp primarily because teachers as an occupational group are simply not located at those points in society where fundamental political and economic decisions are made. There is also something quixotic about changing society by influencing the children and waiting for them to grow up and do something important. Clearly, I do not accept Counts' argument on its face, nor do I believe that it provides an adequate perspective for understanding the occupational characteristics of teaching. Yet, certain themes in it have remained remarkably durable even though their form has changed over the years. In general, he presents us with a portrait of teaching as an activist occupation, at least in principle; but to take Counts seriously, one would have to regard the polity as the occupational arena of teaching, and this is clearly not the case.

The activist tradition continues, but in modified form. There is some evidence that during the 1960's people with meliorist concerns entered the occupation. Perhaps for the same reasons that many young people joined the Peace Corps, others (and some Peace Corps veterans) have entered teaching to try and remedy the social ills affecting the central cities. Their aims are not so much to transform the social order (however vaguely that pursuit was defined by Counts), but to deal with specific contemporary urban problems based on the belief that the schools provide a strategic position for coping with them. There is no faulting their good intentions or their good works; at the same time, the modest influx of such individuals has not transformed the occupation to an extent that justifies an analysis of it as an agency of social reform. Even on the (as yet undocumented) assumption that the reformist contingent has increased, the schools remain strongly committed to passing on a cultural tradition. Tradition and reform are not contradictory, but the question remains: how fruitful is it to analyze the *occupation,* as distinct from the whole *educational establishment,* in these terms? The latter has been done (with somewhat dubious results); as for the former, too many important aspects of the occupation would slip through the net.

A case can be made for viewing the occupation in terms of the dramatic changes over the last decade in the nature and conduct of teachers' organizations, in particular, the National Education Association and the American Federation of Teachers. Without question, both organizations have moved toward greater militancy, primarily, though not exclusively, on economic issues. Without too much distortion, one can argue that teaching, an occupation long thought to be respectably middle class, has become a latter-day participant in the craft union movement, fighting aggressively for the well-being of its members. This is as much true of the NEA as of the AFT, even though the former would most likely eschew the indentification. Their successes, particularly in the large cities, have been dramatic, but they have been limited largely to improvements in economic welfare. It is equally important to catalogue what they have not accomplished as well as what they have. For example, beyond attempts to raise the academic levels of preparation and certification, they have contributed little to the basic rethinking and redesigning of teacher preparation.

Although they have fought for the diminishing of classroom enrollments, against the assignment of teachers to subjects they are not prepared to teach, and for the improvement of on-the-job working conditions and grievance procedures, they have scarcely addressed the problems of teaching technology. This is not a failure on their part; it simply has not been a salient part of their agendas. In other words, the NEA and the AFT have achieved gains for teachers but have done little to change the character of the occupation, as distinct from the welfare of teachers, even at its weakest points.

One observer of the educational scene, Robert Schaefer, has concerned himself with precisely those occupational issues that teacher organizations have ignored (in action, if not in rhetoric); foremost among them is the intellectual aridness of the teacher's occupational life. The problem, he argues, has several origins: the bureaucratic organization of schools and school systems in which teachers become passive recipients of administrative rules and prescriptions, and routine purveyors of curricular materials; the absence of a viable colleagueship among them; and more recently a trend toward curricular reform, academic in origin, in which new materials are designed to be "teacher-proof." The premises underlying the latter trend are perhaps the most pernicious because they are based on the assumption that teachers have nothing of intellectual merit to offer in the process of instruction and that academics, by cutting teachers out of the circuit, can "speak" directly to pupils in the language of their intellectually respectable disciplines. Schaefer states:

> It is relatively easy to agree that the conditions of modern society demand schools which are primarily, but not exclusively, concerned with the intellectual development of students. To assume, however, that mere agreement on intent or an easily achieved "return" to the academic disciplines will achieve the desired transformation is grossly to underestimate the complexity of the problems involved in enticing the elusive intellects of children.[2]

It is the task of enticing children's intellects that Schaefer believes is the most serious challenge to the occupational life of teachers, an intellectual challenge to teachers that has hardly been identified as a problem let alone addressed as one. Accordingly, he deplores the fact that "Society has not expected the school to be systematically reflective about its work—to serve as a center of inquiry into teaching . . . ,"[3] that schools have been regarded as dispensaries.

I find myself in substantial agreement with his indictment, his diagnosis of symptoms, and his proposed remedies.[4]

Finally, teaching has long been discussed in the context of the professionalization of occupations. Unfortunately, this line of inquiry has been one of the least illuminating primarily because it has been limited to the question of whether teaching is or is not a profession. That some occupations having a certain constellation of properties are publicly recognized as professions is somewhat beside the point—at least for my purposes. The social status of teachers and the reasons for teachers being preoccupied with their status (where professionalism is only one indication of status), are both important questions which have largely remained unexamined. I believe there is a great deal of understanding gained by examining the properties of occupations and how those properties fit together.

In short, there is a variety of ways of looking at occupations in general and at teaching in particular. For the most part, I have adopted the perspective of a somewhat cold-eyed sociological observer looking in from the outside; not looking at everything, but at a limited range of occupational issues including the nature of the work setting and of the work itself, the technology of teaching, the characteristics of teacher-training institutions, and the nature of teaching careers. Clearly, there are alternative approaches, both in subject and in perspective. The considerations underlying my selection are (1) that the topics form a unified cluster of related issues, and (2) that they have received relatively little prior attention. The choice of perspective was guided primarily by a desire to avoid taking the posture of a special pleader as much as possible.

It seems odd that in a country where people conventionally identify each other by asking, "What do you do?" that serious attention is not paid to the details of occupational life. The conventional answer to that question is the naming of an occupation, at which point the conversation usually moves to another topic. In fact, very little information is transmitted by naming an occupation beyond a general location of people in the social order. We know very little about the content of other people's work, and our own is so familiar that we can hardly find the language to describe it. For these reasons, I devote considerable attention to the character and elements of the teacher's work because they are so central to understanding the nature and problems of the occupation.

Prior to an analysis of the teacher's work and how it shapes the character of his occupation, I will discuss a variety of viewpoints from which other students of the occupations have looked at work in general.

•

CHAPTER TWO

The Occupational

Characteristics

of Teaching

•

The usual way to view an occupation is to consider the characteristics of the people working in it; and although this is a perfectly legitimate perspective, there are equally defensible alternatives. The approach I adopt here treats the occupation itself as the subject of investigation, and I address myself to a variety of questions about teaching, particularly as it compares to other occupations. The distinction between the worker and his occupation can be clarified by example. Thus, an individual can take a job only to leave it shortly; and if he moves from job to job over a period of time, we can speak of *his* job stability, of his personal work history. Similarly, certain occupations, like many routine blue collar jobs, are characterized by a substantial flow of people into and out of them and can be described as high-turnover *occupations*. Here turnover is treated as an attribute of an occupation. The important distinction is that in the latter case, the occupation itself rather than the individuals in it occupies our attention. Occupations can then be compared in a variety of ways: their size, the nature of the training required for entry, the character of the working environment, the seasonality of employment, strike-proneness, to name a few.

In this volume I am concerned more with teaching as an occupation than with teachers, although one cannot be discussed without reference to the other. Accordingly, I discuss some of the properties of that occupation, such as the characteristics of the workplace, the prevailing state of the art of teaching, the provisions made for training teachers, and the nature of its career lines. By way of introduction I attempt to create a context of three parts in which teaching can be understood: one that considers varying conceptions of occupational life in general; a second that compares teaching with other occupations having important similarities and differences; and a third that considers points of view adopted by various spokesmen for the occupation.

CONCEPTIONS OF OCCUPATIONAL LIFE

Although it is not possible to distinguish sharply between professional and nonprofessional occupations, certain clusters of characteristics are more typically found among those occupations commonly known as professions than among others, characteristics pertaining largely to the nature of work activities and to forms of worker association. It is beyond the scope of this discussion to chart the history of work and occupations, but it is worthwhile to consider several important formulations of occupational life for the light they shed on modern professions and the place of teaching relative to them.

KARL MARX

The Marxian indictment of capitalism consists in part of an attack on the institutions of industrialism, not least among them, occupations. This Marx makes abundantly clear in his famous comment that in a communist society men will be able to follow any pursuit they wish, as they "have a mind," without making an occupational commitment to it: to hunt in the morning and fish in the afternoon without becoming hunter or fisherman. Occupations, like other social institutions, Marx believed, were basically alien to man's human nature; work and labor were essential to man's humanity and should not be yielded or alienated to forces external to him. Not surprisingly, he used the metaphors of "bonds" and "fetters" to describe employment necessary to earn a livelihood. He employs the same metaphors to describe the state, religion, and history—those other enemies of man's natural human condition. Marx would have had men express their true human proclivities through their work—as they had a mind.

One of the central themes in the Marxian scheme is man's relationship to the means of production. The "social relations," he said, "between the producers, and the conditions under which they exchange their activities and share in the total act of production, will naturally vary according to the character of the means of production."[1] But in fact, Marx was primarily concerned with those means of production involved in the manufacture of commodities for sale in markets; accordingly, this type of production meant both the separation of workers from the means of production and the sale of their labor to capitalists for wages. He believed that "every process of commodity production is at the same time a process of exploitation of labor power,"[2] since wage labor produces capital for the capitalist but no property for the laborer himself.

Not all occupations, however, can be readily understood in this way. That is to say, the Marxian formulation is not well-suited to understanding the professions because they are not primarily oriented to the creation of capital from the labor of others, and the element of coercion, so plain in the case of industrial production, is far less prevalent. But at the time Marx wrote, the professions had not yet assumed anything approaching their present importance in the industrial economy. Contemporary writers in the Marxian tradition, as I shall indicate later, tend to force the professions into the Marxian scheme by treating professional persons either as the equivalent of wage workers or as capitalists (or the "tools" of capitalists). Yet, I contend that of all occupations characteristic of industrial economies, the professions afford men the greatest opportunities to determine for themselves the nature of their working lives. No one, of course, is as free as Marx's Natural Man, but if occupations are judged according to the freedom they afford workers to express their interests and proclivities or to exercise self-determination and judgment, the professions provide the widest latitude and the greatest opportunities.

MAX WEBER

In his treatise *The Protestant Ethic and the Spirit of Capitalism,* Weber portrays occupational life in strikingly different terms than Marx. Work, in the Calvinist scheme of things, represents the fulfillment of one's duty in worldly affairs (the glorification of God—this being the highest form of individual activity), a far cry from man sacrificing his humanity to create capital for somebody else. An occupation for Weber is a calling: "an obligation which the individual is supposed to feel and does feel towards the content of his professional activity, no matter in what it consists. . . ."[3] Nothing is promised by this attitude of man toward his work save the sense that he is doing a job well and that he serves God by doing so.

This secular transformation of religious sentiment provides a motivation for disciplined and disinterested work directed more to the accomplishment of a task than to the acquisition of personal gain even though such gain may accrue as an outcome. Weber contrasts the economic activity of work as a calling with its more traditional forms wherein men labor until they have achieved a traditionally given amount of gain. But more importantly, he distinguishes secular economic activity from exploitation and plunder.

Thus, Reinhard Bendix comments in his intellectual biography of Weber:

> "Capitalist" acquisition *as an adventure* has existed throughout history. Enterprises that aim at windfalls, such as piracy, the financing of wars and governments, tax-farming, certain medieval trading companies, and many others, are characterized by an absolute disregard of ethical considerations in relation with foreigners that frequently coincides with strict morality and traditionalism within the community.[4]

This is not the type of capitalism Weber was talking about. Most important here for the understanding of modern professions (to the extent that their normative roots derive from the sense of calling) is the fact that professional activities are designed to be nonexploitative, and ethical considerations in dealing with clients have a high priority in the conduct of practitioners. These considerations, in addition to dedication to the disciplined performance of a task, continue to be central in modern professional life.

TALCOTT PARSONS

Different as the perspectives of Marx and Weber on occupations appear, they resemble each other in one crucial respect: both regard human conduct as influenced by external social constraints. The importance of these external forces has been treated most explicitly and thoroughly by Parsons.[5] It has long been argued that the basic difference between professional men and businessmen is one of economic motivation: altruism and service on the part of the former, personal profit on the part of the latter. That is to say, differences in conduct are attributed to personal motives. Parsons has questioned this notion in a fundamental way. He notices, for example, that both in commerce and the professions, conduct is expected to be rational—based on standards of technical proficiency for accomplishing a task—rather than traditional; to be functionally specific—limited to the particular demands of the task rather than extending to a broad range of concerns involving those performing it; to be universalistic—concerned more with contractual arrangements and types of cases and circumstances than with relationships to particular persons. The point is that both business and the professions have much in common, their similarities being primarily of an institutional nature. They differ not in men's motives to pursue their occupational endeavors, but in the distinct form that occupational activities take in the two cases. One serves the interests of clients, the other produces commodities for a market. The desire for achievement and gain exists in each case, but it is expressed in different ways.

Parsons' emphasis on rationality is especially important for understanding the professions. The particular form that rationality takes in professional life is the technically competent application of a general body of knowledge to a specifically defined area of human problems. The professions, that is, are built around an available set of techniques for coping with the problems that clients present to practitioners. The technological component, the social constraints, and the standards governing conduct are the crucial elements of professionalism in Parsons' formulation.

C. WRIGHT MILLS

It should be clear at this point that the concern of social observers with occupations also reflects deeper considerations on the nature of social life. In particular, the relationship between social constraint and the characteristics of the human condition has been stressed. Those in the Marxian tradition have generally emphasized the coercive character of occupational demands; Mills is no exception even though he differs from Marx in many particulars. One of the main themes of Mills' argument in *White Collar*, his most thoroughgoing statement about modern occupational life, is that the professions have become increasingly centralized as professionals have changed from independent fee-takers to bureaucratic employees. The professional of the old middle class, he contends, governed his working life independently. He regulated his own hours and his position in the market, and set his own fees; he was an entrepreneur. His counterpart in the new middle class, however, differs markedly. He claims that:

> Most professionals are now salaried and fitted into the new hierarchical organizations of educated skill and service; intensive and narrow specialization has replaced self-cultivation and wide knowledge; assistants and subprofessionals perform routine, though often intricate, tasks, while suc-

cessful professional men become more and more the managerial type.[6]

This contention is somewhat misleading even if the dubious assumption about self-cultivation and wide knowledge is granted. Some professionals, teachers prime among them, have long been salaried employees, as have many if not most engineers and accountants. But the independent fee-takers—doctors, lawyers, architects, for example—though undoubtedly *affiliated* to an increasing extent with large bureaucratic organizations are not typically hired, salaried employees. As a portrayal of the dominant trend, I believe Mills has based his argument on questionable evidence. The events he describes have occurred to some extent, but physicians are not characteristically hired by hospitals. Law firms—even the largest—do not typically resemble corporations in their structure,[7] and many of the organizational arrangements through which professional people become affiliated with large organizations actually preserve sizeable areas of independent judgment for the practitioner. Hiring, as an affiliative device, probably does diminish the scope of independence (here Mills is probably correct), but hiring is less characteristic of the contemporary free professionals than it is, let's say, of teachers in the public schools.

Mills, in effect, has adopted a Marxian position concerning man's alienation from his work—it would probably be more correct to place him in the tradition of Veblen rather than of Marx—by stressing the decline of self-determination and severance of the tie between the worker and what he produces (usually associated with the idea of craftsmanship). He attributes the decline to the centralization and bureaucratization of economic institutions and the coercion of man by means of obligations contracted in exchange for a salary. He is undoubtedly correct, however, in documenting the advance of complex technology in many fields and the concomitant growth of large-scale organizations to which professionals have become connected in important ways—though not in ways he suggests.

EVERETT HUGHES

Whereas Marx, Weber, and Mills all concern themselves with the connection between a man's work and the constraints that bear upon it, Hughes, like Parsons, is concerned with the place of professions in their larger societal context. With Parsons, this concern includes the institutional forms and normative standards transcending the professions themselves. Hughes treats occupations in terms of what he calls their "licence" and "mandate." License refers to a societal sanction that justifies the right to some people to engage in certain lines of work and excludes others from doing so; it consists in a definition of legitimate work jurisdictions (as distinct from the more conventional use of license as legal, or legalistic, permission). Mandate refers to the collective right ascribed to members of an occupational group to define for nonmembers what proper conduct is in this special endeavor. "The medical profession, for instance, is not content merely to define the terms of medical practice. It also tries to define for all of us the very nature of health and disease."[8]

Actually, Hughes is more concerned with the division of labor in society than with the nature of occupational life, at least in his paper on license and mandate. As part of that division of labor, the professions raise special problems in social control not only because practitioners have a strong impact on people's conduct but also because they assume an unconventional perspective on matters that touch people's lives deeply: some have access to private and guilty knowledge and claim a kind of expertise that depends on their clients relaxing the customary defenses protecting the private domains of their lives; some also maintain a kind of relativity of perspective that without controls could easily corrode the sense of personal concern, trust, and nonexploitativeness on which the pursuit of the profession depends.

WILLIAM GOODE

The power and legitimacy of the professions, viewed by many as awesome and subject to much public ambivalence, is nevertheless widely accepted. Not only has the professional sector of the labor force expanded, but the importance and the belief in the beneficence of the professions have been broadly accepted. The reasons for this acceptance, despite prevalent opportunities for the misuse of power, are usually attributed to two sets of conditions: the characteristics that distinguish the professions from other occupations, and the peculiar nature of occupational associations.

Many writers have tried to compile a complete list of the distinguishing characteristics of professions; one of the more thoroughgoing was collected by Morris Cogan.[9] Although there is considerable disagreement over what characteristics to include, there is almost unanimous agreement on two. Professions require that their members (1) undergo prolonged training to acquire the technical skills (and the theoretical principles underlying them) necessary for the pursuit of their work, and (2) dedicate themselves to provide service, to put primary stress on the needs of the client. Although much of the literature deals with the question of what distinguishes the professions from the nonprofessions—a singularly sterile question, as I shall explain later—the more important issue is how social power is constrained in occupational life, particularly in the professions, assuming they have the mandate that Hughes says they have. Goode states the issue clearly:

> Professionals seek their own gain as much as any occupational group, and professional associations fight to increase their privileges and advantages. . . . [T]he professional community must create a set of controls such that its members are more handsomely rewarded for conforming to its code of ethics (technical competence and service) than for failing to do so.[10]

He also indicates the importance of occupational associations.

An occupational association is not the same thing as a formal organization, such as the American Medical Association, the American Bar Association, or the National Education Association, all of which are formally constituted bodies designed to promote the interest of their members; nor is it simply a category of all persons engaged in an occupation distinguished from all those who are not (analogous to a census classification, for example, of persons aged sixty-five years or older). Goode has suggested that an occupation can be understood as a social community, albeit a nonterritorial one that does not add new members through biological reproduction. Nevertheless, he contends that the members of such an occupation are associated through: (1) a sense of identity, (2) a permanent or near-permanent commitment to it, (3) a shared set of values, (4) an agreed-upon pattern of conduct among members and between members and nonmembers, (5) a common language (imperfectly understood by nonmembers), (6) a control over the conduct of members, and (7) a control over the selection and training of new members.[11]

Although many occupations have communitylike characteristics, it is the power of professional persons and the vulnerability of clients who seek professional services that put special responsibilities on the occupational association to control the conduct of its members. This control is exercised in several ways, foremost among them being the rigorous selection and training of new recruits, the enforcement of standards of ethics to control the conduct of practitioners, and the continued advancement of the knowledge and technology upon which practice is based. In a sense, the professional mandate (and the powers that go with it) is granted on the condition that members of the community keep their house in order. Accordingly, Goode reminds us, the degree of control an occupation has over its members is inversely related to the vulnerability of its clients. Yet, whatever the particular strengths of such associations, they are not without their weaknesses. The most common threats to the occupational community are (1) the powers of laymen to determine the proper nature of professional conduct and to claim the right to evaluate competent performance and make the evaluation stick, (2) the powers of administrative superiors to control conduct when the work of the profession is characteristically carried out within an organizational context, and (3) the power of a single client who monopolizes most of a practitioner's services.

The community perspective on occupations accentuates the importance of unity and cohesiveness among the members, of internal controls exercised on their conduct, and of defense against external threat. This perspective, however, is not immune from criticism. Rue Bucher and Anselm Strauss, for example, argue that professions become divided into specialties organized around both old and new technologies, and that these technical specialties often represent bases of cleavage within the occupation.[12] Their criticism strikes most directly at the assumption of the unified nature of occupational communities, and, while Bucher and Strauss discuss the case of medicine almost exclusively, many of their comments apply in principle to teaching as well. Yet, the two perspectives may not conflict as much as it appears; both, in fact, have important elements of truth. The Bucher-Strauss perspective, actually, is an internal one; there is no need to sacrifice the notion of community in order to acknowledge both the existence and importance of diversity and cleavage within it. Goode implicitly compares occupations that are more or less communitylike and finds the professions near the community end of the scale; his perspective is more externally comparative.

A. M. CARR-SAUNDERS AND P. A. WILSON

In their monumental treatise *The Professions,* these writers clarify those aspects of occupational associations that define them as peculiarly professional. "The trade union," they say:

> is virtually a single purpose association. The protective function overshadows all others in importance; consequently the search for the strongest bargaining unit becomes the dominant consideration, and efforts are always being made to extend the boundaries. In the professional world . . . it is otherwise. Though the protective motive is present, it is

only one among many and by no means always the most important. In particular the desire *to hall-mark the competent and to foster the study of the technique* gives to the technique such an importance that boundaries are clearly defined and stable.[13]

It is this preoccupation with technology and competence in the application of technique that is so critical in the professions, a preoccupation that accounts in good measure for the elaborate system of training that includes instruction in general principles and theory, in the practice of technique, and for the system of rigorous examination. What distinguishes the technique of professionals from that of craftsmen is the critical linkage between institutions of professional training and universities—the generators, codifiers, and disseminators of abstract knowledge.

OCCUPATIONS AND PROFESSIONS

It is difficult to separate the terms *professional* and *profession* from considerations of relative status, the latter usually referring to high status occupations, the former to persons who pursue them. By and large, professional occupations are associated with high income, high prestige, respect, and power—judgments that follow in part from the fact that professional persons are highly educated, perform demanding skills, and provide valued services. Accordingly, it is not surprising that many persons aspire to become professionals; but more relevant to this discussion, it is not surprising that many occupations attempt to professionalize: to increase the income of their members, restrict entry, demand prolonged and formal training, compete for social power and prestige, and make the public aware of their ascent by changing the occupational symbolism—usually the name. According to Goode, "the spokesmen for almost every recognized white-collar job have asserted that they are professional."[14]

The attempt to professionalize symptomatically involves a concern over whether an occupation is or is not a profession, and while this question may be of utmost importance to the workers, (affecting their income, their style of life, their public reputation), it has little importance as an analytic question for understanding occupational life.[15] The reason for its triviality is that it can be too easily settled as a problem in nominal definition. There are many criteria that plausibly distinguish professions from other occupations. To settle the question of definition—and that is all it is—requires agreement among observers on which criteria to select and on which occupations meet the criteria. Thus, it is only the process of reaching agreement that is problematic. Cogan, for example, in his excellent review of previous definitions, ends with another—and tentative—definition: a new distillate of existing ones with some new wrinkles. The next distiller of definitions will include Cogan's in the mash, but nothing more will be understood about what is problematic about occupations.

The important question, really, is *the nature of occupational life;* and what is problematic about it, both from the analytical perspective of the social sciences and from the more practical perspective of those engaged in the work, is the relationships among its various parts. In my cursory historical review I attempted to identify some of the important characteristics of occupations, in particular, those that have been matters of concern for a long time. That some of these characteristics have become identified with professional occupations is beside the point; what matters, rather, is that they serve as a basis for comparing occupations and that by their presence and absence in any given occupation provide clues to its distinctive properties and problems. For example, it is possible to discuss any occupation—teaching, in this book—according to the following considerations:

(1) What opportunities and arrangements does an occupation provide for individual self-expression, for free exercise of judgment, and for the self-determination of work activities?

(2) What is the state of the prevailing technology, and as a distinct but related question: to what extent do practitioners have access to this technology and command over it?

(3) In what ways is an occupation affiliated with organizations whose operation depends on people engaging in that particular line of work?

(4) What is the nature of occupational association with respect both to formal organization and to the larger community of practitioners?

(5) In what ways is occupational life governed by norms prevailing in society at large and by those norms peculiar to the specific occupation?

This agenda of questions derives immediately from the brief sketch of occupational issues, and I address some of these questions to the occupation of teaching in later chapters.

Perhaps the important question for most if not all occupations, and particularly for the professions and other service occupations, is the competence of practitioners, a question that often gets lost in controversies over professionalism as a sign of status. Whether practitioners can do their work successfully, with efficacy, is a central concern; but this contention must be understood in two ways. First, can the individual members of an occupation do their work well? Second, are there characteristics of the occupation itself that support and enable its members to perform effectively?

OCCUPATIONAL COMPARISONS

One way to learn about the character of occupations is to discover what people have said about them in the past, for one of the advantages of an historical perspective is that it yields information about the more enduring occupational issues. Slightly over a century separates Marx's *The German Ideology* from Mills' *White Collar;* almost a half century separates Weber's *The Protestant Ethic* from Parsons' *Essays.* The central issues have not vanished. Yet history does not reveal all the relevant problems. Another way to view the character of occupations is to compare one with another, to indicate their similarities and differences.

CLIENT-SERVING OCCUPATIONS

One defining characteristic of professions is that practitioners serve the interests of clients; yet literal adherence to this criterion proves troublesome because some professions don't serve *individual* clients in any obvious way. Scientists and military officers are two cases in point; the "client" in both cases is the society at large, and in the former case it is the community of scholars. To some extent, literary figures fall into the same category as academicians in their research though not in their teaching capacities.

Law, medicine, architecture, the clergy, nursing, accountancy, social work, engineering, and teaching are all occupations whose practitioners can serve individual clients directly; the relationship between practitioner and client, however, differs among them. In some, the client presents himself in a position of relative weakness and vulnerability, unable to solve his problem with the resources at his disposal: he may be sick, accused of a crime, in danger of losing his property, or perplexed about his salvation. He seeks someone with the resources to solve the problem, *and* someone who will not use them to make matters worse or to enrich himself. As I suggested earlier, professions whose practitioners serve vulnerable clients exercise control over their members and provide incentives to them to make it worthwhile financially and morally to serve the client's interests. Other occupations, such as engineering and accountancy, serve clients whose expertise in many respects is on a par with their own; the clients themselves may then exert the necessary control (releasing the association to some extent from the obligation to do so). Accordingly, it is important to investigate the power of the occupational community over its members.

The vulnerability of the client is not the only matter of importance. Some occupations confront their clients *en masse*, others one at a time. Teaching is the most well-known case of an occupation whose practitioners deal with clients collectively, but under certain circumstances the same is true for police work, nursing, librarianship, social work, and pastoral church work. The collective treatment of clients raises at least two critical problems for the nature of work activities: those of equitable treatment (as, for example, when patients on a hospital ward become concerned that some are getting special attention from nurses); and those of control, most characteristic of teaching, police work, and group work (as a branch of social work), where the practitioner is outnumbered yet must influence the members of the collective client group even against the more immediate desires of the membership. One critical issue in such occupations is the adequacy of the technology for dealing with collective contingencies.

PUBLIC EMPLOYMENT OCCUPATIONS

There is scarcely an occupation in which some members are not employed at one level of government or another, yet it would be erroneous to claim that public employment is a prime characteristic of all occupations. The term *employment* itself can be misleading because it is generally used to refer both to job-holding *per se* and to a specific type of labor contract in which a worker agrees to contribute a specified effort in exchange for remuneration. I use the term *public employment* here in reference to those occupations most of whose members work for government agencies at any level for wages or salaries; teaching is a prime example (so is librarianship, the military, police work, and other municipal service occupations). There are, of course, members of the ordinarily fee-taking professions who work for governments, but a distinction must be made between those who perform a routine service and those who perform a highly technical service with due allowance for the free exercise of discretion that usually characterizes private practice.

The most conspicuous though not necessarily the most important problem for public occupations is the right to strike against the government. The issues involved are usually of greater interest to the parties to a dispute, to labor lawyers, and to public officials than to students of occupations, who are more concerned with the nature of the work and the setting in which it is performed. Whether the public safety is jeopardized, whether the sovereignty of the state is brought into question, whether the public is subject to great inconveniences are all matters of great social, but not necessarily analytical, importance. Issues other than strikes, though less likely to preempt newspaper headlines, are of equal or greater significance: the nature of the union movement among public employees, of bargaining with employers, of the type of political activity that members of the occupation can engage in, and so on.[16]

More germane to this discussion, however, is the relevance of public employment to the nature of daily work activities. At stake is the degree of control that any employer who pays wages for work can exert over his employees through the content of the labor contract. With this type of control, exerted not through coercion or surveillance but by prior contractual agreement between two parties, the burden of proof rests upon the worker who would expand his area of discretion. In other types of employment, not based as strongly on work for wages, the burden of proof falls more on the employer who would restrict discretion. Of course, these burdens of proof vary in degree; there are fine distinctions along a scale, and never—even under slavery—do they become absolute.

Working for the public, as distinct from salaried employment, raises somewhat different problems of control. If workers, and especially professionals, owe strong allegiance to the occupational community and to the standards of technically competent work, government officials, both elected and appointed, have different and potentially conflicting allegiances. Government officials hold obligations to their constituencies, and to the extent they wish to continue in office, must be responsive to public demands. Constituencies, moreover, are usually diverse both in composition and in the interests expressed by their members; these interests may not be at all consistent with the ethical and technical considerations around which professional and other occupational activities are organized. The case of public librarians is pertinent. As Goode describes it:

> The [librarian's] code urges fairness and wisdom in book acquisitions, a pale and watery exhortation, but does not assert the simple ethical duty to follow professional principle in this central matter and to ignore lay opinion as irrelevant and incompetent. Few clear-cut cases of censorship arise; the librarian avoids the risk. In a high but unknown percentage of instances the librarian does not buy the books which might arouse local critics.[17]

The librarian, clearly, is vulnerable to public scrutiny; equally important is the local library board which constitutes a public board of trustees and is the immediate employer of the librarian. For anyone seeking employment in public library service, the situation must be transparent; no surprise then, to find that those who enter this line of work either accept their vulnerability as an occupational hazard or, turning a danger into a virtue, acknowledge the public's right to oversee.

Although I have chosen my example from librarianship, the parallels with teaching must be obvious: lay boards, diverse constituencies, public scrutiny, not to mention the ideological analgesic that "democracy" demands the public be let in. Municipally controlled social work agencies also confront their employees with similar problems.

MOBILITY-BLOCKED OCCUPATIONS

The term *career* has several different meanings: one refers to a person's work history, the sequence of jobs that fills up the years of a working life; a second to an occupation and the sequence of positions it provides for workers to move through. The two meanings are logically distinct since persons can move into and out of different occupations, and occupations can include persons with very different work histories. I am concerned here with the second meaning. (There are, of course, more than two meanings and much disagreement over definitions.)

Some occupations contain a long sequence of finely graded ascending positions, each carrying greater remuneration, perquisites, responsibilities, discretion, power, and the like. Civil and foreign service appointments in the federal government represent a typical case in point, as does the military. Other occupations such as medicine and law do not characteristically have such graded sequences, but within the confines of one "position," like that of physician, opportunities for social and economic advancement are clearly evident. The career line, then, consists not so much in advancement through positions but through gains accruing to one position over time.

The career line of other occupations, in contrast, is markedly truncated—nursing and teaching representing typical cases. Hospitals provide work for persons in many occupations, but nurses (no matter how bright, how capable, or how experienced) do not advance to positions on the medical staff and only rarely advance to positions on the administrative staff (save within nursing itself). The majority of nurses, even those in low and middle level supervisory positions, come largely under the control of members of the medical profession in the hospital, and like patients, follow doctors' orders (though the orders differ in substance). To the extent that desire for occupational advancement motivates nurses, the advancement opportunities are limited. Many will have no place to go *and still remain nurses* once the available higher positions have absorbed the aspirants for them. The rest will either quit to become nurse-secretaries for private physicians or leave the occupation altogether.

Teaching presents the same problem. The classroom teacher can spend his working life in the classroom reaping the modest benefits of salary increments (according to schedule) and additional benefits when the schedule itself goes up. He can gain in power, working conditions, and in bargaining strength through affiliation with a teachers' association or union; he can teach in a secondary school rather than in an elementary school to accumulate gains in quasi-legitimate prestige. There are not supposed to be any status differences between elementary and secondary school teaching especially since the advent of the single salary scale, but there are. And, finally, he can seek a position in a "better" school where "better" usually means suburban, middle class, untroublesome parents and pupils, where the rigors of teaching are supposedly less demanding than in the rougher, central city schools. The financial rewards of advancement are not munificent nor do they bring dramatically large gains in status. What is more, no significant changes in responsibility or in control over subordinates occur with long tenure in the classroom; and although this is also true of some of the fee-taking professions, they at least provide opportunities for making a lot of money and for gaining esteem among colleagues.

The teacher can opt to leave the occupation altogether, go into nonteaching occupations within education (such as guidance counseling), or advance into administrative positions. All of these possibilities involve entering a different occupation. Administration is the dominant route out of teaching, and although both occupations fall within the field of education, they are vastly different lines of work. Thus, advancement in teaching means small gains; advancement in education means renouncing teaching.

The main issue, then, in mobility blockage is whether an occupation can keep its members, and in this respect, teaching is not altogether unlike employment in mass production industries where advancement in blue collar work stops short of the white collar hierarchy.[18]

BUREAUCRATIZED PROFESSIONS

In modern industrial societies many occupations are pursued within large bureaucratic organizations. This does not mean, as

Mills has asserted, that previously independent professionals have joined the ranks of the salaried employees to do the bidding of large corporations. To say, for example, that physicians have become increasingly dependent on accessibility to hospitals with their advanced technology does not necessarily mean that medical decisions have fallen under the control of hospital administrators. Many kinds of arrangements have been worked out by the various professions to reconcile their occupational interests with those of the organizations with which they are affiliated (not without cost to be sure), but not by seriously jeopardizing the interests either of the occupation or of its clients.

University teaching, medicine, law, scientific research, engineering—all have come to be carried on within organizational contexts. The alliances evolving have been delicate at times but viable nonetheless. Medical practice, in which traditional forms of treatment involved a doctor and a patient in relatively private contact, has moved into the hospital in a way that grants the physician considerable control over the management of a case. He maintains substantial independence through the arrangement of "hospital privileges" which give him the right to use hospital facilities in treating private patients; but he is not typically hired by the hospital, an arrangement that would subject him far more to administrative pressure than would privilege. The physician who practices in a hospital, however, is far from unfettered because such practice exposes him to the review and scrutiny of his colleagues who gain a far better perspective of his competence than if his practice were restricted to his private office. Moreover, such scrutiny tends to keep him alert and up to date. The pressure, then, originates more from professional colleagues than from administrative superiors, probably to the benefit of the patient.

The problem in medicine is to preserve two important values: the doctor's concern for and loyalty to the patient, and his free exercise of judgment based on the requirements of the case; both values are vulnerable to the demands of administrative pressure. The situation in academic settings, in research institutes, and in large corporations is much the same. Although the device of privilege is not typically used, other devices designed for the preservation of free inquiry, the maintenance of loyalty to clients, and the release from production schedules are often employed. Even in the military, perhaps the prototype of bureaucratic organizations, changes in the technology of warfare have resulted in greater reliance on technical expertise, even in the noncommissioned officer ranks, than on strict military discipline in the old sense. The ranks of the technically competent have swelled at the expense of the lowest ranks of the order-followers, and the style of discipline has shifted so that less emphasis is put on domination and obedience, and more put on influence, manipulation, and holding out positive inducements. This is not to suggest that the changes have been easy. According to Morris Janowitz and Roger Little:

> there exists a deep source of organizational strain in military organization because the authority structure does not articulate with the skill structure. . . . The basic dilemma centers about the staff officer who, despite his expanded functions and specialized skills, is defined as subordinate to the commander.[19]

But again, given its history, the military should not be expected to make this kind of transition easily; the point is, however, that it appears to be moving in this direction.

It is not uncommon for bureaucracies to be described as coercive organizations where people occupying positions high up in the hierarchy give orders to their subordinates and expect unquestioning obedience from them. Professions, in contrast, have been portrayed as occupations consisting of individual practitioners who apply expert knowledge, free from administrative control, to the particular problems presented to them voluntarily by clients. We have no difficulty conjuring up images of the loyal clerk stuck to his chair in a business firm or of the infantry soldier in basic training, on the one hand, and the AMA's traditional doctor of the year, the canny independent general practitioner, wise man, and friend of man, on the other. These are, of course, stereotypes, not to be taken too seriously. But it would be erroneous to claim that bureaucracy—an organizational form based largely on the exercise of authority by virtue of one's position in a hierarchy and on the subjection of members' conduct to administrative rules— is inherently inimical to professional practice based on expertise, despite their real differences (rather than their caricatured ones). In fact, the two principles of organizing people and conduct— professional and bureaucratic—both conflict with and resemble each other; perhaps the resemblance makes it possible for the two principles to coexist under the same organizational roof despite prevailing strains. The main differences lie in the areas of authority —expert knowledge or administrative rules—and of members' loyalty—to the community of practitioners or to the particular organization and its superordinate officers.[20] They resemble each other in that both are organized within specific spheres of technical competence and universalistic, disinterested conduct toward those served. Despite the often-heard indictment, from both the political right and the political left, that professionals cannot flourish under bureaucratic conditions, the fact is that they do.

The main problem in the juxtaposition of professional and bureaucratic modes of organizing conduct is the strain generated between the nature of technology and the form of authority. This issue can be resolved to some extent both by organizations and by individuals; the nature of the solution will vary with the type of organization and the particular occupation involved.

WOMEN'S OCCUPATIONS

The things that men and women do together are familiar enough, yet probably all societies distinguish conventionally between men's and women's work. In American society, nurses, social workers, librarians, teachers, bookkeepers, cashiers, secretaries, private household workers, persons who wait on tables, and textile manufacturing workers are overwhelmingly women. Theodore Caplow, citing the United States Employment Service, notes that only 10 percent of American occupations are filled by both men *and* women, the remainder predominantly by men *or* women.[21]

Occupations in which women predominate as workers allow some provision for the fact that married women are usually expected to run a household and raise children, expectations conflicting with the demands of holding a full-time job. In order to remain employed, especially during the child-rearing years, a woman must either have money to pay someone else to raise her children (if she can rest easily with that arrangement), hold a part-time job, hold a job in which she can regulate her working hours, or work at odd hours of the day and night. With the exception of part-time employment, these working arrangements are usually either impossible or considered undesirable; accordingly, the common pattern is for women who have entered the labor force to leave it either permanently or temporarily. Many high level occupations, particularly those conventionally numbered among the professions, presume that those who join the community of participants will remain for the better part of a lifetime. This presumption is not simply a matter of foolish occupational pride especially in those lines of work where it is necessary for members to "keep up" in order to do their jobs competently. Moreover, occupations that are easy to enter and easy to leave belie the importance of the credentials they require for entrance.

Although occupations open to women cover a wide range of the occupational spectrum, they do have a cluster of properties, particularly at the higher levels, that distinguish them from male occupations. (At the lower end of the scale, women's occupations tend to be subordinate in much the same way that blue collar, men's jobs are; the difference lies primarily in the amount of physical exertion involved.) Whatever their obvious differences, nursing, social work, librarianship, and teaching have certain characteristics in common. To oversimplify, they all appeal more to the heart than to the mind. Each is an occupation that provides a personal service; that is, a service designed to reach the person himself rather than what belongs to him. The work contains a significant element of nurturance, of caring for, of personal attachment between worker and client within the limits that the technical requirements of the task allow. These characteristics, of course, do not apply across the board; they are more typical of social work than librarianship, more typical of medical than of surgical nursing.

These four occupations also have characteristic patterns of subordination. Their work is carried out in organizations (none of them has a tradition of private practice) in which members serve as hired employees. Although each is based on a set of more or less precisely defined techniques (e.g., administering medication, interviewing, disciplining children, using book retrieval systems, teaching reading, and the like), other people—usually men in superior positions—initiate the main work activities. Superiors do not define the content of the job—the actual activities that workers perform—but rather the times and occasions when they shall be performed. This is not to say that nurses, social workers, librarians, and teachers have no autonomy or no opportunities to exercise judgment and imagination; rather that doctors, social work supervisors (many of whom are women), head librarians, nursing supervisors (most of whom are women), and school principals have much to say about what these workers do and when.

It is both insufficient and inaccurate to claim that professionalism is incompatible with feminization in an occupation even though some observers have asserted just this. The issues raised by feminization concern the stability of the work force in high level occupations and the means for scheduling activities that derive from competing demands—issues whose resolution depends on the nature of the accommodation worked out between the demands of the life cycle and those of occupational employment. Strains clearly exist between partially incompatible forces, but their prevalence does not imply a complete incompatibility between job and household for women.

OCCUPATIONS WITH INTANGIBLE PRODUCTS

It is characteristic of a craftsman that he works with tangible materials and turns them into a final product whose dimensions and qualities can be ascertained and judged. He may or may not be able to describe all the steps of production verbally, but anyone can see what he has done if not exactly how he did it. Even when the materials of an occupation are intangible or symbolic, it is still possible to determine what has been produced. Lawsuits are won and lost, music composed, bank statements issued, plans for urban renewal developed, research undertaken. In some occupations, however, where practitioners produce something, nobody knows exactly what it is or how it was accomplished. It is not difficult to discover whether a clergyman has led a successful fund drive to build a new church, but has he saved any souls? A patient can sit and talk to a psychiatrist for an hour a day for five years, but do changes in the patient have something to do with his treatment?

It is precisely in those occupations, teaching among them, where a personal service is performed for people that the problem of recognizing intangible and long-term outcomes arises. Perhaps, unlike the work of the craftsman, the outcome does not appear with the conclusion of activity but ten years later when a dozen other things may also contribute—in unknown ways—to its appearance. And then, after all that time, the outcome appears not as something one can take hold of but as a change in attitude, in perspective, in style—all difficult to define however important they may be.

The problem raised by these occupations is the difficulty of establishing expertness based on a technology. This difficulty is particularly troublesome in an occupation that calls itself professional, because a profession's claim to both license and mandate is predicated on the capacity of its members to produce a detectable solution to a problem. If practitioners have difficulty demonstrating their expertise because the available technology does not permit them to do so, then nonpractitioners need not acknowledge their special claims. Moreover, if practice is loosely based on an ill-defined and poorly developed set of techniques, by what process other than trial and error and its seat-of-the-pants derivatives do new members of the occupation learn their trade?

EDUCATIONAL OCCUPATIONS

In certain respects, teaching has more in common with noneducational occupations such as social work, librarianship, and the ministry than it does with occupations supposedly in the same general area, such as guidance counseling, school administration, and college teaching. Counseling, despite the claims of some observers that it is integrally related to the teaching process, usually involves contact with clients on a one-to-one basis (rather than on an aggregate basis), contact that is relatively fleeting. Counseling, moreover, is based much more on psychiatric practice and social case work than is teaching (which is based more on techniques of group management and instruction).

School administration is basically a managerial occupation concerned with the internal politics of schools and school systems, and with the politics of relating schools to the community and to the labor markets that provide school system personnel. Within the school, administrators have primarily supervisory obligations. The one thing they don't do is teach; teaching, after all, is the occupation they left in order to become administrators.

College teaching has obvious similarities to school teaching; both depend largely on techniques of instruction, however undeveloped. But the academic profession, especially in large universities, is very different from school teaching because research activities accompany those of instruction. The importance of research alters the priorities of college teachers because they know that advancement in their careers depends more on what they produce than it does on how well they teach. Aside from the obvious facts that academicians do much less actual classroom teaching than their primary and secondary school counterparts and that the classroom situation itself is much less demanding once the substantive material to be taught has been prepared, instruction is simply one component of an academician's job—and in many universities, a small one at that. The contrast between the two instructional occupations is related to differences in the functions of the organizations that employ them. Although both schools and universities have responsibilities for dissemination, only the universities have responsibilities for the creation and advancement of knowledge. To put the case starkly, teaching has little in common with this whole range of educational occupations even though all of them fall within the same institutional category.

SUMMARY

I have cast much of this discussion in the language of professionalism, using the professions not as a criterion by which to judge but as a lens through which to examine. Logically, I might as well have taken a formulation of blue collar jobs and compared their properties with those of other occupations. Though logically defensible, such an approach would have been analytically unfeasible because too many characteristics of teaching would remain unexposed through the comparison.

Although questions of occupational status inherent in the

idea of profession are of great importance to the members of an occupation, and the process by which occupations professionalize is of great interest to social scientists, *my purpose is to describe those parts of an occupation that give it a distinctive character and to indicate how those parts are connected.* Historical and comparative analysis has already indicated what some of them are: the unity of the association of workers, the relationship between workers and the organization to which they are affiliated, the arrangements for the independent exercise of judgment and the self-determination of work tasks, the nature of the career line. All of these, and many more, are closely tied to three broad concerns in occupational life: (1) the social characteristics of the setting in which work is performed, (2) the characteristics of the setting in which workers are trained to do their jobs, and (3) the sequence of positions and organizations comprising the work career. It is around these three concerns that the remainder of this book is organized as well as a fourth which cuts across all three: the nature of the technology underlying occupational practice.

TEACHING FROM THE PERSPECTIVES OF ITS SPOKESMEN

The nominal criteria for identifying professions are both widely known and widely accepted; this does not mean, of course, that there is agreement on which occupations are professions and which shall succeed in becoming so. No one should take the rhetoric of occupational associations at face value. Characteristic of the many lists of distinguishing characteristics is the one presented by Myron Lieberman; few would take exception to what he includes while some might add criteria that he omits. Professions are occupations that:

1. provide a specific social service;
2. emphasize intellectual techniques in providing it;
3. require a prolonged period of preparation;
4. afford broad autonomy both for practitioners and for the occupation as a whole;
5. expect practitioners to accept personal responsibility for their judgment and actions;
6. emphasize service rendered rather than gain received;
7. govern and control the conduct of members; and
8. formulate and expect adherence to a code of ethics.[22]

He might well have mentioned control over entry and responsibility for the generation and advancement of knowledge relevant to practice.

Although these statements are framed as characteristics of occupations, most of them actually refer to persons who are members of occupations. Thus, it is not medicine that provides a specific service, but physicians. Even though occupations consist of all persons who provide the service in question and possess all other relevant characteristics, they consist of much more. Occupations have characteristics in their own right in addition to the aggregated characteristics of their members, and the former frequently are neglected.[23] The distinction is important and affects one's perspective both in analyzing occupational life and in making policy for occupational change.

Perspectives on the nature of occupational life in teaching are numerous; most center around the question of professionalism. But professionalism, at least for my purposes, is incidental; more important is the conception of occupational characteristics. Rhetoric (an occupation's statements about itself, pride in its strengths, seriousness and sympathy about weaknesses, optimism about the future) provides a fragmentary, though moderately useful, picture of occupational life. Accordingly, I treat here four internal perspectives on the occupation, two based on publications of leading teachers' associations—the National Education Association and the American Federation of Teachers—and two based on the writings of concerned, sympathetic, but critical observers—Myron Lieberman and James B. Conant.

NATIONAL EDUCATION ASSOCIATION

In 1963 the NEA prepared a statement pertaining to all those occupationally engaged in the educational enterprise (teachers and administrators at the school and college levels, educational specialists, and government personnel), delineating their obligations to man the educational establishment and to provide educational services of the highest quality. The statement deals primarily with the problem of selecting new members; preparing them for work; assuring their continued engagement in training throughout their working lives; maintaining standards in the occupation through licensure, accreditation, and proper work assignment; and advancing the development of theory and research.[24] This is a standard bill of fare for any occupation that attempts to follow the road to professionalization. The NEA, of course, has been doing more than moving along the lines described here; partially in response to the gains in membership and power of the teachers' union, it has increased its militancy in its fight for better pay and working conditions.

Keeping the gate and maintaining standards are traditional concerns of many occupations, particularly the professions. The NEA, accordingly, has recently shown increasing interest in problems of teacher training (prior to the first job and subsequent to it), probably in response to a series of investigations, carried out largely by the U.S. Office of Education, that document the absence of a lifetime commitment by teachers to their occupation. Along these lines we find two substantial publications: *The Real World of the Beginning Teacher*, and *The Development of the Career Teacher*. The NEA acknowledges that its interest in the lifetime career of teachers is relatively new-found, and that it has spent much of its energy and resources in the past on problems of undergraduate preparation. Implied in the NEA's *modus operandi* is a strategy for developing professionalism among teachers: The assumption is that the process can occur piecemeal, one problem at a time, rather than on a broad front of interrelated problems.

The NEA links two prevalent dropout problems together: those of pupils and teachers. "Conditions that will cause pupils to want to stay in rather than leave school will also cause teachers to want to remain in rather than leave teaching."[25] The conditions in question are opportunities to establish close personal relationships between pupils and teachers, the availability of stimulating curricula, adequate teaching resources, and so forth. The logic of this contention will not stand too close scrutiny because evidence documenting teachers' lack of career commitment indicates that it is related to forces outside the classroom. As far as remedy is concerned, this formulation of the problem of retaining teachers implies that schools should improve their resources and that teachers should try to be interesting so that pupils will want to remain in school without making the teacher's job intolerable. This remedy is not a very potent brew; but as I shall indicate shortly, the underlying premises of this approach to professionalism are very similar to those underlying the approach to continued in-service training.

The NEA states that teachers, to be considered professionals, must be broadly and liberally educated as well as trained to do their jobs; yet, at the time they complete their formal training they are neither completely trained nor completely educated. That the NEA sees the need for the continuing education of teachers is not as important for this discussion as the programs it recommends for meeting these needs. After all, most high level occupations provide, formally or informally, for the continued development of their members (to keep them up-to-date and to maintain their commitment). But among teachers, commitment poses an acute problem. The NEA, in response, leaves its solution primarily up to each teacher. Thus: "In-service education is primarily an affair of the individual; it progresses or fails according to his initiative or desire. . . ."[26] The role of the school and the school system is primarily one of making opportunities available for teachers to improve themselves and to provide internship programs with competent and sufficient supervision for new teachers. Underlying these remedies is a self-help conception of career development.

The NEA's approach to professionalism is essentially that the schools should continue doing what they have been doing in teacher education all along, but do it better: the misassignment of teachers should cease, teachers should communicate with each other more, school districts should encourage experimentation by teachers and should encourage "a climate conducive to intellectual growth," and so on. No one, of course, can take exception to these recommendations, but they indicate a conception of professionalization based largely on the efforts of individual teachers to bring about their own self-improvement and on the facilitative contributions of school systems by opening up opportunities for teachers to act on their own.

The NEA's concern with the advancement of professionalism clearly includes the further development of knowledge on which teaching is based and of the competent performance of activities predicated upon that knowledge. Not surprisingly, then, it calls upon the universities. Beyond the traditional plea for the maintenance of high standards, the NEA asks for:

> close coordination and cooperation among school districts, colleges and universities, state departments of education, professional associations, and learned societies [as] essential to the planning, financing, and conducting of sound programs of continuing education.[27]

In addition, it asks for the participation of universities in the development of instructional materials, in providing courses in up-to-date content and methods, and in the advancement of research on teaching techniques and on teacher training.

The worthiness of these goals remains beyond dispute, yet the NEA says very little about what the relationship between schools, school systems, and universities should be; and if the histories of other professions is at all instructive, the nature of this relationship is particularly crucial for the advancement of technology.

The *explicit goals* of the NEA follow the traditional professional pattern, yet the image of the occupation coming from its publications is that of private individual members acting to become more competent as workers, not of an occupation changing its character. But an occupation is not simply the sum of its members. The development of an adequate technology, for example, is not the same as individuals becoming more skilled in their work, nor is establishing new relationships with universities the same as individuals going to college and graduate school. Individuals now have the opportunities to improve themselves as teachers, and undoubtedly, school systems can become more responsive to the needs of teachers to improve their competence. Unfortunately, the NEA's ideology takes one's eye away from the collective occupational strategies for the advancement of teaching competence, while the history of other high level occupations points precisely in that direction. If radically different relationships between schools and universities need to be invented, efforts should be made to invent them; but the thinking must occur on an occupation-wide basis, not just on an individual one.

It would be misleading to leave the impression that the NEA eschews collective action in the interest of advancing the position of the occupation. Despite its individual self-help rhetoric, the organization in recent years has become dramatically more militant by putting pressures on those states and school systems that have tolerated conditions inimical to the competent performance of teaching activities. It has done so through the application of "sanctions"—a form of black-balling. In situations where working conditions are bad—low salaries, overcrowding, hiring of under-qualified teachers, too many teachers offering subjects in which they lack preparation, and the like—the NEA has urged new recruits to the occupation to avoid accepting employment, and teachers already employed to seek work elsewhere. It has urged schools of education to refuse sending the *vitae* of their graduates to such states and systems. The strategy has been effective in many cases; and when conditions have reached acceptable standards, the sanctions have been removed.

No one would argue that these measures are unrelated to professionalism; they are predicated on the principle that professional workers can do their jobs properly only under congenial conditions. The underlying assumption, however, is that teachers already possess the professional competence and that the main problem is to assure the maintenance of conditions conducive to its expression. In short, the use of sanctions takes the prevailing state of competence in the occupation for granted—and to that extent resembles the strategy of the union to strike—and does not deal directly with the more basic problems of the occupation: the state of the art, the low level of occupational commitment, the advancement of knowledge, and the establishment of alliances with the universities.

The NEA, traditionally, has been a confederation of diverse organizations representing classroom teachers (in their variety), school administrators (through the American Association of School Administrators), educational researchers (through the American Educational Research Association), university teachers and administrators (through the American Association for Higher Education), as well as others. These organizations clearly have different interests and constituencies. Over the past few years the organizational composition of the NEA has changed markedly: the AERA has become independent, and both AASA and AAHE have become "associated organizations" *vis-à-vis* the NEA rather than "departments" or "national affiliates" of it. This means, in effect, that their programs and policies need only be "compatible" with those of the NEA, that NEA review of activities pertain to compatibility only; but most importantly, AASA and AAHE members need not join NEA, and these organizations have become financially independent. In contrast to their prior positions, their programs need not be "consistent" with those of NEA, nor are their members obliged to promote NEA membership, both minimum requirements of affiliate and department status.

The message seems clear. The NEA appears to be evolving into a classroom teachers' organization devoted to the interests of a single occupation. Whether this trend is a response to union activity, or to forces indigenous to the NEA (particularly its prior heterogeneity of composition), or both is not entirely clear; but the NEA seems to be moving in the direction of a national teachers' association rather than of an educational association.

AMERICAN FEDERATION OF TEACHERS

In the fiftieth anniversary issue of *The United Teacher*, the official newspaper of the United Federation of Teachers (Local 2 of the American Federation of Teachers, New York), Charles Cogen (ex-president of both the UFT and the AFT) described the goals of teacher unionism as follows: to bring about (1) economic and professional improvements, such as salary increases, grievance procedures, the reduction of classroom size, duty-free lunch periods, fringe benefits, and job security; (2) increased teacher participation in the control of working conditions and educational policy, such as increases in the extent of guidance services or the reduction of class size (again); and (3) participation in social change, including the support of such programs as Head Start, More Effective Schools, and Job Corps, and the support of social welfare and civil rights legislation.[28] In addition, Cogen describes the union's direct participation in political action: influencing the legislative process at the state level by lobbying and lending support to liberal and prolabor candidates for public office. Clearly, he presents a picture of a union deeply concerned both with bread-and-butter issues and with events in the wider political community that impinge on the work of teachers. Equally interesting is including the issue of reducing class size as an aspect of both professionalism and working conditions, a point that touches one of the union's central ideological dilemmas: how to be both a labor union and a professional association at the same time.

The dilemma of professionalism consists of several parts. First, spokesmen for the union have attacked what they consider to be a specious kind of professionalism that emphasizes middle class status, loyalty to superiors, silence about deficiencies in the schools, and "dedication" construed as a kind of occupational subservience; this does not mean that the union opposes adequate salaries, urges disloyalty, or favors washing dirty linen in public. Second, they stress the idea of competence: "the thing which distinguishes a professional from other workers is the fact that he is required to exercise his expert judgment in the performance of his work."[29] And third, they connect the idea of professionalism with economic gains:

> When the NEA spokesmen raised the issue [of professionalism], the rejoinder of the UFT was, "There is nothing so unprofessional as working for less than professional salaries under less than professional working standards."[30]

A professional salary is one that will attract enough qualified people into the occupation, particularly to staff the more difficult schools. The argument, as least in ideological terms, goes further: unionism and professionalism fit together naturally—they are more than merely consistent.

The difficulty with the union's position on professionalism is that it really amounts to a question of status and represents part of the more general American phenomenon of occupational aggrandizement that includes teachers but is by no means peculiar to them. Many occupations try to improve their economic and social standing by a variety of collective economic, political, and symbolic strategies. The assumption underlying the union's position, however, is that once collectively organized teachers have achieved working conditions that meet so-called professional standards, the competence of teachers (presumably fettered by poor working conditions) will become liberated, dormant talents will emerge, and desirable learning outcomes will appear in pupils as a result. One might call this the "latent talent" argument. Although it might be true that a highly competent professional—in any field—will be seriously hampered by intolerable working conditions, creating desirable working conditions will not necessarily release hidden talents unless a high level of technical competence exists in the first place.

Although both the NEA and the AFT are far from indifferent about teacher competence, neither organization follows the courses of action that other professional groups have designed to develop technical competence in their members: extended and concentrated apprenticeships, close affiliation with universities, and development of research programs and means for disseminating research among practitioners. Neither the NEA's self-help nor the union's latent talent approach deals with the competence issue directly or sufficiently. To say this, of course, is not to deny the value of self-help or of creating good working conditions, but merely to indicate the remoteness of their programs from the problem of technical competence.[31]

What distinguishes the AFT's conception of teaching (particularly from that of the NEA) is its emphasis on the employee status of teachers; the composition of membership is the central issue. The president of New York's Local 2 (UFT) states the case most explicitly in a printed debate in which he opposes the establishment of a separate supervisor's local under the aegis of the AFT:

> Many people are sympathetic toward unions without actually being members of unions. Basically, unions are *employee* organizations and it is the employee status (not the particular sympathies of individuals), which determines membership eligibility. There can be no doubt that, with respect to teachers, supervisors are managerial personnel.[32]

What follows from this line of argument is that if teachers are employees, they should act like them. Accordingly, unionized teachers have adopted a strategy of collective bargaining based on a statement of the conditions under which they will and will not work—nothing is added or explained by calling these conditions professional; what is important is whether they are conducive to teachers' getting the job done—according to the formula of "no contract—no work." Teachers are not especially prone to strike; they much prefer bargaining over working conditions and remuneration, a procedure that at least potentially brings them into disputes over the distribution of power. And although observers have noted the increasing militancy of teachers—and it is undeniable as they have become increasingly unionized, especially in the big cities—equally noteworthy is the fact that both the NEA and the AFT have adopted similar tactics, and that there has been recent talk about merging the two organizations which remain opposed on both organizational and rhetorical grounds.

The AFT is not basically a combat organization, yet it tends to be organized around a set of interests defined in opposition to those who occupy managerial positions in school systems. On this point it differs most sharply from the NEA which fastens more on the community of interests among those engaged in the educational enterprise and subdues the conflicting interests distinguishing managers and workers. The AFT, moreover, is not categorically opposed to school administrators; rather, its policies mark off those interests on which it is opposed to them and those on which it is not at any given time. Basically, it takes the state of occupational technology as given and works primarily at the local and state levels to achieve those conditions it considers most advantageous to the working lives of its members.

MYRON LIEBERMAN

Most discussions of professionalism in teaching consider, with more or less emphasis, at least some of the following aspects of the occupation: the nature of political control, characteristics of the workplace, the state of the prevailing technology, the nature and quality of training and of training institutions, the contributions of universities to occupational life, and the characteristics of the work force. Observers and spokesmen for teacher organizations differ on what aspects they consider most important. Where the NEA puts most stress on the individual teacher and Conant on the quality of teaching skills and the contribution of universities, Lieberman concerns himself primarily with the relationship between teachers and administrators, both in the schools and in the councils of occupational associations. The main issue is the relationship between administrative power and teacher autonomy:

> if [the school administrator] is to be responsible for the operation of the school system, it is necessary that he be given power to control the behavior of teachers. It is difficult to see how such power can be reconciled with professional status for teachers. The teachers will be too subject to administrative control to be regarded as professionals. They will lack the direct and personal responsibility of professional workers to their clients if primary responsibility for the quality of their services is lodged with educational administrators.[33]

Lieberman makes his case against administrator control on at least two grounds. First, he argues that administrators dominate teacher associations; in particular, the NEA and that branch of it concerned with the accreditation of teacher training institutions, the National Council for Accreditation of Teacher Education (NCATE). The crux of his argument is that accrediting agencies should not be controlled primarily by representatives of the institutions they are charged with accrediting but rather by representatives of an association of practitioners. The reasoning is simple enough; if raising standards of training means the investment of large amounts of money for the improvement or elimination of marginal institutions, one can hardly expect representatives of those institutions either to acknowledge serious weaknesses in their own establishments or to preside over their liquidation. The NEA, he claims, is dominated by school and college administrators, and this domination is reflected in the composition of NCATE with its small teacher representation. However, as is well known, it is often difficult to determine how people will act if all one knows about them is the organization to which they are affiliated.

Second, Lieberman finds more direct evidence for administrator control over the operation of schools. This control arises because teachers are hired to engage in activities whose content is defined by hierarchical superiors who themselves hold obligations to the larger community through the school board. Lieberman correctly points out that administrators, in meeting community pressures, must often exercise power over the teachers.[34] He goes further in stating:

> The barrier to the professionalism of teaching lies precisely in the fact that administrators *have* broad powers over teachers; as a practical matter, administrators who possess power are seldom able to resist the pressure to exercise it.[35]

He does not, however, contemplate the possibility that administrators will play one group off against another to give teachers autonomy, and some do just that.

For Lieberman, however, professionalism is not simply the absence of administrative control. It means the use of autonomy for providing technically competent and ethically defensible service to clients—as in the independent fee-taking professions. More than Conant, he stresses the importance of the relationship between teacher training and university research. Thus, he argues:

> Professors in teachers' colleges contend that these institutions are ideal for teacher training because, unlike the uni-

versities, they concentrate upon training instead of research. This is a completely antiprofessional point of view. The best professional schools, whether they be in medicine, engineering, dentistry, psychology, or anything else, are located in the universities which are centers of research.[36]

Training institutions, then, should turn out competent practitioners versed in the techniques and scientific foundations of their calling. Accordingly, at least two major areas of decision making should be removed from the jurisdiction of administrators and representatives of the lay public: what to teach and how to teach it.

Lieberman's writing leaves the distinct impression that he has overestimated the power of administrators at the school level and has drawn the lines of conflict between teachers and administrators too sharply. He has sensed correctly that school boards and administrators are often in a position to lay down school policies that ought to fall within the jurisdiction of teachers by virtue of their expertness. Yet this is not the same thing as formulating the nature of the relationship between professional workers and administrators, and that is the basic question. All organizations staffed by professional workers are directed in one way or another by administrators. However, the relationship between the two cannot be formulated simply in terms of autonomy and coercion as Lieberman tends to define it; its content must be specified. Administrators do in fact have obligations to parties other than teachers: to the community at large, to a board of trustees, to state and federal agencies, to sellers of school supplies, and so on. These obligations are real and cannot be put aside, and their existence is bound to affect the relationship between administrators and teachers. He seriously neglects the important question of how much *direct* influence administrators actually exercise over the work of teachers since the latter are both numerous and spatially scattered. School principals, in fact, characteristically complain that they cannot perform what they claim to be their primary job: supervising teachers in their classrooms. Yet while overstating his case and stating it more vaguely than he should, Lieberman has nevertheless raised a key issue in the occupational life of teachers: What *is* the character of the relationship that should prevail between professional workers and their administrative superiors? Whether Lieberman continues to maintain his views about administrator dominance, in the light of recent changes in the NEA, is a matter of conjecture.

JAMES B. CONANT

Although much of the discussion about Conant's volume on the education of teachers deals with the respective jurisdictions of states and universities over teacher training, the theme of his message is teaching competence. He quotes a statement of the Massachusetts Board of Education in 1838 claiming that a skill is involved in teaching and that it can be imparted and mastered. "What," he asks, "is this skill and how can one communicate it to others? This question remains the hard core of the issue."[37] Indeed, it does, and many of Conant's recommendations are directed in one way or another to learning and performing teacher's tasks.

One of his recommendations suggests the creation of a new— new in education, anyway—position in training institutions: the clinical professorship. Beginning with the correct premise that there has long been a chasm between the knowledge and interests of those involved in the scholarly and disciplinary fields (mostly the behavioral sciences) that underlie the practice of teaching and those who actually teach in the schools, he urges that clinical professors establish a linkage between the two. They should be, as Conant puts it:

> prepared by training to understand what the other specialists have to say, and inclined to listen to them, and prepared by continuing experience in the elementary and secondary school to demonstrate in concrete teaching situations the implications of expert judgment.[38]

Essentially, he proposes a scheme for direct occupational training of students by apprenticeship based on a medical school model where faculty members with clinical appointments apply knowledge derived from academic research in the physical and biological sciences. It is precisely this problem of linkage between knowledge and practice that the NEA ignores (though it pays lip-service to some of Conant's ideas).

His recommendation that the training of primary, elementary, and secondary school teachers should differ again reflects his concern with competent performance. For Conant, these three levels of teachers represent different degrees of specialization, in ascending order, based on the assumption that teaching tasks at each of them make different demands on teachers, and that they should be trained to cope with these demands. His diagnosis of the problem may or may not be correct; we don't really know whether elementary teachers should be more specialized than primary teachers. But the more basic point is that training should be directly tied to tasks. Similarly, his recommendations about salary schedules and their connection to additional preparation indicate a similar concern. Salary policy should be formed to reward those who advance themselves through degree programs "designed by the teacher and his university advisor for his specific purposes"[39] rather than those who pick up isolated courses, catch-as-catch-can, in order to turn them into cash. The rationale behind the recommendation is clear. Financial reward should benefit those who do what is most relevant to advance their own competence; and under the prevailing system, obtaining systematic training under the auspices of a university program should be most relevant. Again, the approach differs from that of the NEA. A financial inducement is attached to improving competence; the teacher is not simply advised to go out and improve himself in some morally desirable way.

Conant does not use the language of professionalism nor does he look at the nature of occupations and professions; rather, he addresses himself to specific problems of training teachers. Behind his formulation, however, is an image of what an occupation is, or should be. In contrast to the NEA's picture of self-improving individual professionals (along with the occupation acting militantly when it has to), Conant's concern is teaching skills and their efficacy. At one point he lists some of them: teachers must be able to disseminate information, make their material appropriate for the pupils they are instructing, carry on their activities in a collective setting, and establish and maintain discipline.[40] Teacher education, accordingly, should be designed to create competence in their performance. The scope of Conant's concern, however, excludes broader questions about the nature of the occupation. One finds little or no mention of the teaching career, and perhaps if teachers find that their occupation does not provide gratifying working lives over the long run, then even financial inducements offered in salary schedules will not be sufficient to guarantee that they will avail themselves of opportunities for continued training. Moreover, he pays little attention to occupational associations. The actors in his drama are states, school systems, and universities (in particular, training institutions). Their role in the accreditation of training programs he acknowledges, and he admonishes them to give greater voice to representatives of the scholarly disciplines that underlie the skills of teaching. But for the most part he envisions an advisory contribution for these associations. A far broader conception of the occupation, I would submit, is necessary because the improvement in the core instructional activities (Conant's main concern) has wide ramifications, and only a broader scheme can take them properly into account.

•

CHAPTER THREE

The Teacher's Work Setting

•

Most institutions for occupational training operate on the assumption that the nature of the job for which candidates are being prepared is known. To think otherwise can be unsettling, for how can people be prepared to perform a task of unknown dimensions? This question raises the issue starkly but also overstates it. Only at the lower end of the occupational scale can jobs be defined in anything approximating their entirety; at the upper end, some, perhaps most, of the component tasks can be described in a way that a program of training can be designed. But for a variety of reasons, there are bound to be areas in which workers confront problems for which their training has left them unprepared. Not all contingencies can be anticipated; training to be at all realistic must cover general *types* of cases and situations rather than every possibility, and new technological developments render prior training obsolete. Most jobs are predicated on assumptions about the direct contribution of work toward some desired outcome. That is, occupations involve means-ends sequences over the long and short run, and training is designed to provide experiences and activities related to this sequence.

Consider the case of a physician doing a "work-up." The task requires that he interview the patient, asking about his medical and social history, his daily round of activities, how he feels generally, and specifically about any symptoms. The questions are not casual but are designed to elicit information not only about general health but about specific maladies whose proper identification and diagnosis require inquiry by triangulation and by process of elimination. A work-up also includes a physical examination and measurements and observations yielding information about the state of health and illness. Although it can be understood as a sequence of specific procedures leading to one or alternative diag-. noses and ultimately to treatment, it is also much more. It requires not only mastering the component procedures but also creating a climate in which the physician elicits relevant information, listening for incidental comments that may reveal incipient problems ostensibly unrelated to the current visit and putting the information together to draw proper inferences from it. While training programs for physicians can cope readily with the means-ends sequences, the other tasks are less easily translated into definable training procedures.

Occupations differ in the degree to which their activities can be explicitly formulated, but work is not simply the summation of activities. Jobs are performed in settings that differ in their social and ecological arrangements, and what is apparently the same work carried on in two different settings may actually represent two very different jobs. With teaching, most investigations of the training process assume that the nature of the work is known, that its properties, if not reduced to formal job description, are at least sufficiently well understood to justify the content of training programs. But even if we acknowledge this dubious assumption, training seldom incorporates preparation for those aspects of the job that are related to the character of the workplace: the school. It is to the properties of the *work setting* that I now turn.

What kind of a place is a school to work in? This vastly complex question is approachable from two sides: first, it can be answered by describing the relationship between schools and their external environments—political, economic, and social; second, in terms of their internal structure—ecology, characteristic relationships of authority, and technology. Forces originating both inside and outside the school impinge on the work of teachers, and although there is no logical priority between them, I shall put greater emphasis on the internal forces.

THE EXTERNAL SETTING: THE SCHOOL IN ITS ENVIRONMENT

SCHOOL SYSTEMS AND THE COMMUNITY

Legally, school systems are agencies of state government.

States provide some measure of financial support, usually based on average daily school attendance, and set standards for licensure and accreditation. In some cases they legislate that certain parts of the curriculum shall be mandatory. There are variations and complexities from state to state in the state-school system relationship, but these fall outside the scope of this discussion. Although American education is not governed by a national ministry, the federal government does provide financial aid and does support educational programs at the local level (e.g., the recent Elementary and Secondary Education Act). Perhaps the paramount fact about American school systems is that they are agencies of local government: financial and political control over the actual operation of school systems resides in municipalities. Their immediate governing agencies are school boards composed of elected or appointed laymen whose task is to determine educational policy. The political control of the educational system is always a controversial question: should schooling be controlled by an elite, or more directly by the people? If the latter, does the central government or the local government represent the "people's" interests better? And by "people," do we mean parents of school-age children or the whole electorate? There are, of course, no clear-cut answers. National governments can be notoriously tyrannical; their tyrannies, however, are often matched and exceeded by those of local governments. Yet, local governments can be highly responsive to the needs and interests of districts immediately surrounding the schools. National governments can be extremely inflexible and unresponsive, but they can also protect people from local tyrannies. Wherever political control rests, school systems are subject to multiple pressures reflecting the interests of diverse groups in a community, and they vary in their vulnerability to them. Not least among these groups are the teachers themselves, who are interested in maintaining their freedom to offer instruction unfettered by the demands of those who press for the priority of special interests.

   Special interests aside, the key question is the extent to which school systems should be representative of and responsive to local, state, or national constituencies, and the extent to which their operation should be governed by an independent, professional teaching force. The British, by means of a centralized national ministry, have made the schools part of a national constituency and have supported a relatively independent teaching profession. The American case differs markedly; the general power to make policy lies in the hands of lay school boards, and democratic ideology enjoins the local citizenry to participate directly in matters pertaining to the operation of the local schools. Thus:

in England . . . the *content* of what is taught in the schools is virtually never discussed save in professional gatherings of educators, whereas in America constant efforts are made, through citizen committees and parent-teacher associations, to insure that what is done in the schools is done with the "authority" of lay opinion.[1]

Teaching in America, then, is not simply an occupation of public employees; it is one in which members of the lay public have a voice in deciding how the teacher's work shall be performed and what he shall teach, although communities (and the individual schools within them) differ in the extent to which teachers are exposed to lay participation. As long as an element of parity obtains between teachers and laymen about what to teach and how to teach it, a question about the technological adequacy of the occupation will remain. At issue here is the teacher's "licence" in the sense that Hughes means it—the extent to which "the society" acknowledges the occupation's right to prescribe what is good for everybody—an issue joined at the meeting point between teaching competence and political authority.

SCHOOLS AND THEIR ADMINISTRATIVE SETTING

If municipalities are the *politically* immediate external environment of school systems, school administrations constitute a more closely surrounding environment. The work of teachers is affected by the properties of both. Educational policy in school systems flows from the school board within constraints determined by more or less flexible state legislation. School superintendents, the hired executive officers of school boards, interpret and formulate policy in terms that ultimately influence the work of teachers. The basic operating units of school systems are schools that serve, in the usual case, residential districts, and which in turn are administered by an executive officer, the principal, whose major formal responsibilities are directing its instructional program and supervising teachers. Between the superintendent and the principal exists an intermediate echelon of administrative officers whose jurisdictions follow either geographical or functional divisions (and sometimes both).

In design the administrative structure of school systems approximates the pyramid of classical bureaucratic organizations; the close resemblance to the pyramidal model, however, is extremely misleading because the pyramid does not represent any simple principle of subordination and superordination. Conflict often originates at the top. A policy-making board composed of laymen hires a superintendent who, on the basis of his expertise, is expected to effect policy throughout the system. Although the superintendent is legally the subordinate of the board because the board can hire and dispose of him, he is the superior of the board in expertise; and out of these two distinct bases of authority —legal status and expertness—a variety of political balances of power develop, some peaceful, some turbulent. Symptomatically, these power struggles often take the form of accusations of encroachment between board and superintendent (depending on whose ox is being gored). Rhetorically, the distinction between policy and administration is at stake, a distinction that totally misses the real point: the contrasting principles of authority.

Because of the complexity of teaching activities, putting educational policy into effect by passing directives down the line is all but impossible. Difficult as this process is even in industrial organizations that have a far more tangible product and a more clear-cut technology underlying the production process, the directives are even less effective in the schools because the outcomes of educational programs are indistinctly defined and protean in character.

Although the organizational charts of school systems indicate clear lines of office hierarchies, this clarity is partly an illusion. The subordinates of a superintendent actually represent both distinct and overlapping constituencies that extend to some degree beyond the formal bounds of the school system. Some systems, for example, divide their middle-range administrative personnel into jurisdictions governed by school level; other systems are organized by functional jurisdiction based on curriculum, business, personnel, and the like; still others are divided into combinations of the two. No matter how these jurisdictions are sliced, each is internally diverse because schools serve districts whose demographic composition varies immensely (ethnic, religious, racial, and economic diversity tends to be especially marked in the large cities). Because school systems are agencies of municipal governments and because organized interests have an acknowledged right to influence educational policy, those whose job it is to effect policy must be sensitive to a diversity of interest groups, more or less highly organized, within their jurisdictions. The racial desegregation and community control issues have brought this problem of school system management into stark relief.

Because of their ostensibly pyramidal structure, school systems, at their upper administrative levels, are ill-designed for the expeditious transmission of policy decisions to the points where work activities are carried out. They have many of the trappings of bureaucratic organizations which are best adapted to the performance of routine and repetitive tasks, and they suffer from many of the organizational strains usually subsumed under the pejorative term *bureaucracy* (red tape, resistance to change, proliferation of forms and records, and so on).

Schools, then, as operating organizations cannot be understood simply as the last stop on the transmission line of school system policies. Although principals and teachers are constrained by system-wide directives prescribing curriculum and teaching methods (with substantial variations among systems and between schools within systems), they also have some autonomy. Though a principal may have little control over hiring his own teachers and over the size and allocation of the school budget, depending on the system and the power of the principal within it he can have much to say about policies internal to his school. He gains some independence from the central office to the extent that he justifies his actions according to the needs of the district that his school serves. However, he must often buy his independence from the system at the price of commitments made to local interests within his district.

If *school systems,* down to the level of the schools themselves, can be described as approximately bureaucratic—with the qualifications noted above—the pyramidal bureaucratic model represents a gross distortion when applied to the *school,* despite appearances to the contrary. The crucial fact about schools is that they include two distinct categories of members who are affiliated with the organization in radically different ways. Principals, their administrative subordinates, and teachers all represent extensions of a bureaucratic hierarchy since all are employees of the system and obligated through employment contracts to carry out system-wide policy. Pupils, in contrast, are something akin to clients of the school or conscripted beneficiaries, to be more exact. They are consumers of an educational service, not functionaries obligated to effect policy. Although pupils' attendance can be coerced if necessary, it is the task of teachers to win the pupils' voluntary participation in the instructional program; that is, at the minimum, to do their work and act properly.

Secondary and elementary schools differ in their patterns of organization. The former tend to be departmentalized by subject matter, often with academic heads of department, and staffed with administrative officers below the level of the principal. Guidance counseling is usually performed as an ancillary specialized service. Whereas the various educational activities are allocated by means of a specialized division of labor at the secondary level, the variety of school functions at the elementary level falls much more within the jurisdiction of teachers; hence, elementary schools tend to have a flat hierarchy usually consisting of teachers and a principal. Only in the largest elementary schools does one find a more elaborate administrative component.[2]

One of the traditional hallmarks of bureaucratic organization is the prevalence of rules as guides and standards of conduct.[3] Although schools are often criticized because of their proliferation of rules, rule domination is much less compatible with the performance of school activities than it is with, for example, the management of industrial production of tangible goods and services. School rules pertain more to the specific problems of managing the organization and controlling pupils' conduct and decorum rather than to the central instructional activities that represent the core of the teacher's work. Although teachers may have to follow syllabi handed down from the superintendent's office and follow directives issued by the principal and his administrative subordinates, many, if not most, of their day-to-day activities are governed by the exigencies and pressures of the classroom. The modes of coping with these problems do not usually consist of matching specific policies and procedures to specific problems, but rather, of following loosely defined patterns of conduct roughly geared to both the short- and long-run events occurring in classrooms. And this type of job performance does not readily lend itself to determination by rules which presuppose clearly definable and regular patterns of activities. This is not to say, however, that teachers cannot be constrained by all kinds of rules and regulations —even some that affect the method and content of what is taught. But the core activities of classroom management and instruction over extended periods of time cannot readily be governed by rules because of the irregularity and flexibility inherent in these activities.

Similarly, the governance of classrooms does not lend itself to the widespread applicability of rules. Teachers *do* impose and enforce certain rules for pupil conduct, but particularly in the earliest grades, teaching pupils to follow and obey rules is itself a problematic issue—that is, pupils must learn the nature of rule-defined conduct—which means that rules cannot be taken for granted as guides to conduct. Moreover, the diversity of pupils in a classroom and the range of differences in interest and capacity they present make carrying out the main instructional activities according to rules exceedingly difficult because rules work best in more standardized situations.

Thus, despite the pyramidal structure of school systems, the hierarchy extending down to the level of pupils, and the importance of rules in some aspects of school system operation, these systems depart in many critical ways from the classical model of bureaucracies, and it is these departures that relate closely to the peculiarities of the teacher's work. Perhaps the distinguishing characteristic of school systems is the vague connection between policy formation at both the high and middle levels of the hierarchy and its implementation at the level where instruction takes place—the classroom.

Schools and school systems do, however, have many of the trappings of bureaucracy: regulations that do not mean anything, a steady flow of trivial memoranda, forms to fill out and file, and so on through a long list of inane rituals. These phenomena are partly a charade common to most large-scale organizations, and partly, and more importantly, attempts by those occupying managerial and supervisory positions to exert some degree of control over unpredictable exigencies and over people why may be inexperienced or inept, yet insulated by the privacy and dispersion of classrooms.[4]

SCHOOLS AND OTHER ORGANIZATIONAL SETTINGS

Schools, universities, hospitals, and law firms all resemble each other as client-serving organizations staffed by professionalized practitioners; each contains different levels of positions, some of which define career lines. But beyond these properties, most similarities end. Law firms and hospitals are staffed by free professional workers who maintain many of the traditions and techniques of solo practice within the organizations that house them. With the advance of both medical and legal specialization (and in the medical case, the enormous development of technology), professionals have carved out a niche in large organizations which permits them to carry on many of the traditions and techniques of private practice—including relief from coercive administrative control—while using the resources of the organization.

Both teaching and academic life have developed in organizational settings which did not require securing a preserve within an administrative apparatus because of loyalties to individual clients. The case of academicians, however, is more complex than that of public school teachers, for though they were never really private practitioners, they have long adhered to a tradition of academic freedom that has protected them from certain administrative pressures. College faculties, moreover, often constitute strong political entities within the colleges.[5]

Whereas schools tend to be single-hierarchy organizations (with the qualifications I mentioned earlier), hospitals and universities are multi-hierarchy organizations in which professionals constitute one among several hierarchies organized separately from the administrative component of the organization. In these two cases, professional workers maintain important ties to powerful associations of fellow workers in a broad community not tied to particular hospitals or universities but cutting across all of them. In the medical case, for example, doctors are usually more strongly identified with each other as fellow members of the same professional community than they are with a particular hospital to which they bring their patients for treatment. Academicians are often more strongly tied to their colleagues in the same discipline than to the university that employs them; though clearly there are exceptions to these generalizations in both the medical and university situations. In schools, by contrast, where there is a single administrative hierarchy and municipal political control, teachers tend to be more responsive to administrative superiors attached to their place of work than to a colleague community whose boundaries extend beyond any one school or school system. In medicine, in academic life, as well as in the law, administrators have substantially less control over the work activities of practitioners.

According to Amitai Etzioni, the usual conception of large-scale organizations consists of three propositions: that (1) staff authority (deriving from technical expertise) is subordinated to line authority (based on a chain of command for organizing and regulating central goal-serving activities); (2) organizations are directed by (line) managers rather than by experts; and (3) organizations have a single center of authority.[6] While this formulation provides a rough approximation of school organization, it applies poorly to organizations whose main work is carried out by professionals. According to Etzioni:

> Although manager orientations are suitable for the major goal activities in private business, the major goal activity of professional organizations is, in its nature, expertness. Managers in professional organizations are in charge of secondary activities; they administer *means* to the major activity carried out by experts. In other words, if there is a staff-line relationship at all, experts constitute the line (major authority) structure and managers the staff. Managers give advice about the economic and administrative implications of various activities planned by the professionals. The final internal decision is, functionally speaking, in the hands of the various professionals and their decision-making bodies.[7]

Again, to use the hospital as an example: the main group of technically expert workers is doctors; but they are not staff in the advisory sense. That is to say, their duties are to perform the central activities: caring for patients expertly. They do not advise hospital administrators who in turn give orders to subordinates down the line. Doctors, in effect, are the "line," and when they need advice they turn to their medical colleagues.

When teaching is compared with law, medicine, and university instruction (and correlatively, schools compared with law firms, hospitals, and universities), several of the occupation's distinguishing characteristics emerge clearly. First, the policies governing many of the teacher's central activities originate from the general guidelines set by a lay school board and from the directives of administrative superiors, not, as in the case of the fee-taking (but organizationally affiliated) occupations, from a developed craft tradition and a codified body of knowledge shared by the community of practitioners independent of the organizations to which they belong.

Second, advancement and promotion in teaching follows administrative lines of authority based on judgments of competence (among other things) by line superiors. Other occupations, in contrast, provide alternative routes for advancement; practitioners can choose whether to advance by accumulating wealth, responsibility, power, or renown. Moreover, advancement usually involves more thorough exposure to and dependence upon colleagues than is true in teaching (although administrative superiors play more than a negligible role in other occupations).

Third, teaching has an exceedingly simple division of labor with almost all facets of the work falling within the jurisdiction of teachers. (There are, by way of exception, ancillary educational workers who serve on something like a consulting or referral basis.) But in comparison to medical practice, to legal practice in large firms, to university research (particularly since the advent of computer technology), and to architecture with its linkages to engineering, teaching activities do not involve the division of work into components that are farmed out to sub- and para-professionals.

These, in general terms, are some of the broad characteristics of the occupation and its setting in the workplace, characteristics that will serve as reference points in later sections of this book.

THE INTERNAL SETTING: THE SCHOOL AS A WORKPLACE

The familiarity of schools often gets in the way of understanding them. Their division into elementary and secondary levels (and frequently the further differentiation of secondary schools into junior and senior high schools), the predominance of women as elementary school teachers, the subject-matter specialization of high school teachers—all of these are too common to receive much attention. Further, the business of schools is known to be instruction; and when private citizens, government officials, spokesmen for minority groups, social critics, local taxpayers, college admission officers, or college professors analyze the schools, they usually challenge whether pupils are learning enough about the right things (whatever *enough* is and whatever the right things are). In any case, most controversies about schools end up with statements, whatever their merit, about classroom instruction. This approach presents a basically correct but highly conventional picture of schools; a picture that usually represents the implicit model underlying much research on school organization and the schooling process.[8] My purpose in presenting this image is not to impugn it, but to suggest that the schools, the work of teachers, and the problems endemic to both can be seen from different perspectives.

This section purports to discuss the school as a workplace, as a setting that provides both opportunities and constraints for the work of teachers; it does not concern the usual questions of instruction and teaching methods. Some questions have been largely ignored or underemphasized: those pertaining to school *ecology*, the arrangements of space and the implications of its distribution; the modes of *affiliation* with schools; the character of *authority relations* between school administrators and teachers, between teachers and pupils, and between parents and teachers. Nobody reading these pages will learn anything about how to teach, but rather will be exposed to some ideas that may define and locate some of the critical problems of teaching, problems incorrectly attributed—usually—to the "orneriness" of human nature.

THE ECOLOGY OF SCHOOLS

Like most words that distinguish large chunks of human experience, *ecology* has a breadth and superfluity of meaning; accordingly, for a discussion such as this to be useful, it is better to employ a specific usage of the term rather than attempt a complete definition. By ecology, I refer to the internal spatial arrangements of schools; my interest extends beyond description of those arrangements to some of their implications for the work and career development of teachers. The most obvious characteristic of schools is their division into isolated classrooms, each containing an aggregate of pupils (from about ten to fifty at the extremes, and averaging near thirty) under the direction of one teacher. This fact in itself determines much of what happens in schools.

Because they occupy isolated classrooms, teachers work separately from each other for most of the day; and since there is a prevailing taboo that teachers abstain from observing each other at work, they learn very little *at first hand* about what their colleagues are doing and how well they are doing it. (There are, of course, exceptions to this generalization.) This situation contrasts sharply with other occupations with clearly definable work groups (as in many industrial and commercial firms), where colleagues establish both working and informal relationships with each other. Thus in teaching, those with the most intimate knowledge about the work and its problems, and with the best qualifications to judge it, are afforded few opportunities to come together because of the geographical properties of the workplace. Teachers do talk about their work and its problems, at least at one level—by talking shop—but without benefit of direct observation. Academicians, one might argue, also seldom see each other teach—the same taboos obtain—and they talk about their work in much the same way that teachers do. Despite superficial similarities, the differences between the two teaching occupations are plain. Teachers *talk about* their work with colleagues; academicians, whose work consists of research as much as it does of teaching, often actually *do their work* when talking with colleagues.

A teacher who works in an isolated setting, performing tasks for which he has almost sole responsibility, does not require a division of labor with tasks broken into components and later synthesized through the coordinative efforts of managers. Except in a limited way, teachers do not depend on specific prior contributions of other teachers; and although they may complain that their predecessors of the previous year have not prepared their pupils adequately, this amounts to a flimsy indictment because it is so difficult to pinpoint with any precision what actual contributions a teacher makes to the achievement of a pupil or a whole class.[9] Compared to other occupations requiring coordinated collective efforts, as are found in certain types of industrial production and medical practice, teaching does not depend on the successful completion of specific prior contributions to a sequential effort; that is, few *demands of the job* encourage the cohesiveness and mutual dependence of the teaching force within a school.

Because the classroom is an aggregation of pupils, the teacher is charged with responsibilities to instruct and maintain control over them *both individually and collectively.* In this respect, teachers have much in common with clergymen and jail keepers. All preside over congregations whose members have diverse needs and interests which cannot find the same degree of expression that is possible when practitioners take clients one at a time. The teacher must serve some individual interests, but he cannot do so to the extent that he jeopardizes his hold over the members collectively by treating individuals as special privileged cases and thus raising questions of inequity. In a sense the teacher and the jailer have more problems in common than either has with the clergyman because they are specifically charged with effecting changes in individuals (hopefully for the better), but have only a collective setting in which to do it. The clergyman has better opportunities to serve his parishioners individually though he must also placate potentially warring factions in the congregation to keep his job. In all three cases the same problem grows directly out of the spatial and numerical properties of the work setting.

Patterns of school ecology are also related to the characteristic relationship between schools and the districts they serve. Despite the current controversy in large American cities over the concept of the neighborhood school and its implications for *de facto* segregation, the fact remains that most elementary schools draw their clients from the surrounding residential area; accordingly, the smaller a school district, the more homogeneous it will be in social composition. Moreover, school populations, until pupils reach the legal school-leaving age, consist of conscripts—or captive audiences, so to speak.[10] For the instructor, the major implication of distinct social composition is its relationship to the distribution of those psychological capacities most relevant to level of achievement. On the average, the larger the district, the greater the range of achievement-related capacities represented.

A diverse school population contains within it a variety of pupil interests, aspirations, talents, and stages of maturity; and since classrooms are collective settings, such diversity presents problems to teachers in carrying out their instructional tasks. One of the chronic problems of school organization is how to deal with diverse capacities (both in terms of instruction and the maintenance of order) in a situation which encourages treating people alike. The conventional ideological solution of "meeting individual differences" is plainly ridiculous because it denies the existence of a real dilemma, and to that extent cannot meet the demands of the situation. The current strategies of "grouping" (e.g., tracking, nongraded classes, and the like) simply deal with a fragment of the problem of heterogeneity. At the elementary level, teachers have experimented with loosely constituted and fluid ability groupings and with moderately adventurous attempts at nongraded classes spread over two and sometimes as many as three conventional grades. At the high school level, the more highly institutionalized and rigidly organized track system has emerged as the most common solution, one that has come under intense public and professional criticism because certain minority groups tend to cluster in both the upper and lower tracks so that the system looks suspiciously like a not-too-subtle form of discrimination. There is no question that ability-grouping and tracking are conspicuously vulnerable to such criticism and that they can be used more or less deliberately for discriminatory purposes; but their emergence has usually been an attempt to solve problems of an ecological nature, and no one yet has come up with a fool-proof solution. It is the nature of dilemmas that they defy easy resolution.

MODES OF AFFILIATION WITH SCHOOLS

People who hold jobs are said to be employed, but the term *employment* in its conventional meaning conceals *the different ways individuals attach themselves to organizations,* usually by exchanging effort for remuneration. This rough definition of employment covers a range of phenomena, but at its core it refers to engagement in work to earn a livelihood. At one extreme, novelists, poets, and composers of music are employed even though they are characteristically unconnected with organizations and depend for their remuneration not on any explicit arrangement of exchange but on the unguaranteed response of a consuming public; their case minimally falls within the definition. In common usage, however, employment refers to hiring by agreement to a labor contract between an employer, often an organization, and an employee who contributes his efforts in exchange for wages (or salaries) and fringe benefits. The contract sets both the amount of remuneration and the nature of the employee's duties and privileges. Between these extremes of examples lies a multitude of alternative arrangements, some involving no employer (in any strict sense), no formal contract (which is not to deny the existence of mutually recognized obligations), and no hiring (in the sense of work directly exchanged for pay, even though individuals both work and get paid).

Teachers are salaried employees; they agree, through a written (or unwritten but formal) contract with a school board, on what tasks they shall perform in exchange for pay. The employment of teachers follows the well-known guidelines of *hiring* as a means of affiliating individuals with an organization.

The meaning of hiring as an affiliative device becomes clear when compared to other devices prevailing in different occupations. In private medical practice, for example, the patient is not so much an employer as a client even though he pays for services. Even in hospital practice, physicians are not typically employees;

they affiliate themselves by means of hospital privileges, a device that frees them considerably from administrative pressures that might interfere with the medical aspects of patient care. Although physicians must adhere to general hospital policies, their decisions about patient care are governed more by technical considerations derived from the principles of medical practice, by occupation-wide standards of ethics, and by loyalty to and concern for patients.[11]

In law, men recently out of law school are generally hired in junior positions in law firms or take jobs as clerks for judges; their mode of employment closely resembles hiring. But as they advance in their careers, they can become "entrepreneurs" (solo practitioners), establish small partnerships, or rise in the larger firms as junior and senior partners; many, however, do remain hired employees. Partnership, however, is not a form of hiring but a collegial mode of affiliation in which associated lawyers use the common resources of the firm and draw their share of the firm's monetary intake according to the amount of the firm's resources they have used and to the amount of the firm's earnings they have attracted. The law firm, like the hospital, provides arrangements for members to serve client interests in a relatively independent manner without subjection to heavy administrative demands. Partnership is the affiliative analogue of privilege (among physicians) and hiring (among teachers); the architectural case resembles law with solo practitioners and small firms predominating.[12]

Academicians present a different affiliative pattern. In the smaller and weaker colleges their position resembles that of school teachers hired to teach. In large universities, as well as in strong liberal arts colleges, faculty work is divided in varying proportions between teaching and research. Strictly speaking, college instructors are hired employees; they are hired to teach but expected (not hired) to do research. Research institutes hire men to do research; but they are not universities (although there have been complaints within academia these days that universities are becoming research institutes). While academicians are not paid (on a contractual basis) to do research, they do it. In fact, it is widely acknowledged that advancement in academia depends in some inscrutable way on scholarly output. How, then, is the faculty member affiliated with his university? Partly by hiring (to teach) and partly by patronage (to do research), where patronage is an arrangement whereby an individual can follow independent scholarly pursuits (advancing knowledge, as the expression goes) without administrative pressures determining what he shall study and how, and without the demands that production schedules impose to produce something useful in the short run. The linkage between academic freedom and the affiliative device of patronage is not difficult to see.[13]

Hiring, after this excursion through other affiliative arrangements, has contrasting properties. To overdramatize its meaning somewhat, it belongs with those phenomena falling under the rubric of the proverb: he who pays the piper calls the tune. For teachers, affiliation by hiring means a special responsiveness to the expectations of school administrators who define what teachers shall do within broad or narrow limits, depending on the school system, the school, and the particular administrator in question. It carries the implication of dependency on superiors also characteristic of the neophyte members of most occupations. Further, it is the status of the hired employee that is both celebrated and defended by teachers' unions, a status that sets the occupation off from others whose work requires—or at least sometimes seems to require—a measure of independence (e.g., loyalty to a client, free inquiry, or whatever).

None of this discussion should imply that doctors, lawyers, architects, graduate engineers, accountants, and the like cannot ply their trades effectively and without encroachment as hired employees or as members of organizations having a strong administrative apparatus. Doctors do practice good medicine in the army, and lawyers practice good law. Similarly, though teachers are hired employees, the nature of their work and its organizational setting provide many opportunities for the exercise of free judgment and independent action. I do imply, however, that autonomous occupational activity requires some kind of protection from administrative action that impinges directly on its *substance*.

The fact that teachers and pupils are members of schools means that there are two affiliative problems to consider. I turn now to the problem of pupils. Pupils are conscripts but only in the sense that school attendance is legally mandatory up to a certain age. The school situation is distinct; the administrative apparatus of schools and school systems, at least in intent, exists in part to provide services for the benefit of pupils. Teachers, then, not pupils, represent the lowest level of educational *functionaries* in schools.[14] The affiliative status of pupils is that of conscript-clients, the direct beneficiaries whose presence justifies the existence of the organization (though not necessarily all of its bureaucratic pathologies).

One of the earliest items on the school's agenda in the primary grades is *establishing* the basis of affiliation. To state the issue differently, the earliest affiliation of pupils with the school constitutes a problem in motivation: getting them to like school enough to assure at least minimal willingness to do the work and follow the instructions of teachers.[15] The problem is complex and pertains most centrally to methods of teaching, a topic to be discussed later. Schools, then, have a two-fold problem of affiliation. Teachers are attached to the organization as hired employees—functionaries—and must develop some way of working out a resolution between the autonomous exercise of a craft and the administrative imperatives affecting them through the contractual obligations associated with hiring. Pupils, in contrast, are conscripted clients, not functionaries. Their affiliative position is such that teachers must exact individual and collective compliance (in the interest of maintaining order) while serving individual interests and problems.

AUTHORITY RELATIONS

Because teachers and pupils are affiliated with schools in different ways, it comes as no surprise that the characteristics of their respective relationships of authority should also differ. I treat authority relationships between school administrators (principals) and teachers, and those between teachers and pupils as distinct problems; both, however, represent central characteristics of the teachers' work and are determined in large part by the properties of the school.

Discussions of authority relationships between administrators and teachers—I am concerned here with administrators whose jurisdiction lies within schools and those based in the central office whose jurisdictions extend across schools—usually begin with statements about the desire of teachers for autonomy in their work. "Professionalism," according to Ronald Corwin, ". . . represents the efforts of a vocation *to gain full control* over its work and to enhance its social and economic position in the society in the process."[16] Neal Gross and Robert Herriott, arguing along the same lines, state that since teachers are professionals—and they speak specifically about elementary school teachers—"they . . . may interpret efforts of administrators to influence their performance as *invasions of professional prerogatives.*"[17] I shall say more about the tenability of these contentions later. For the present, the important point is that the so-called professional autonomy problem is one fragment of the larger question of authority relations between teachers and administrators.

I have treated questions of ecology and affiliation as issues distinct from authority; their implications for the exercise of administrative authority are that teachers work in separate classrooms and remain responsive or at least exposed to the pressing problems arising within them, and that certain administrative prerogatives—in principle if not always in practice—derive from the fact that teachers are affiliated by hiring rather than by other devices. But there are other authority problems.

First, the exercise of authority depends on the social composition of schools, particularly of the teaching staff, where the age, sex, and experience of both teachers and principals define in good measure the nature of the issues. According to the NEA, figures reported for 1965–1966 indicate that men represent 31.6 percent of all public school teachers, 14.8 percent of elementary and 53.6 percent of secondary school teachers.[18] The principalship, however, is a more male-dominated occupation.[19] It has long been part of the American folklore that men take orders from women superiors reluctantly, yet in elementary schools, by virtue of the distributions of men and women in teaching and administrative positions, a sizable contingent of men is subordinate to women. Even though the nature of the teacher's work is such that direct order-giving, common in occupations based on routine activities, is not predominant, women administrators still have much to say about male elementary teachers' prospects for advancement. Whether the folklore actually expresses the true state of things remains an open question. According to Caplow:

> the case records of every major investigation in industrial sociology contains a mass of relevant details [about the undesirability of men being subordinated to women]. Yet, it cannot be denied that the distribution of these attitudes in the population at large has never been directly checked.[20]

Caplow's assessment of the folklore is thus one of skepticism. Yet for various psychological reasons, strains are known to arise when men and women work together on certain jobs, and when women possess the authority to give men orders (whatever the basis of that authority). Schools, particularly at the elementary level, contain structural arrangements conducive to producing such strains.[21] Whether they take the form of resentment or apathy on the part of male teachers, of reticence or overbearing control on the part of women administrators, all these symptoms, not to mention others, have been observed.

Sex and age differences among teachers contribute to additional problems of authority. According to data collected in the National Principalship Study, 37.7 percent of male elementary principals are forty years of age or under; that is, the elementary principalship is a job frequently taken by young men. (Fifty-three percent of them are forty-five or under, while only 20.9 percent of women elementary principals are that young. In the secondary principalship, women are exceedingly few in number; and the proportion of young men declines at the higher school levels.) Among teachers, age is comparatively independent of level taught; but at the elementary level, 61.3 percent of the teachers are forty-five years of age or older and the overwhelming proportion of them are women.[22] In other words, many elementary schools put young men in positions of authority over older women, women who may greatly exceed their superiors in both knowledge about and experience in elementary schools. At the higher level schools, with older male principals predominating, the elementary school anomalies of authority appear less frequently.

It is important to remember that I am describing the situation in the larger urban school systems (those which educate most of the youth), but not necessarily the situation throughout the country. Yet one of the peculiarities of school organization, particularly at the elementary level, is that it contains authority situations widely regarded as unconventional, at least according to the prevailing folklore. Whatever the validity of that lore, there is something far more discomfiting about the relatively inexperienced having formal authority over those with greater experience even when the relationship between experience and competence is difficult to establish. Age and experience often serve as rough indices of competence even though one can be seriously misled by so construing them. However, schools are so composed that sometimes embarrassing, sometimes resentful, and sometimes indignant reactions arise from confrontations between the young and the old—both according to and in reverse from the conventional order.

Second, authority relations between principals and teachers center around a cluster of activities known as supervision, a concept whose vagueness and multiplicity of meanings almost defy definition. Where the connotations of the term *supervision* are considered too harsh, the vague euphemism *instructional leadership* takes its place. The principal's primary obligation is to effect system-wide policy in his school. Actually, systems vary in how freely a principal can direct the program of his school; but flexible policy is still policy. Similarly, the implications of alternative policies for directing the work of teachers depend in large measure on social constraints originating in the character of the teaching force: the experience of the staff, their morale, the principal's obligations to particular faculty members, the number of new teachers, pupil enrollment, and so on.

In terms of actual tasks, supervision involves getting teachers to act according to policy, however flexibly that policy is defined (i.e., informing teachers about what their duties are in terms of curriculum and method, determining whether they are doing their jobs properly, and helping them). Policy-making, surveillance, and help, then, comprise three basic components of the principal's supervisory responsibility; and while this array of tasks appears straightforward, it actually contains myriad problems and allows various approaches to their solution.

Most obvious among the problems is the absence of clear and standardized guidelines for judging teacher performance and the quality of the school's product. Readily observable and easily rated activities may have little or no defensible connection with such desired outcomes as pupil achievement. Principals, for reasons legitimate or illegitimate, are usually constrained to make fragmentary and infrequent observations of classroom activities which are seldom comprehensive enough to put observed classroom activities in their proper context or to provide adequate information for proper evaluation. And although rhetoric puts supervisory activities at the core of the principal's work, the manifold parts of their jobs, the unanticipated (and often unanticipatable) contingencies faced in the course of their daily work means that teachers must accept major responsibility for the events of the classroom, even for those beyond their effective control. The same conditions that frustrate principals as supervisors also make it difficult for them to help teachers; and obvious difficulties also arise when one person has primary responsibility for both evaluating and helping.

For my purposes, the characteristics of the principal's authority should be seen from the teachers' vantage point: they are seldom observed in the course of their work by persons who must judge it; they are expected to ask for help yet are enjoined to assume major responsibility for what occurs in the classroom; and their requests for help can easily be interpreted (or worse, misinterpreted) as incompetence. Moreover, their work, with its imprecise definition, may be viewed out of context. Given the peculiarities of teacher subordination, it is not surprising that remuneration follows seniority and the acquisition of academic credentials, both of which represent criteria unclearly related to the character of the work. They also account in good part for teachers' traditional opposition to merit pay; pay really only indirectly related to performance despite its rhetorical connotation. How does one reward merit in a job whose component tasks defy clear description?

Third, like most managers of large-scale organizations, principals have multiple obligations which, in the setting of the school, can easily become polarized into (1) those pertaining to the operation of the school as an administrative and productive unit, and

(2) those pertaining to the work of individual teachers. The former consist of many parts: responding to system-wide policies, directing the instructional program of the school, dealing with problems presented by parents both individually and collectively, and the like. These are obligations that can cause principals to give greater priority to the interests of the whole school than to those of particular teachers (of course, such problems of management are not peculiar to schools). Problems in the principal's exercise of authority originate more directly inside the school—from teachers. Foremost among the issues in his exercise of authority is the inchoate notion of professional autonomy among teachers. Although this question will be discussed in greater detail later, it is important to recognize here the sense in which classrooms are the private domains of teachers. The presence of managerial or supervisory personnel can immediately change the character of a classroom from a relatively private setting (from the perspective of those in it) to a public one; it is well known that private and public conduct may change radically even when there is nothing to hide. One frequently observed phenomenon in classrooms is pupils "protecting" a teacher when a supervisor appears, even pupils whose ordinary habit is giving teachers a "hard time." What the supervising principal sees is a favorably distorted picture of classroom events, a perspective that may work to the long-run detriment of the teacher whose problems may be real and easily remedied, if the principal has a fair look at them and benefits the teacher through his undistorted observations.

Once inside the classroom, what can the principal do? Become as inobtrusive as possible? Correct minor errors or violations of school procedure on the spot? Tell the teacher what and what not to do while the class is in session, or wait until some later time (perhaps so much later that the immediacy of the situation and its important details become lost)? The prescribed procedure for dealing with the situation is for the principal to make his observations and then communicate them to the teacher in privacy soon after the class and in a helpful way. Yet clearly, the whole procedure of classroom visitation for the purpose of supervision is fraught with ambiguities and places the teacher in a position of considerable vulnerability.[23]

Evaluation of Classroom Teachers. Although balancing the interests of teacher autonomy and administrative supervision admits of a viable solution, the situations in which principals exercise authority over teachers not only raise problems of delicacy in the relationships between people, but raise other difficulties as well.

According to an NEA study dealing with the evaluation of class-room teachers, the time available for "accurate evaluation" exists in short supply.

> Despite the differences in their schedules and in their as-signments to different size school systems, the principals in all groups came very close to the average of 55 percent who said they did *not* have enough time for accurate evalu-ation of classroom teachers.[24]

One can only speculate why over half of the principals surveyed report insufficient time, or whether the *amount* of time available is the critical consideration; but the NEA paints a gloomy picture based on teachers' reports of how much they were observed at their work. The data pertain to classroom visits of five minutes or more during the first half of the 1962–1963 academic year. Of all teachers surveyed, 27.1 percent (N = 1105) report *no* class-room visitations by any supervisor. Probationary teachers are visited more than continuing teachers, but almost one-fifth (18.6 percent) of the probationary teachers received on visits (32.8 per-cent of the continuing, or more experienced, teachers received no visits). Moreover, 51.4 percent of the probationary teachers received between one and three visits of five minutes or more during the semester, while of their continuing counterparts, 44.4 percent received visits. Of those visited, the median number of visitations was three for each group of teachers (not many, espe-cially for those new to the occupation.)[25]

The NEA also asked teachers to report on the last supervisory visitation received during the semester. The median length of that visit for probationary teachers was twenty-six minutes which, when multiplied by the median number of visits for the semester, gives a rough median estimate of a little over an hour of observa-tion (assuming all observations to be of similar duration) over a period of about 450 working hours. Again, this is not much ob-servational supervision for the teachers who need it most; and, as expected, the more experienced teachers receive even less super-vision. As to the outcome of those visits, 52.9 percent of the pro-bationary teachers report that the visit was followed by a confer-ence with the observer; 51.2 percent report that they were helped by the observation (and, presumably, its aftermath).[26] All of these figures decline when the whole year (rather than the semester) is taken into account, but they do not drop much.[27]

Not surprisingly, general dissatisfaction with teacher evalua-tion prevails. Among probationary teachers, only 11.1 percent express strong confidence in the system (14.8 percent of continuing teachers); and 46.1 percent of all teachers (the differences between probationary and other teachers are negligible) express either doubt or negative opinions about it.[28] Principals express greater confidence in the system than teachers (with the degree of confidence varying directly with the size of the school system); but even among principals in the largest systems, where confidence reaches its zenith, only 28.3 percent answer, "yes, certainly," to the question: "Does your present system of evaluation enable administrators to make a sound evaluation of a teacher's work?"[29]

Supervisory Authority. Fairly substantial evidence of the difficulties in the principal's exercise of supervisory authority apparently exists, then, especially where it involves classroom visitation; and according to the findings of the National Principalship Study of large urban school systems, the supervisory function lies at the core of the principal's job.

Anne Trask reports—and her observations are supported by interviews held as part of the National Principalship Study—that the supervisory aspects of authority are defined both in terms of activities and rhetoric.[30] Although principals, in describing what their jobs should be, indicate the importance of observing teachers directly through classroom visitation and discussing their observations with teachers shortly after, and of holding meetings with teachers in which classroom problems are discussed, advice is given (both solicited and unsolicited), and samples of pupils' work and their standardized test scores are checked, some include a wide range of activities under supervision which are exceedingly remote and trivial, such as the distribution of books and supplies. In sum, the various activities that pass for supervision look very much like attempts to resolve a dilemma consisting of the obligation to supervise by direct observation, the most essential component of supervision according to many if not most principals, and the manifest difficulties of actually doing so: the touchy problem of entering classrooms, of telling teachers what to do when their subject specialty gives them competence not shared by the principal, of acknowledging the sense in which a classroom is the teacher's private domain.

The situation is not too different from one that Smigel finds in large law firms and concerns a superior's confidence in the good judgment of his subordinates. According to Erwin Smigel:

> many lawyers used the words "good judgment" when trying to explain why their firm was effective. "Our men have good judgment." An analysis of their statements reveals that to be considered having good judgment, an associate

[a lawyer subordinate to a partner] must either have the ability to determine the idiosyncratic behavior of the partner he is working for or the ability correctly to interpret and codify the difficult rules. Partners prefer associates who can do both.[31]

The inability of a teacher to do the same thing puts the principal in a difficult position; hence, possibly creating the various strategies for handling the situation obliquely. The question of autonomy, then, is really a two-sided one consisting of the teacher's desire for command over his own bailiwick, keeping it free from intervention, but also including the principal's expectation that teachers will do the job on their own. The issue, moreover, is more one of internal school politics than of expertise. The skills of teaching are as undeveloped as those of organizational administration; hence, supervisory activities cannot readily be based on claims to superior expertness. Although considerations of technique are far from absent, the principal's problems often consist of gaining the cooperation of his teachers. This fact goes some way in explaining recent proposals for selecting principals through election by the tenured faculty, a technique that provides more evidence of teacher *support* for the principal than *recognition* of his expertness as a supervisor.

Training of New Teachers. A critical problem in running a school is the indoctrination and training of new teachers, one that on its face does not appear as a problem of authority at all. Yet, both Weber and Barnard, as well as other students of authority, have recognized the importance of a sense of duty, of voluntary cooperation (or of a range of synonymous phrases referring to the same thing), as essential to relationships of authority. Teaching, for a variety of reasons, is a high-turnover occupation; many of its members leave or plan to leave in the earliest years of their careers and must be replaced by newcomers who for the most part are inexperienced. Moreover, both their undergraduate and graduate preparation (including practice teaching) frequently leaves teachers unprepared for the rigors and sometimes overwhelming problems arising from their first classroom confrontation. Unlike medical training institutions, institutions that train teachers do not provide anything approaching a system of supervised apprenticeship; thus, many new teachers start their first job green—and then do it alone. According to an NEA survey of teacher opinion, between two-thirds and three-quarters of those responding claim that they were adequately prepared in their subject-matter fields (general education and developmental psychology), but 40.6 percent said they learned too little about teaching methods; 49.1 percent felt they had learned about the right amount.[32] The principal's job (and that of members of his administrative staff, if he has one) includes the task of making competent workers out of green recruits, teaching them not only "the ropes" of working in the school but also the skills of running a classroom and the massive problems sometimes accompanying that task.[33] Despite the existence of employment contracts that obligate teachers to perform their classroom duties, they can only do so if their capacities are sufficient to the tasks; and since one important component of authority is willing compliance, capacity to do the work becomes a critical issue. A willing worker is one who at least can cope with the demands of the job (although the converse of that statement is not necessarily true). Training the new and inexperienced teachers on the job, then, represents a particularly acute problem for the principal; for if he cannot successfully settle his newest recruits into their jobs so that the gratifications from the work—and teaching is not a high-paying occupation—outweigh the frustrations, he finds himself caught in a vicious circle of high turnover because the earliest years of a teaching career are critical in determining whether teachers will remain in the occupation.

In this situation the principal's role of helper and trainer becomes particularly important, especially if rates of turnover are high (which they can be for a variety of other reasons having nothing to do with the adequate inculcation of new recruits). The responsibility for this task falls largely upon the principal and competes in priority with other demands on his time and energy because the experienced teachers can only make a limited contribution to the development of their new colleagues.

Resources of Authority. Consider the principals' resources in their exercise of authority. As agents of the school board and its hierarchy of administrative employees, they are responsible for effecting policies and procedures laid down by superiors, a subordination that varies from school to school according to what power they have been able to carve out for themselves. Principals share only some of the prerogatives of industrial managers; they can seldom hire and fire, and in many systems they have little voice in selecting newly recruited teachers to work in their schools. They usually have the power to dismiss only nontenured teachers, at least in large urban systems where teacher tenure actually means something. Depending on the system, principals can sometimes arrange for the transfer of teachers out of their school and can apply negative sanctions by assigning them difficult classes or onerous clerical and custodial tasks. However, there are obvious weaknesses in these procedures, especially where teachers' unions are strong and where the particular teacher has a personal following among his colleagues.

On the more positive side, principals exercise power through the judicious use of praise and encouragement, and can reward by assigning desirable tasks; but these procedures, like their negative counterparts, contain self-limiting features such as accusations of favoritism. Principals are almost universally unable to provide financial rewards because salaries are determined by systemwide schedules, but they can use sponsorship as a means of helping individual teachers advance in their careers. In many systems, however, one often finds costs attached to such sponsorship, with teachers undertaking petty, onerous, and unpleasant assignments for the principal.

As noted earlier, teaching tasks are often difficult to reconcile with a rigorous chain of command (of the industrial type), given the difficulties of observational supervision. In short, the principal's resources of authority are relatively weak compared to those of managers in other types of organizations; and as Dan Lortie puts it succinctly: "organizational control over teachers is accomplished through selection-socialization and subtle mechanisms which refine bureaucratic rule."[34] He adds, and I think correctly, that the authority relationship between principal and teacher represents the last rung of a bureaucratic hierarchy in which the occupant of each position has the power to reduce the free options of those occupying positions immediately subordinate. It is not surprising, then, to find in schools the prevalent use of a rhetoric of school "philosophy" and "goals," terms that imply the near impossibility of precise definition, rather than a language of authority, control, and accountability. In fact, among school people one finds almost a preoccupation with avoiding terms like *authority* and *power* to describe relationships that are obviously part of a hierarchical system.

Teacher Autonomy. The old and complex issue of teacher autonomy and control (really two sides of the same coin) is couched in terms of the general problems of professional workers in bureaucracies and has received both ideological and empirical answers. On the ideological side, Mills has been a representative exponent of the position that the autonomy of professionals has gradually diminished with the growth and centralization of bureaucratic organizations during the first half of the twentieth century. Essentially the same position is taken by Robert K. Merton, in his well-known essay, "The Role of the Intellectual in Public Bureaucracy,"[35] where he argues that intellectuals (among whom he includes "specialists in the field of social, economic, and political knowledge"), especially the politically minded among them, become converted into technicians by virtue of their conditions of employment in public bureaucracies. His reasoning is grounded not so much in ideology as in classical Durkheimian theory: "In describing the process whereby the intellectual in a bureaucracy is converted into a technician, we proceed on the assumption that perspectives and outlook are largely a product of social position."[36] Although one must not attribute to him the view that publicly employed intellectuals inevitably turn into faceless cogs in a machine, Merton nevertheless argues that in the confrontation between the individual and the large-scale organization, the individual generally comes out the loser.

Since the publication of Merton's paper and Mills' *White Collar*, a number of investigators have directed their attention to the question of what happens when the intellectual and the professional become involved in bureaucratic life; the results turn out more complex than either of these earlier formulations had anticipated.

It is clear from Harold Wilensky's analysis of trade union intellectuals and professionals that one cannot speak simply of intellectuals or professionals but only of various types of them who respond differently according to the nature of the job they perform in the union, the structure of the union, and the way in which these men conceive of their jobs. [37] That is, men bring their own personal orientations to their work; their sentiments are not simply the products of organizational constraints. Wilensky states that:

> All of these . . . role-orientation types can be seen as directions toward which the mentality of the intellectual and staff experts who enter a social movement *develop. Some* orientations are appropriate to the demands of the movement *at a given stage of its growth;* others are not. Conflicts between the meanings the experts assign to their activity and the functions they fulfill *exert a strain toward change* in both person *and organization.*[38]

In a study that comes closer in content to the situation of teachers, Mary Goss discusses the supervision of physicians in hospitals. In discussing an occupation in which the norm of professional autonomy is highly developed and well defended, Goss discovered that the norm of autonomy:

> did not require, as is sometimes thought, that each phy-

sician be autonomous in every sphere of his activity, but only that he be free to make his own decisions in professional matters [those concerned primarily with the medical aspects of patient care] as opposed to administrative concerns. Nor, even in the professional sphere, did the norms rule out the possibility of supervision; so long as supervision came from a physician and took the form of advice, it was within normatively acceptable bounds for physicians.[39]

Finally, Donald Pelz, in his investigation of medical research men (not practicing physicians) working for a government agency, reports that:

performance [among junior level men] is highest when independence from the chief *is combined* with frequent contact with him—when the individual has frequent contact with the chief, but also has considerable voice in the final decisions.[40]

His findings suggest that productive research activity hinges upon independence and autonomy but in a context where the chief provides both support and guidelines, and that is different from *laissez faire* autonomy, where men are left alone.

The autonomy of teachers is complex and not adequately summarized by the statement of Gross and Herriott, cited earlier in this chapter.[41] Ideologically speaking, most professional occupations defend the right of their members to exercise technical judgments free from lay and administrative interference; their claims to professionalism are based primarily on their members' possessing an esoteric expertise (though the claim either to professionalism or to expertise is not always acknowledged by the public). Ideology aside, what is the situation with teachers and principals? Here, some previously unreported data of the National Principalship Study shed interesting light.

The description of how these data were collected has been described elsewhere in detail,[42] and it would not benefit this discussion to review it other than to say that they were gathered by the methods of survey research from teachers, principals, and central office administrators in forty-one urban public school systems in cities with a population of fifty thousand or over. Answers to questions were obtained through a forced multiple-choice format in which school personnel at various echelons checked statements about what *principals* should do in various aspects of their jobs. Table 3.1 summarizes the content of the questions, to whom they were asked, the response alternatives, and the findings.

TABLE 3.1 *Teacher, Principal, and Administrator Sentiments Concerning the Principal's Supervisory Activities, by School Level*

Questions

Principals: What obligation do you feel as principal of your school to do the following activities?

Teachers: Do you feel the principal of your school should engage in the following activities?

Higher Administrators: What obligation do you feel the principals under your jurisdiction have to do the following activities?

Response Alternatives:

1 Absolutely Must and Preferably Should (AM, PS)
2 May or May Not (MMN)[a]
3 Preferably Should Not and Absolutely Must Not (PSN, AMN)

	Percent Responding					
	Teachers			**Totals**		
	Elem.	*JHS*	*SHS*	*Prin.*	*Tchr.*	*H.A.*

1. Require that teachers discuss their major classroom problems with the principal.

	Elem.	*JHS*	*SHS*	*Prin.*	*Tchr.*	*H.A.*
AM, PS	69.4	57.0	50.4	68.2	60.0	75.6
MMN	24.3	32.3	35.5	23.9	30.1	20.5
PSN, AMN	6.2	10.6	14.1	7.8	9.9	3.9
Mean[b]	2.17	2.41	2.56	2.24	2.36	2.01
S.D.	0.85	0.91	0.95	0.85	0.91	0.80
Number	1340	971	1010	497	3321	127

2. Ask teachers to report all major conferences with parents to the principal.

	Elem.	*JHS*	*SHS*	*Prin.*	*Tchr.*	*H.A.*
AM, PS	69.7	53.3	46.4	54.1	56.7	55.1
MMN	24.0	31.8	37.2	35.4	30.3	33.1
PSN, AMN	9.1	14.9	17.4	10.5	13.0	11.8
Mean	2.19	2.47	2.60	2.44	2.40	2.41
S.D.	0.95	0.99	0.97	0.90	0.98	0.95
Number	1339	966	996	494	3301	127

[a]The "May or May Not" response category presents problems of interpretation. The respondent who checks it may be expressing a middle position among the alternatives, or may use that category to say, in effect, that his answer depends on certain conditions not expressed in the statement. A large MMN response on a given question, then, tends to "pull" the mean toward the middle category, a fact that may tend to diminish the differences between groups of respondents.
[b]The summary statistics, mean, standard deviation, were calculated from the raw data, not from the groupings shown in the table.

Percent Responding

	Teachers			Totals		
	Elem.	*JHS*	*SHS*	*Prin.*	*Tchr.*	*H.A.*

3. Require teachers to keep the principal informed of "problem" children in their classrooms.

AM, PS	76.1	65.9	54.7	62.6	66.7	75.8
MMN	20.8	28.3	34.8	29.0	27.2	21.9
PSN, AMN	3.1	5.8	11.1	8.5	6.1	2.3
Mean	2.04	2.21	2.44	2.31	2.21	2.09
S.D.	0.76	0.84	0.88	0.89	0.84	0.70
Number	1342	960	995	494	3297	128

4. Closely direct the work of teachers who are likely to experience difficulty.

AM, PS	85.7	81.6	76.1	87.3	81.6	93.0
MMN	11.6	12.4	18.5	10.9	13.9	6.2
PSN, AMN	2.6	5.9	5.5	7.8	4.5	0.8
Mean	1.86	1.93	2.05	1.75	1.94	1.56
S.D.	0.74	0.83	0.83	0.72	0.80	0.65
Number	1336	974	1012	497	3322	128

5. Require that teachers' classroom behavior conform to the principal's standards.

AM, PS	54.9	57.1	55.9	54.6	55.9	51.2
MMN	26.3	25.6	26.4	34.7	26.1	26.0
PSN, AMN	14.7	17.3	17.8	10.6	18.0	22.8
Mean	2.50	2.45	2.49	2.47	2.48	2.65
S.D.	1.07	1.08	1.04	0.90	1.06	1.08
Number	1331	965	1015	498	3311	127

6. Check to see that teachers prepare written lesson plans.

AM, PS	37.2	35.4	24.2	53.3	32.7	55.5
MMN	37.9	40.8	41.3	36.4	39.8	38.1
PSN, AMN	24.8	23.8	34.5	10.2	27.6	6.4
Mean	2.83	2.84	3.15	2.41	2.93	2.29
S.D.	1.01	1.01	0.99	0.93	1.01	0.90
Number	1326	971	1003	497	3300	126

Percent Responding

	Teachers			Totals		
	Elem.	*JHS*	*SHS*	*Prin.*	*Tchr.*	*H.A.*

7. Know what is taking place in most classrooms during most of the day.

	Elem.	*JHS*	*SHS*	*Prin.*	*Tchr.*	*H.A.*
AM, PS	76.5	70.8	66.9	66.9	71.9	62.6
MMN	19.4	24.1	26.8	26.1	23.0	34.2
PSN, AMN	4.2	5.1	6.2	6.8	5.2	3.2
Mean	2.06	2.15	2.24	2.28	2.14	2.30
S.D.	0.80	0.83	0.83	0.82	0.82	0.70
Number	1335	968	1009	495	3312	123

8. Closely supervise new teachers in the school.

AM, PS	87.3	87.8	85.4	70.4	86.8	97.7
MMN	9.6	8.7	11.9	2.8	10.1	1.6
PSN, AMN	3.1	3.5	2.7	0.2	3.1	0.8
Mean	1.74	1.73	1.78	1.33	1.75	1.30
S.D.	0.75	0.78	0.76	0.54	0.76	0.54
Number	1338	974	1013	500	3325	128

9. Visit classes on a regular schedule to determine how well teachers are carrying out their jobs.

AM, PS	48.1	55.5	51.9	62.3	51.3	67.2
MMN	32.3	27.8	31.5	24.0	30.8	25.8
PSN, AMN	19.6	16.8	16.6	13.6	17.9	7.0
Mean	2.61	2.45	2.54	2.36	2.54	2.16
S.D.	1.04	1.02	0.98	0.98	1.02	0.90
Number	1342	975	1018	499	3335	128

10. Limit supervisory activities primarily to those teachers with classroom problems.

AM, PS	28.1	25.9	27.0	11.9	27.1	6.3
MMN	24.0	21.9	23.8	16.4	23.4	7.0
PSN, AMN	47.9	52.1	49.2	71.7	49.5	86.7
Mean	3.28	3.37	3.32	3.87	3.32	4.15
S.D.	1.06	1.09	1.07	1.04	1.07	0.86
Number	1318	963	1011	495	3292	128

What does it indicate about teacher autonomy? In oversimplified terms, teachers tend to be somewhat negatively disposed to autonomy (given the range of sentiment implicit in the questions). That is, teachers *favor* (more than they oppose) principals' efforts to maintain control and surveillance over teachers' activities, a finding that in general terms contradicts the folklore of professional autonomy (at least for this particular occupation). A closer examination of Table 3.1 will clarify this finding.

First, in eight of the ten questions, over 50 percent of all teachers (disregarding school level for the moment) acknowledge that principals *should* exercise the various kinds of control expressed in the questions. (In one of the two exceptional cases, Question 10, almost half, 49.5 percent, favor control over their own activities.) Opposition to the principals' supervisory activities never exceeds 27.6 percent, and on five items it does not exceed 10.0 percent. The outstanding exception to this generalization is Question 6 (the inspection of written lesson plans), an extremely close form of supervision that teachers frequently resent.[43] And although teacher support for such close surveillance drops to 32.7 percent, the proportion in favor still exceeds the 27.6 percent opposed. Questions 4 and 8 draw overwhelming support for obvious reasons. There is widespread acknowledgment throughout school systems that new and inexperienced teachers and those having trouble need close supervision. But for teachers to expect the principal to know what is going on in most classrooms most of the day (Question 7) implies a kind of omnipresence that almost denies privacy (unless, of course, the teachers answering the question attribute an almost trivial meaning to it—that math is taught in math classes, for example). The solidity of teacher support for their own supervision is undeniably arresting.

Second, does the evidence support the proposition that administrative supervision is inversely related to professionalism based on specialized expertise? Here the relevant data are not the aggregated teacher responses, but those responses distinguished by school level. On the basis of formal educational preparation, a case can be made for the proposition that secondary teachers are more professional than their elementary-school counterparts. The NEA, for example, reports that 12.1 percent of elementary teachers in its sample hold no college degree while only 1.6 percent of secondary teachers do not. Both levels of teachers hold bachelor's degrees in almost identical proportions (elementary: 62.2 percent; secondary: 61.6 percent); but secondary teachers hold master's degrees, the hallmark of specialization in teaching, more than twice as frequently as elementary (35.4 percent and 13.9 percent, respectively). The proportion holding doctorates is negligible.[44] The same argument can be made on the basis of subject-matter specialization, particularly in terms of the teacher's expertise compared to that of the principal. Secondary teachers, and particularly those in high schools, characteristically have a subject-matter mastery, requiring graduate training, that exceeds the principal's knowledge of the subject. At the elementary level, teachers and principals have similar knowledge and skills primarily because elementary schools are not departmentalized by subject.

Despite the logic of arguments based on training and subject specialization, the data indicate a weak inverse relationship between sentiments toward supervision and school level. When mean scores (rather than percentages) are taken as measures of teacher sentiment, in seven of ten items high school teachers show greater opposition than teachers at the other two levels (Questions 1, 2, 3, 4, 6, 7, and 8). However, the difference in mean scores between high school teachers and whatever other group happens to be lowest on those seven items is very small, ranging from .18 to .41, and in no case amounts to more than one-half the magnitude of a score representing the "width" of one category (1.00). Thus, even though senior high school teachers express greater opposition to supervision (expect more autonomy on the job) than their junior high school and elementary school counterparts, they express very little more. Among senior high school teachers, favorable sentiment toward supervision falls below 50 percent on only three questions (2, 6, and 10).[45] Clearly, these figures present no clear-cut picture of teachers' desire for autonomy (for exemption from administrative supervision), and although the findings support the expected inverse relationship between professional specialization (as indicated by level taught) and the desire for autonomy, the relationship is weak and occurs in the context of generally favorable sentiments toward supervision.

Some caution must be exercised in interpreting these findings. They can only be understood in terms of the specific content of the questions asked. True, they covered a variety of supervisory situations, but not a very broad selection; and clearly the questions were not entirely free from ambiguity. Also, the questions as framed took the commonly prevailing supervisory arrangements in schools for granted; that is, school administrators do the supervising when it is done. Teachers, in other words, were not given the opportunity to entertain the idea that supervision might well be or become a collegial function; hence, the responses were in part an artifact of the questions asked. But with these qualifications, teachers generally appear to want administrative supervision, under existing arrangements, for any number of possible reasons: that the job's insecurities give rise to a need for help, that teachers are dependent on their superiors for sponsorship and promotion, that they simply enjoy adult contact as relief from their near-constant involvement with pupils, and the like.

Finally, how do teachers' sentiments about autonomy compare with those of their administrative superiors (principals and those based in the central office of the school system)? Since administrators have responsibilities broader in scope than teachers—principals being charged with the operation of schools, and school-wide administrators with the management of several schools—and since they are both dependent on teachers for the successful performance of *their* tasks, one would expect them to favor reducing teacher autonomy (though the exercise of the principals' supervision), more than teachers would. In general, the findings in Table 3.1 support this contention, but not dramatically. On Questions 1, 4, 6, 8, 9, and 10, teachers want more autonomy than their administrative superiors think they should have. There is practically no difference among echelons on Question 2; and on Questions 3, 5, and 7, teachers are just as favorable to supervision (or more so) than at least one echelon of superiors. Among the six items on which teachers express greater opposition to supervision than their superiors, differences in means range from .35 to .83, the latter figure representing a difference approaching the magnitude of one response category.

These data provide no clear support for any general conflict of interest between teachers and administrators on the issue of autonomy (which is not to deny the existence of important cleavages on other issues). In comparing the absolute value of mean differences between teachers and administrators who have the closest score on any item, and the mean differences between the two echelons of superiors (principals and higher administrators), the following pattern emerges:

(1) On four questions (6, 7, 8, and 10), the differences between teachers and administrators with the closest score are larger than the differences between principals and system-wide administrators; that is, only on these four items can one speak of an "administrative position" that differs from the position of teachers, and oddly, on Question 7 teachers express sentiments more in opposition to their own autonomy than do their superiors. Thus, on only three of these four items can one speak of an administrative position *opposed to* teacher autonomy.

(2) On three questions (1, 3, and 5), there is a greater difference between principals and system-wide administrators than there is between teachers and the administrative echelon closest to them in mean score, an indication of greater cleavage *between* admin-

istrators than between at least one administrative echelon and teachers. (3) On three questions (2, 4, and 9), there is virtual agreement across the board. Thus, whatever the issues that teachers and administrators disagree on, and there are plenty of them, teacher autonomy is not one.

These findings—and some may find them surprising—do not lend themselves to easy mobilization by teacher interest groups to find support or lack of it for cherished ideological positions. As they stand, providing only broad comparisons among echelons in the school-system hierarchy and among levels of teachers, they do not necessarily support the contention that the interests of teachers and administrators are similar; neither, of course, do they lead to the opposite conclusion. In fact, the summary measures of sentiment (mean scores) indicate the existence of patterned sentiments, but not an interpretation of them; the interpretive question remains open.

Perhaps the questions themselves do not tap the most important elements of the hierarchical situation. Each group of respondents may interpret the questions differently so that they do not all speak to the same phenomenon. Important divisions of opinion may exist within echelons so that internal divergencies cancel each other out. These possibilities all emerge from the measurement and comparison of sentiments in different groups of respondents. It is also possible that forces operating within the school systems militate in favor of similarity in outlook: administrators were once teachers and may continue to hold teachers' sentiments after they have moved into a different job. Perhaps teachers believe that advancement in their careers depends on their adherence to the viewpoint of administrators on whom they must depend for promotion. Or teachers may find the rigors of the job so great that they welcome almost any form of administrative involvement up to the point where it becomes seriously oppressive.

Teacher-Parent Relations. Parents, as taxpayers, as members of organized groups (like PTA's), and as holders of an ideology encouraging participation in school affairs, should be considered part of the authority structure of schools (since schools are agencies of local government). Recent trends, especially in ghetto areas of the large cities, provide additional justification for this formulation since organized parent groups have penetrated more deeply than ever into the policy-making functions of school organization. In the past, parent involvement has included primarily paying taxes, participating in PTA meetings, and raising issues with teachers and administrators about their own children. These actions have represented the customary forms of parental involvement; less legitimate forms of parental influence, of course, have also been part of American school history.[46] Parental involvement in school governance, however, is relatively new, and although it derives in part from the desire to promote special interests (from those groups, primarily, who have received less than their share of educational goods in the past), its growth has also included pressures for its legitimation as a proper source of influence. One of the peculiarities of schools (unlike other organizations such as stores, law firms, insurance companies, and industrial establishments) is that the organization's clients must be included in any reasonably complete discussion of authority; that is, the exercise of authority in schools is not solely an internal matter.

In recent years, a trend of bringing parents into the classroom in quasi-instructional capacities has emerged, a trend with potential dangers. A layman in a classroom, working at tasks that usually fall within the professional jurisdiction of teachers, can pose a threat originating from several sources. First, a possible threat to a teacher's status may arise from the question: if a layman can do the job, wherein lies the teacher's *special* competence? The teacher need not be threatened, however, if he establishes control over those classroom activities most centrally related to the core tasks of the job and delegates to para-professional parents the noncritical and burdensome tasks (such as certain clerical chores).

The threat deriving from overlapping jurisdictions may prove more serious. Here the issue is not relative competence and invidious status comparison; it is: who controls the division of labor within the classroom? The experience of certain Massachusetts school systems with "contract correcting" provides a case in point:

> The contract correcting program . . . was designed to utilize the services of women . . . as *assistants* to teachers of English in composition. They were the lay readers who *worked for teachers* by doing the routine tasks of evaluating student prose.[47]

Scattered throughout the report are references to the teachers' need to maintain control over the program—to make clear (presumably with civility) who is boss, what constitutes an encroachment on the teacher's prerogatives, and when the pupil's personal relationship with the corrector is proving detrimental to the teacher. Although these jurisdictional boundaries appear easy to demarcate in principle, they are difficult to maintain in practice, particularly where the lines are obscured by questions of personal preference that lend themselves to easy misinterpretation by both teachers and correctors. There is also the question of "errors at work," an issue that Everett Hughes has discussed with great perception.[48] He indicates that workers in most occupations do not like to be watched by their clients. Workers in all occupations make errors, but they also correct them in characteristic ways easily misinterpreted by uninitiated members of the public. Although errors can appear damaging and the methods of correcting them nefarious, appearances do not necessarily coincide with realities, and most practitioners of crafts prefer the luxury of privacy in both making and correcting mistakes. Parents in the classroom, even when defined as helpers, leave the teacher exposed to the purview of laymen even though the laymen in the contract correcting case are engaged in a similar enterprise. What looks bad to a layman, when the event is taken out of context, may indeed represent highly defensible practice. Thus, several issues combine to arouse the opposition of teachers to procedures that allow too deep a penetration of laymen into the major work of the school.

Teacher-Student Relations. The concept of bureaucracy (a clear demarcation of offices hierarchically arranged, contractual provisions for salaried employment, orders issued by superiors, and the obligation of subordinates to follow them) provides rough guidelines for understanding relations of authority within school systems if it is applied to those segments of school hierarchies that include the administrative component and the workers engaged in the main activities of instruction—teachers. The school picture does not correspond at all points to the classic formulation of Max Weber (based largely on his observations of the German industrial, military, and civil-service establishments), yet one will not go disastrously wrong in applying—with caution—this model to the appropriate segments of school systems. But as a scheme for describing authority relations in the *classroom*—the area where teachers and pupils come together for instructional purposes—the distortions outweigh the parallels; for what the bureaucratic model takes for granted, the classroom makes problematic.

Classrooms have several properties that distinguish them from the bureaucratic segments of schools and school systems.[49] First, they are aggregates in which the teacher faces the members collectively as well as individually. This puts the teacher in a position not really analogous to that of the principal who also occupies a superior position over a group of individuals. Seldom does he confront his teachers collectively; rather, he presides over them as they perform their duties in substantial isolation from each other. The teacher's work consists more of the management of a mass than of the coordination of individuals performing tasks separately. Second, the teacher's charges are not employees bound to the organization by contractual agreement; they are conscripted clients whose allegiance must be won by a subtle combination of good will, coercion, persuasion, control, and command over curricular materials and techniques of instruction. In the coarsest terms an incompetent teacher can be fired (though with great difficulty, given genuine rules of tenure and/or a strong union), while an incompetent pupil cannot; the pupil is legally bound to attend school. This is not to suggest that all pupils chafe at the mandatory nature of school and would rather be elsewhere; rather, the situation makes it incumbent upon the teacher to deal with pupils whatever the number or proportion who resent attending, and to do so without the prop that a written contract provides.

Finally, schools differ according to level; and in addition to the various organizational properties that vary with school level, there are concomitant variations in the characteristics of the student body related to age, social background, personal characteristics, and future educational and occupational prospects that affect the character of authority relationships between pupils and teachers. The affiliation of pupils to the school is different, therefore, from that of any other class of school membership; it is different not only because they occupy a client status, but also in the closeness and intensity of their relationship to those in immediate positions of authority. None of these peculiar characteristics of the pupil-teacher relationship fits the traditional bureaucratic model of authority.

Although definitions of authority abound in the literature and are distinguished from each other by subtleties of meaning and variations in emphasis,[50] there is a central core of meaning that usually pertains to how persons, without resorting to direct coercion, control the conduct of others. To understand the exercise of authority in a given situation, one must take into account hierarchical arrangements, principles of legitimacy, the applicability of rules, subordinates' sense of duty and obligation, and the availability of sanctions and their use both by superiors and subordinates. The case of the classroom poses special problems.

Little is known about how to affect the conduct of people assembled *en masse;* ask any clergyman. Yet in the workaday world of the classroom, this is what the teacher must do. He must present a program of instruction seeing to it that the pupils absorb an acceptable minimum of the material, and he must maintain reasonable order among them. Although this may not appear too formidable a task, prevailing conditions make it a particularly demanding one. First, classrooms are usually composed of individuals whose interests and capacities differ—sometimes widely—and the teacher must make some effort to cope with the variety in a collective setting; that is, he cannot adopt the posture of the physician, the lawyer, or the architect who deal with each client case by case, free of the influence of other clients. Second, he has a double responsibility: to the classroom as a whole (a problem in management), and to each individual in it ("meeting the needs of individual pupils," to use the prevailing cliché). This responsibility presents a dilemma with no easy solution; for what is good for the members of a classroom considered collectively may prove damaging to the interests and needs of individuals within it. Particularly where matters of discipline and grading are concerned, doing right by an individual may pose problems of equity for others and for the class as a whole. Does the teacher, for example, make the punishment fit the crime (at the risk of hurting the individual who commits it), or does he adhere to standards of discipline that apply across the board so that pupils will consider his treatment of them as fair? Similarly, does he assign a high grade to the poor work of a weak pupil who has made a tremendous effort to give him encouragement, or does he grade according to general standards, letting the chips fall where they may, even if doing so results in the continuing deterioration of that pupil's attitude toward school and toward his work? Obviously, there are no clear answers since the dilemmas are built into the collective setting and are aggravated by the fact that the classroom is a public place and events occurring in it are highly visible to its members.

Although schoolmen prefer not to regard their work in terms of power and discipline, these terms apply appropriately. (The old argument that discipline problems disappear when teachers appeal to the real interests of pupils crumbles when one realizes that pupils have many interests that schools cannot cater to, and that they may not be interested in the activities that schools make available to them.) It becomes relevant, then, to consider what resources teachers realistically have at their disposal and how they use them to establish and maintain order, because part of the teacher's job is to create an environment in which learning can take place. Although it is difficult to state precisely what the appropriate conditions are, it is reasonable to assume that chaos is not one of them.

Rewards and punishments are two such resources, but which acts are actually rewarding and punishing is far from obvious. The conventional wisdom has it that grades for work completed are staples of the teacher's trade; but where do they derive their sanctioning quality, especially for the youngest pupils whose previous experience has been limited largely to the household and its immediate environs where performance is not characteristically sanctioned by symbols applied continuously and systematically to specifically defined tasks? Many pupils undoubtedly begin school receptive to the achievement-grading system based on their earlier experiences in the family, but such receptivity cannot always be taken for granted. Thus, in the earliest grades a critical part of the teacher's task is to instill in pupils a willingness to accept the rules of a regime—really, to establish the regime—based on grades as rewards and punishments for achievement on assigned tasks, a regime that in many cases represents a marked departure from that of the family. The teacher, moreover, must transform otherwise neutral symbols (grades) into sanctions in the eyes of his pupils; make rewards rewarding and punishments punishing so that pupils acknowledge and feel their effects. Only when this transformation has occurred—and there is reason to believe that in many cases it does not—can a teacher of older pupils take the efficacy of grading for granted. More simply stated: if a pupil does not care about grades or even considers good grades something to be ashamed of, he will neither regard high grades as rewarding nor regard low grades as an impetus to do better work.

Grades customarily apply to the instructional activities of the classroom; their use as sanctions for pupils' conduct in nonacademic areas is problematic. Should a pupil, for example, who does excellent work academically receive low grades if his conduct disturbs other members of the class? Should sanctions other than grades be used when the conduct in question falls outside the academic area; and if so, what other resources does the teacher have at his disposal? Here the issue is not the encouragement of academic performance but the maintenance of order. Corporal punishment is legally proscribed in many school systems (even though the proscription may be honored in the breach); but whether permitted or not, does the teacher's use of corporal punishment solve the problem presented by the disruption of the classroom or the violation of rules? Teachers can reprimand, publicly or privately; send pupils to the principal's office; call in the parents; or resort to a variety of other remedies all designed to keep order. In all cases, however, appropriateness, equity, and efficacy are as important as short-run effectiveness; the teacher, in exercising authority, must deal with both the individual and collective aspects of the problem (which do not necessarily lend themselves to solution by the same course of action), take into account the phenomenon of diminishing returns (i.e., whether the same punishment meted out on successive occasions does not lose its efficacy), and remain aware of the actual potency of his actions—in short, take stock of his actual position of power within the classroom. A major component of the teacher's exercise of authority concerns his success in winning the voluntary allegiance of the pupils to the school and to himself; that is, successfully establishing good will among them.

The physician, the lawyer, and the architect all have more vulnerable clients than the teacher; often, in fact, the teacher is more vulnerable than his assembled clients. In part, the professional's position of power *vis-à-vis* his clients is determined by the efficacy of the technology available to him (the topic of the following chapter), and by his control over sanctions. A physician may literally be able to tell his recalcitrant patient: "It's your funeral"; a lawyer can convince his client to reveal to him the incriminating parts of his conduct so that he can prepare a stronger defense. In both cases, part of the practitioner's resources is his ability to control or predict the likely future course of events that may crucially affect the client's welfare (this in addition to the technical skills he has mastered as part of his craft).

In comparison, the teacher faces his clients in a far weaker position. He lacks the highly developed technology, he cannot reliably predict whether future events will be sanctioning nor can he control their occurrence, and he must therefore fall back upon resources of a highly personal kind such as "personality," charisma, and reputation, which are difficult to define and to master as reliable skills of the trade. In many respects, then, the teacher's position of authority in the classroom is weak; he must rely on personal skills and capacities most difficult to define (and hence difficult to build into a program of job preparation), and must sustain close personal contact with his clients over an extended period of time (more so in the elementary than in the secondary grades), a situation that tends to preserve the consequences of errors throughout a school year.

The authority relations between teachers and pupils in classrooms, then, are largely nonbureaucratic in character (which is not to deny the existence of bureaucratic elements in classrooms), for reasons having many origins, not least of which is the great potentiality that classrooms provide for the unexpected, nonroutine events that so typify groups of young people gathered collectively.

•

CHAPTER FOUR

The Technology of Teaching

•

In one perceptive analysis of teaching, Bryan Wilson points to the "living process in which the establishment of rapport, the impact of personality, are necessary to the stirring of the imagination and the awakening of enthusiasm involved in the learning process."[1] Although this statement sounds suspiciously like some of the woolly-headed and sentimental descriptions of teaching, the important and somewhat jarring point is that it comes up in a discussion of occupational technology, technology being a term with meaning and connotations very different from the key words in the statement: rapport, personality, imagination, enthusiasm. But the juxtaposition raises the central issue: technologies, in common usage, refer to specific linkages between ends and means for the accomplishment of tasks.

THE PROBLEM OF DEFINITION

Common usage, unfortunately, gets in the way of understanding what technology means in a discussion of teaching. In recent years the term come to summon up images of teaching machines, language laboratories, and computer-assisted instruction, that is, the newly fashioned hardware of teaching. For this reason, I have so far defined technology in the broadest terms—linkages between means and ends—without identifying particular means, ends, or linkages. It is most important at this point to establish the idea that technology pertains to the means of getting a job done, whatever the means and the job happen to be. Hence, we should not equate technology with hardware, nor exclude hardware from the definition of technology, for the latter is a very general concept.

If Wilson is correct, and I think he is, teaching activities consist in part of spontaneous, diffuse, and ill-defined elements—the very antithesis of what technology is commonly taken to mean; yet one can argue that these activities constitute important aspects of teaching technology, and herein lies one of the critical problems of the occupation. "Diffuse roles," like that of the teacher, "are likely to embody internal role-conflicts because of the absence of clear lines of demarcation whereby the role-player knows when he has 'done his job.'"[2] The technological difficulties found in teaching are not limited to that particular occupation but are found more widely in lines of work whose central activities involve providing a service to persons treated in their psychological entirety: social work, certain aspects of nursing, and both psychiatry and pediatrics among the medical specialties.

Lortie has described this characteristic of the work as "the relative indivisibility of the teacher's tasks."[3] Richard Simpson and Ida Simpson make much the same point in stating that "the main intrinsic appeal of the semi-professions [among which teaching, they maintain, is one] is to the heart, not the mind."[4] This is not to argue that teaching is mindless or devoid of activities in which means can be related to ends in achieving some specific outcome, but that compared to other occupations the linkages are hazy and difficult to define; nor is it to argue that the constituent activities of the occupation cannot be rationalized in a technological sense. To the present, however, such technological development has not taken place to any marked extent, and it is with the present state of the occupation that I am concerned.

In addition to the fact that teaching activities lend themselves to description in a language of diffuse terms—rapport, inspiration, respect for individual differences, and the like—there is also an educational rhetoric that emphasizes the softness of the prevailing technology and places only loose boundaries around the core elements of the work, in contrast to other occupations in which distinguishing characteristics and boundaries are more prominent. Thus, one speaks of *philosophies* and *traditions* of education, and the *art* of teaching, all terms that emphasize the difficulty of defining precisely what teachers do at work. It is as much an error to underestimate the technological competence of teachers as it is to overestimate that of physicians. Although occupations vary in their state of technological development, there is a substantial amount of flying by the seat of the pants in all of them. Involved here, in addition to the precise definition of activities, is the degree to which the theoretical bases of occupational action have been codified; and in teaching, codification has not proceeded very far (for reasons to be discussed later).

Teachers, along with those engaged in a variety of other occupations, professional and otherwise, are primarily concerned with providing a service, the nature of which is more to help persons than to provide a specific service directed to some clearly definable problem that people present for solution. The contrast between the two types of service is clearly found in nursing, where parts of the job consist of performing specific medical procedures (such as administering medication or assisting with a surgical procedure), and where other more nebulous parts involve expressing the various emotions of caring.

TECHNOLOGY AND STRUCTURE

Many observers have noted the connection between occupational technology and the structural characteristics of organizations. Foremost among these characteristics are those of bureaucracy, particularly the extent to which work is governed by explicit rules.[5] Both the technical and popular literature on school organization provides reasonably convincing if not rigorous evidence for the prevalence of rules in the operation of schools. At the same time, the proposition that schools are rule-dominated organizations must be taken with caution. School boards and school administrators have been known to restrict the conduct of teachers with a proliferation of rules ranging all the way from minute curricular prescriptions to restrictions on teachers' social activities outside of school; similarly, the conduct of pupils is often hedged about with rules regulating proper decorum, dress, passage through hallways, smoking, and so on.

Despite variations in the pervasiveness of rules from school to school, it is important to distinguish between rules that apply to members of the school at large and those that apply within the classroom where most of the work of the school takes place. With the exception of curriculum content, syllabus, and textbook use, instructional activities as well as those concerned primarily with maintaining order within the classroom tend to be governed not by rules but rather by the personal resources of teachers, teaching lore, and personal strategies for running classrooms. The teacher's task, then, is to *create* a set of beliefs:

> The teacher gives directions and the pupils follow them. . . . [T]he development of this belief system [in one classroom situation] seemed to capitalize on several aspects: (1) the requests themselves were individually quite *insignificant;* (2) they dealt mostly with activities in which teachers are expected to be involved; (3) they were *asked of everyone;* consequently to refuse would be to cast oneself in a special light; (4) the situations were *cloaked with individual attention, warmth, and humor.*[6]

I have emphasized the phrases that reveal one teacher's personal style of establishing classroom order; obviously, there are alternatives, and just as obviously his conduct is concerned more with rule creation than with following rules already in force.

There is no denying the prevalence of fairly standard procedures for coping with specific classroom situations. The fact that teachers work in relative privacy from each other and from administrators frees them considerably from the constraints of rules and standards that apply in principle to everyone, but at the same time isolates them from the sources of a craft tradition most likely to emanate from contact with colleagues. (One can also argue that it is this isolation from colleagues that inhibits the development and codification of a teaching technology in the first place.) Thus domination by rules, according to the conventional bureaucratic perspective, applies only partially to the school; it occurs primarily outside the classroom—in parts of the school where instruction and classroom management are not the first orders of business.

ALTERNATIVE APPROACHES

It may be correct to assume, as Lortie has maintained, that the tasks of teaching are indivisible, that the division of labor perhaps has gone about as far as it can. Yet this conclusion might be premature; teaching may be only *as yet* undivided. Perhaps it is more fruitful to think of the occupation in terms of several distinct technologies associated with different aspects of the job than about some unitary global technology. One of the obvious characteristics of the occupation that suggests such a possibility—even if it ultimately proves incorrect—is the distinction among teaching tasks associated with school level. Elementary and secondary school teachers do very different things with their pupils, despite certain clear similarities in their activities, because they deal with pupils at different stages of the life cycle. For example, a high school teacher may count on grades, more or less successfully, to induce good school work; but such reliance is predicated on the assumption that pupils already acknowledge the rewarding and punishing properties of grades, and for some high school pupils, this assumption may not be tenable. By implication, then, part of the elementary school teacher's job is *to establish* grades as sanctions. There is no reason to assume *a priori* that grading schoolwork is the same kind of activity as getting pupils to accept certain words, numbers, and letters as sanctions and to guide their conduct by them.

What are the alternatives to regarding teaching as a unitary occupation with a global technology? One, clearly, is to reject the importance of technology and instead regard the occupation primarily as an "art" in the sense that the teacher guides his conduct according to his "feel" of the situation and to the knowledge he has gained through his accumulated personal experience, an alternative that places primary reliance on the teacher's personal resources, sensitivities, and intuition. The job then emerges as an aggregation of activities essentially private in nature. Undoubtedly teaching will always contain private, idiosyncratic, elements; but this is true of most other occupations as well, especially those where uncertainties and unpredictable contingencies are inherently involved. But as a general conception, this formulation leaves much to be desired; it neglects the elements of craft and technique implicit in the term *art,* for none of the occupations conventionally considered as arts—poetry, music, and painting—consists solely or even predominantly of personal expressiveness. Expressiveness is clearly built on the mastery of technique, and to regard teaching solely or primarily as art is really to avoid explicit consideration of the techniques involved.

A second alternative is to consider teaching a bureaucratized occupation in which teachers occupy the lowest rung on a hierarchy and are expected to follow directives that descend from points higher on the scale. This conception rests largely on the assumptions that the employee aspect of the occupation predominates and that the essence of the job is to follow the syllabus and the rules and to minimize the exercise of discretion. Undoubtedly, some school systems operate this way, but as a general formulation of the occupation, it ignores too many facets of the job. Teachers, even though they are hired functionaries in a formal organization, must deal with the vicissitudes of particular classrooms determined largely by the composition of the membership (each classroom develops its own unique history of events), and by the variations between one class and another within the same school. It is most unrealistic to believe that any system of administrative rules and edicts can provide adequate guidelines for the conduct of teachers who work in settings characterized by so much variation and diversity, unless, of course, those rules and edicts make ample provision for the exercise of discretion—a qualification that negates the underlying principle.

A third alternative is to consider a tentative list of teaching technologies that together comprise the main elements of the occupation. This alternative must be viewed in the context of conditions prevailing in the occupation and in the structure of school organization: that the outcomes of schooling are difficult to identify both in the short- and long-run; that it is difficult to distinguish the contributions of the teacher, of the classroom setting, and of influences originating outside the school; that the "products" of teaching are in good part intangible; and that teachers must balance the individual and collective interests of pupils. But given these conditions, it is still possible to distinguish several distinct areas of teaching technology, and that is the alternative I adopt here.

AREAS OF TEACHING TECHNOLOGIES

At least four aspects of teaching can be identified in terms of their technological elements: (1) *the instructional process*, where questions of technology concern methods of presenting curricular materials and designing classroom activities; (2) *motivation*, the means by which teachers engage pupils willingly in instructional activities and establish favorable sentiments toward school and the schooling process; (3) *classroom control*, managing the assemblage of pupils, maintaining order, and creating a climate conducive to learning; and (4) *changing social arrangements* within classrooms and developing new arrangements, both within the school and without, that do not depend on the use of classrooms. This list clearly does not exhaust the full range of teaching activities (its technologies), but its components are both familiar and obvious. Though it refers to parts of the teacher's job that are both central to the occupation and the subject of considerable research in the past, there is not a single area included which has well-known and established modes of proceeding such that means, outcomes, and appropriate conditions can be related systematically. That is, teaching is still carried on primarily according to uncodified rules of thumb and through accumulated individual experience amounting to little more than lore. At the same time there probably exists enough knowledge and experience stored in individual heads to provide the basis for sophisticated technologies—were that knowledge and experience ever brought together, codified, tested for efficacy, and communicated to teachers both in training programs and on the job.

Technologies of instruction vary with the nature of the material to be learned, with the setting in which learning occurs, and with the characteristics of pupils. Blanche Geer, for example, in her studies of trade schools, describes a school that provides training in the use of calculators and other business machines.[7] The learning outcome is a routine, mechanical skill; the technology for imparting it, highly explicit. The pupil is supplied with a machine, a manual for operating it, and an instructor who tells him precisely what to do. The activities are clearly described and arranged sequentially; and the machine identifies errors of performance in a diagnostic fashion by jamming in ways indicative of the type of error the student makes. In effect, the business machine school provides a good working example of the dictum, "learning by doing," a strategy having a clear meaning only when instructional activities are the same as those of the work itself. The learning-by-doing principle has a fuzzy meaning at best in the usual classroom situation—where it is ostensibly applied—because a high order of complex inference is required to link classroom events with anticipated and actual outcomes. Given the complexities of classrooms, the question of whether what is learned is a direct outcome of what is done remains problematic especially when that outcome is intangible and may take a long time to appear. Clearly, then, the business machine school represents a limiting case of instructional technology precisely *because* the linkages between ends and means are so clear.

With some oversimplification it can be argued that instruction has two major components, the first consisting of curriculum content and the second consisting of procedures teachers use to present that content to pupils. In recent years there have been serious attempts to revise the content of curricula within the boundaries of traditional disciplinary areas. The products of these efforts have been the "new math" and new curricula in the physical and biological sciences all designed to bring the content of what is taught in elementary and secondary schools more into line with the basic conceptual apparatus of these fields as understood by academicians. Not surprisingly, the impetus for these curricular changes originated in the universities, from academicians acting as exponents of their disciplines, who felt that the schools were presenting materials too remote from current thinking and knowledge. The efforts were prodigious; not only did they produce new curricula, but they also spawned new agencies that continue to produce them.

Jerome Bruner, one of the high priests of contemporary curriculum reform, states the principle underlying recent attempts to change the nature of curricular material: "Grasping the structure of a subject," he claims, "is understanding in a way that permits many other things to be related to it meaningfully. To learn structure, in short, is to learn how things are related."[8] Although the statement is couched in the language of learning process, in fact it is a statement of outcome; it leaves open the question of what things a teacher must do in order that pupils can grasp the structure of a subject and use that knowledge to relate things to each other. And that open question *is* the question of technology.

Actually, Bruner acknowledges the undeveloped state of teaching technology. He comments: "There is a surprising lack of research on how one most wisely devises learning episodes for children at different ages and in different subject matters."[9] But in his statement about current inadequacy, he suggests—and this is actually stated more explicitly in other parts of his book—that a workable technology must include what he calls "learning episodes." Activities (from which pupils learn the structure of disciplines) must be adapted to the differences in mental abilities associated with age (or better, maturation).[10] Bruner goes on to discuss the considerations that must go into the formulation of learning episodes: questions of reward and punishment, and the timing and sequence of presenting materials.

It is plain from Bruner's comments on instruction that he is bent on setting the agenda (for himself and others) but has not yet begun to develop the technology. Accordingly, one finds him arguing mostly by illustration (and appropriately so, given the current state of our knowledge), with instances drawn from mathematics and physics showing, for example, how pupils (at least highly talented ones) evolve general formulations of quadratic equations from experience in manipulating specially prepared pieces of wood and balance beams.

In a later statement he speaks of criteria for setting up a theory of instruction, and from the context it is clear that what he means by theory is really a technology consisting of four parts: (1) a definition of experiences that stimulate a predisposition to learn (this aspect I have called "motivation," and treat it separately from instruction *per se*); (2) the structuring of a body of knowledge so that it can be readily grasped by the learner; (3) the establishment of sequences for presenting material most effectively; and (4) the identification of rewards and punishments and their appropriate scheduling (another aspect I have included under motivation).

What Bruner omits from this list (and from his books) is as conspicuous as what he includes: first, the activities of the teacher (except as he presents learning materials—whatever "presents" means in this context); and second, consideration of the character of classroom settings, particularly their collective nature. His discussion is couched in the context of *a* teacher and *a* learner when actually teaching involves contact with learners one at a time *and* collectively, a condition that alters the nature of the technology markedly. In effect, Bruner has largely restricted his perspective on the instructional process to the nature (and to some extent the presentation), of *learning materials* and has thereby left many other questions unexamined. The impact of this perspective, which is held by others besides Bruner, has manifested itself in the creation and revision of curriculum materials, a necessary but partial aspect of the instructional process.

The cost of the curriculum-revision approach to instruction has appeared in the widespread misgivings about the efficacy of the new curricula. It is difficult to locate exactly the reasons for this apprehension, but very likely it stems from the fact that teachers often don't know what to do with a new curriculum once they have it, and in many cases they simply do not have command over the materials. Particularly when those who fashion a new curriculum are not the same persons who use it (the cleavage and mutual suspicion between academicians and classroom teachers are notorious) there is a tendency for developers to consider the job done once the new materials have been produced and not to worry about how the new curriculum gets into the heads of teachers, into the programs of schools, and then into the heads of pupils— problems of politics, administration, and instruction. Curriculum reform and development, then, no matter how important, is but one component of instructional technology, and we know painfully little about the other parts. Symptomatically, one hears of curriculum developers who *do* use the materials of their *own* creation in the classroom and who express a sense of excitement and optimism about them but lament that they "don't work" in the conventional classroom settings within which other teachers operate.

There is obviously more to instruction than the nature of curriculum materials; most important are methods for their presentation and the design of classroom activities. Harry Levin and his colleagues have reviewed some of the important research on these questions; it provides leads but scarcely takes us as far as we want to go. He reports, for example, on the work of Cogan, who showed that where pupils see their teachers as warm and friendly, they complete more required and self-initiated work than where they see their teachers as less warm and friendly. No relationship was found between the extent to which pupils find teachers rejecting and the amount of self-initiated work. The absence of positive findings in the second case might be explained by a tendency among pupils to agree more about a teacher's friendliness than about whether he is rejecting.[11] The findings, however, do not indicate the conditions under which pupils learn more or less, nor do they show whether a teacher's expression of warmth is associated with other outcomes. Levin also reports the results of a study by Ackerman indicating:

> that a child taught alternatives is able to approach new problems in a more flexible fashion; that he will attempt more types of solutions, if he has once learned that problems can be solved in more than one way. By trying more solutions, the child was also able to solve more problems correctly.[12]

This method of instruction, however, is costly in time, and pupils solved fewer problems than they did when taught to approach problems with one type of solution.

The general conclusion of Levin and his colleagues emphasizes the limitations of available knowledge linking teaching methods and learning outcomes:

> We have seen that at least one kind of teacher behavior, namely, warm and friendly behavior, is related to how much work students perform. But what of the many other teaching behaviors and the many different consequences such teacher behavior can have in terms of teaching outcomes? The research literature includes a modicum of work which is relevant to the problem, but we venture to say that for the majority of the teacher behaviors which typically are regarded as "good" and "desirable," there is little evidence that they have significant effects on student performance.[13]

MOTIVATION

There is bound to be overlap between the various technologies I have selected for discussion; and although the boundaries between instructional and motivational activities may be hazy, there is ample justification for treating them separately. Although definitions of motivation can become extremely complex, I am concerned here with a relatively simple notion: pupils' desire to do their school work well. The technology of motivating them, then, refers to teacher activities designed to elicit pupils' voluntary engagement in doing school work. The technological question in its simplest terms is concerned with what teachers do to get them interested in performing.

Speaking about the technology of motivation requires the usual disclaimers: not much is known about it, and the research is scanty. The broad outlines of the task are described by Bryan Wilson: it involves effecting "new attitudes of mind, new values . . . and new motivations which are not forthcoming in the home context of most children."[14] It is this last phrase that puts a particular stamp on the teachers work, for motivating children at school takes place within the structural context of classrooms which are markedly different from the household.

The experimental work of Robert Rosenthal and Leonore Jacobson sheds light on what appears to be a disarmingly simple method of motivating pupils. In a six-grade elementary school with eighteen classes, three at each grade, the investigators armed each teacher with the "information" that about 20 percent of the pupils (with the children identified) in each class were "academic spurters" according to test results that ostensibly indicated future academic promise. *In fact,* the test administered to all pupils measured general ability (a form of I.Q., not future promise). The names of children identified as spurters were selected at random; thus any systematic differences between the spurters and the others were initially in the mind of the teachers. Pupils were retested at two subsequent four-month intervals, and the changes in several types of I.Q. measured by the test were compared between the two groups of pupils (potential spurters and nonspurters).[15]

The findings of this research are far more complex than I can report here, but some of them bear directly on the question at hand. Rosenthal and Jacobson report that:

> The children from whom intellectual growth was expected were described as having a significantly better chance of becoming successful in the future, as significantly more interesting, curious, and happy. There was a tendency, too, for these children to be seen as more appealing, adjusted, and affectionate and as lower in the need for social approval. In short, the children from whom intellectual growth was expected became more intellectually alive and autonomous, or at least were so perceived by their teachers.[16]

What happened to the I.Q. scores in each grade over the eight-month testing period? First, I.Q. scores increased among *both* the control (nonspurter) and experimental (spurter) groups. Second, in grades one through four, the gains of the experimental groups exceeded those of the controls; in grades five and six, the scores were almost identical with the controls doing very slightly better. Third, only in the first and second grades did the experimental groups gain significantly more I.Q. points than the controls (15.4 percent more on the average in the first grade and 9.5 percent more in the second grade.[17] Evidently, a teacher's *belief* that some of her pupils have intellectual promise (that may not manifest itself to her in the short run) can affect the magnitude of intellectual performance (as measured by an I.Q. test) over an eight-month period; the impact of this belief tends to be greatest in the earliest grades. The greatest effect of the teacher's belief is on those identified as spurters, but it is not restricted to them, a fact suggesting that however this belief "works" in a classroom, the mechanism is somehow mediated to everybody because of the public nature of the classroom, not just to those singled out as possessing academic potential.

The motivational technology in this study appears simple enough: pupils will do better work, at least of the kind that shows up on an I.Q. test, if the teacher holds certain beliefs, real or fictional, about what they can produce. *How* the technology works and under what conditions (beyond those built into the design of the study) is not known. Does the teacher assign more demanding work in the belief that her pupils can do it and by the same means express confidence in them? Does she change her methods of instruction (thereby implying a close connection between instructional and motivational technologies)? Does she communicate something by gesture, by mood, by the expression of optimism? The mechanisms are not known nor are all the conditions under which the technology works (and fails).[18]

The unconventional work of Rosenthal and Jacobson contrasts sharply with the more familiar approaches to motivational technology found in the educational literature. Consider one of the standard treatments of the motivational question:

> Sometimes . . . the pupil may have no particular emotionalized attitude toward a new learning experience which is being approached. In fact, his feelings for it may be negative and resistive. When this condition exists, the teacher may find it necessary and desirable to utilize methods and techniques to build up the interests or motivation which is needed to make learning most effective.[19]

In their textbook treatment of how a teacher might proceed,

Harold Massey and Edwin Vineyard suggest that when pupils show no particular interest in science, a teacher might, for instance, provide some dramatic demonstration that reveals the wonders of science. They go on to warn, however, that teachers should be wary of "special motivations" of this kind (gimmicks, essentially) that amount to temporary expedients for drumming up interest.

They proceed with a list of "helpful hints" for teachers to arouse the motivation of pupils, from which I have extracted and summarized several illustrations: (1) know the pupils, their interests, the current state of their knowledge, and their capacities; (2) show enthusiasm for the subject matter and for the pupils; (3) use diverse methods; (4) provide opportunities for each pupil to succeed and to gain the approbation of his peers and of adults; (5) use humor appropriately; (6) inform pupils of their progress; (7) commend good work and criticize unobtrusively; (8) establish a friendly and firm relationship with pupils; (9) dress appropriately and use a pleasing voice; and so on.[20]

Many descriptions of teaching technology consist of statements of this kind: helpful hints, remedies for what to do in particular situations, in short, practical advice—nothing very "theoretical" or high-flown—that will help the teacher through some of the rough spots in running a classroom. Just how teachers provide opportunities for each pupil to succeed at something, win the approval of others, and establish friendly but firm relationships with pupils is not discussed; yet, the advice that Massey and Vineyard offer represents a fair description of how the technology of teaching, in general, and of motivating pupils, in particular, is formulated: loosely stated rules of thumb and suggestions about how to act so that teachers don't get into too much trouble. This is common sense, practical stuff; but one should not look too hard for underlying theoretical principles or precise statements about conditions under which certain procedures influence one outcome or another. What teachers actually do in a classroom once they are equipped with this knowledge is another matter; what is relevant here, though, is how the task of motivating pupils is formulated. Massey and Vineyard provide no evidence that their hints are actually helpful or are more likely to produce certain results rather than others.

CLASSROOM CONTROL

There has long been a reluctance to consider seriously the problems of teachers in managing a classroom full of pupils. To view these problems as matters of "control" or "discipline" has seemed both harsh and old fashioned; and, at least in the rhetoric of progressive educators, the words themselves sound antidemocratic. (But why classrooms should be run as democracies—assuming it were possible—has never been adequately explained.) The problem of maintaining order remains even though it is difficult to specify the *types* of order conducive to various learning outcomes. Although most people would agree that classrooms should not be chaotic, absence of chaos will not do as a definition of appropriate classroom atmosphere. The nature of the problem in general terms has been defined by Jackson:

> The teacher who has "lost control" of his class, as the expression goes, cannot compensate for that deficiency by doing an especially good job of evaluation or by spending extra time with his remedial reading group. In an educational sense, when group control is lost, all is lost. . . . Order, though desirable, is not enough, and when carried to extremes it may no longer even be desirable. Once a teacher has mastered the mundane, though fundamental, business of managing the social traffic in his room he is still confronted with important problems that bear upon students' attention. . . . The crucial problem is what to do once the room has grown quiet and all eyes are on the teacher.[21]

The classroom conditions making the establishment of order problematic are various and include the following: (1) with schooling compulsory most classrooms are bound to contain some pupils who would rather be elsewhere and who express that desire through disruptive activities. (2) In any classroom of twenty-five or more pupils it is likely that at least one brings with him symptoms of psychological disturbance sufficient to upset the proceedings. (3) If it is true that academic standards have risen over the last ten years, the less intellectually endowed pupils are likely to find school a source of increasing frustration and declining rewards; and frustration generated within the classroom may well manifest itself in disturbances directed against both school and schooling. (4) Young people, when their conduct is directed by adults, are often inclined to test the limits of acceptable conduct; a simple way to do this is to misbehave in school. (5) In any collective situation where certain kinds of conduct are defined as misbehavior, the violation of prohibitions must be identified correctly if the system of sanctions is to remain intact and credible to the members. In a classroom this means that the teacher must be able to find the actual culprits—not simply the suspects—and mete out punishments fairly. Pupils are usually better able to observe clandestine activity than the teacher, they often know exactly who starts trouble and whether or not the teacher has caught the right person; moreover, they are particularly sensitive to questions of justice and injustice when disciplinary action is taken.

I have put the matter of classroom discipline in rather unpleasant terms; but teachers confront these problems in their world of work, and using a more benign rhetoric doesn't make them go away. The fact remains that very little is known about how to establish and maintain control in groups the size of classrooms, in which pupil membership is mandatory, and in which the teacher, occupying a formal position of leadership, is outnumbered and has few resources for keeping order (particularly if his charges are not inclined to maintain it themselves).

Massey and Vineyard, as well as others, rely on listing specific techniques: "tips on class control," as they call them. They suggest, for example, that teachers should have standard procedures for handling classroom routines, plan their work before entering the classroom, show "enthusiasm and vitality," keep the whole class occupied, maintain classroom discipline themselves rather than passing problems on to school administrators, avoid the use of low grades as punishments for nonacademic infractions, administer punishment in private, make the relevance of rules known and understood, and deal with classroom offenses by keeping both the nature of the infraction and the personality of the pupil in mind.[22] To some extent they have carried their discussion of discipline away from a rule-of-thumb formulation and toward a more systematic and technological one. Accordingly, they enunciate a general principal underlying the withdrawal of privileges as a means of discipline:

> In general, any penalty which is a natural consequence of undesirable behavior and which bears a direct relationship to the offense is a good penalty to impose. Whenever this relationship exists, and when the privilege is one that is definitely desired by the pupil, the teacher will find withdrawal of such a privilege a very effective and psychologically sound disciplinary procedure.[23]

They go on to list a variety of disciplinary measures subsumable under this general principle. This is not to claim that the principle is necessarily correct under all circumstances even though it sounds plausible, but that the disciplinary procedure is more than an *ad hoc* reaction to a particular event.

Anyone who visits a variety of classrooms can observe that some teachers maintain better control than others (which does not necessarily mean that pupils in the more controlled classrooms learn more). But if there is any doubt about the extent of our ignorance about classroom control, one need only listen to the graduates of the elite schools of education, who serve their brief apprenticeship mostly in suburban communities, describe their helplessness when confronted with the problems of tough, urban school classrooms; for were there an adequately developed technology of control available, one would expect to find it most highly developed in teacher-training programs of university-affiliated schools of education with strong research traditions.

The NEA, in its 1964 nationwide poll, asked 1093 teachers whether, in their personal experience, "maintaining pupil discipline has become more difficult than when you first started teaching?"[24] More than twice as many teachers (45 percent as opposed to 20 percent) found maintaining discipline harder than when they started. With the sample partitioned among those with 5–9, 10–19, and 20 or more years of experience, the length of teaching time was *positively* related to difficulty in maintaining discipline. For example, 62 percent of those with 20 or more years experience reported greater difficulty than when they started compared to 25 percent of those with 5–9 years; similarly, 12 percent of the most experienced teachers had less difficulty than when they started compared to 31 percent of the less experienced teachers. Those finding no change in difficulty drops from 43 percent among the least experienced teachers to 25 percent among the most.[25] These findings are not easy to interpret: particularly among the most experienced teachers, social conditions that might affect the severity of discipline problems would have changed the most; rates of school retention have increased with the result that pupils who previously would have left school now remain; and increases in the academic demandingness of school, related to changes in the composition and requirements of the labor force, could reduce the relevance of school for the intellectually less able pupils. Although the available data do not offer an adequate explanation of the NEA's findings, it is reasonable to assume that maintaining discipline remains a substantial problem in the work of teachers; certainly there is no evidence in the figures that increased teacher experience reduces the severity of the problem.[26]

The relative absence of discipline problems in college classrooms (though not in other spheres in college life) suggests that the voluntary presence of students and their motivation to attend and do the work are usually sufficient to maintain order. (Students usually respond to the irrelevance of college teaching by cutting classes rather than by disrupting them, although the range of responses expressed in opposition to irrelevance has expanded lately.) The maintenance of classroom order is largely nonproblematic at the college level.

In the absence of adequate research it is not possible to formulate here the components of a motivational technology; yet a plausible case can be made for identifying some of its dimensions. First, and particularly in the elementary schools, teachers must create a sense of goodwill among pupils, a sense of diffuse attachment to the teacher, the classroom, and the school. In other words, a teacher must create a feeling that school is a desirable place to be (at least as desirable as competing alternatives) and that schoolwork is worth doing. Creating this kind of sentiment, particularly in the lowest grades, is very different from meting out rewards and punishments (e.g., praise, grades, admonitions, and the like) on a *quid pro quo* basis in exchange for specific acts of academic performance and nonacademic conduct (such as writing a good English theme, getting math problems correct, taking on extra responsibility in the classroom, and the like).

Second, grading, rewarding, punishing, and assigning responsibilities (all of which pertain to specific acts of classroom and school performance) must be equitable in the sense that they apply across the board to *types* of situations (e.g., classwork of a given quality or certain kinds of misbehavior), and should not reflect arbitrary or capricious acts by teachers. Equitable treatment would not be as difficult to carry out were teachers not enjoined to take both the unique as well as the aggregate characteristics of pupils into account. The technological issue involved in equitable treatment, therefore, is not simply one of applying a general standard of fairness, but of coping with a dilemma arising out of the teacher's double obligation: to the class and to each individual within it.

Third, there is the problem of creating credible and workable sanctions. Even if one assumes sufficient goodwill, the task of making sanctions rewarding or punishing remains. Concretely, this means that if a teacher assigns a good grade to a good piece of work, the pupil will construe the grade as a reward if he values good grades. Similarly, a teacher must know if keeping a pupil after school is regarded by the student as punishment. Again, the initial confrontation with the task of sanctioning arises at the elementary level; secondary teachers usually assume that the problems inherent in the task have been solved. One difficulty in the use of sanctions lies in their applicability both to academic and nonacademic conduct. This means that teachers must use sanctions to create and preserve an atmosphere conducive to learning and at the same time avoid resorting to punishments that undermine that atmosphere. Yet, little is known about how to balance the standards of appropriateness and severity as they apply to punishments.

Another difficulty is the repeated use of sanctions over time. The indiscriminate use of praise, for example, makes it meaningless after a while; and punishments, when used too frequently, reach a point of diminishing returns. The latter point is particularly troublesome whenever it becomes plain to pupils that the most formidable punishments in the teacher's arsenal turn out to be quite bearable. Finally, when classroom control is transformed into a problem of the frequent use of rewards and punishments, the weaknesses in the teacher's position of power become easily recognized, and knowledge of them often becomes widely diffused throughout a school.

The teacher's position of power is hardly one of great strength; in addition to the limitations on his powers noted above, he must rely mainly on the lessons he draws from his *own* experiences, correctly or incorrectly, because there is little or no codified knowledge to guide his judgments and actions. His working conditions, moreover, make it difficult to distinguish between those effects of his actions that are "his fault" or "his doing" and those that are inherent to the situation and remain realistically outside his control. It is easy for teachers to make mistakes early in the school year and not be aware of them (or if aware, not be able to rectify them). And, of course, knowledge of an error does not necessarily imply knowledge of an appropriate remedy, so that a new confrontation with the situation may prompt an alternative approach but not necessarily an effective one. This is not to suggest that teachers receive no help and have no resources to avoid repeating the same error; administrators and colleagues are available, but not always often enough or at the right times. In addition, one should not underestimate the social complexity of classrooms and the inherent difficulty for a teacher in recognizing his own contribution to classroom problems when he himself is both participant and observer and when many contributing events occur beyond his purview and his control.

Working in relative isolation, often without efficacious sanctions at his disposal and in the absence of a codified body of knowledge with which to judge the appropriateness of his actions and to remedy his errors, the teacher may find himself in a position where he cannot readily distinguish the symptoms of classroom disorder from the reasons for them, or cannot understand why he seems to be making little or no headway in his instructional efforts. He works largely with "soft" resources consisting in large measure of the personal relationships he establishes with members of a class. The plight of the teacher, and particularly new ones to the trade, is aptly summed up by Dwight Allen and Kevin Ryan:

> Myriad problems that they only vaguely anticipated become searing realities. They did not realize that teaching was so complex. They had not anticipated that they would have to be doing so many things at once. They have a hard time finding the proper level of communication to use with students. They have difficulty planning, and, further, they have difficulty translating their carefully worked-out plans into classroom activities. . . . When things go right, they do not know why they are right, and when things go wrong —particularly when they go wrong—they do not know why they do.[27]

CHANGING SOCIAL ARRANGEMENTS

The remarkable thing about American schools is that they have changed so little since the demise of the one-room schoolhouse. There are few schools left in which one teacher instructs children in six or eight grades in one room; this older arrangement has been supplanted by a setting known as the self-contained classroom in which one teacher (or several sequentially) provides instruction for a group of pupils of similar age assigned to a particular grade. Over the decades of this century there have been numerous attempts, both architecturally and socially, to vary classroom design: by unscrewing desks and chairs from the floor, by permitting pupils to move more or less freely around the room, by dividing the members into numerically smaller units to provide ability and interest groupings, by introducing more than one teacher into the classroom, by introducing inanimate teaching components (such as teaching machines and computers), and by widening the age span of pupils assigned to one teacher. Some changes have involved temporarily removing pupils from the classroom: taking them on field trips and assembling them in large aggregates to hear lectures, watch dramatic productions, or see movies; others have involved alternative modes of classroom management where the balance between teacher direction and pupil initiation of activities varies. Although changes in the dominant pattern are undeniable, the general observation that *plus ça change, plus c'est la même chose* [the more things change, the more they remain the same] would not be far from the mark, for the precept of the self-contained classroom has been engraved into the architecture, however much the outward form of school buildings has changed and no matter how many sliding partitions have been set into them. Moreover, teacher training has been adapted to the architecture since most teachers are trained to run a classroom and offer instruction in that setting. Most attempts to change the educational enterprise by altering social arrangements seek to do one of several things: increase the school's contribution to its traditionally purported outcomes (such as academic achievement), challenge the importance or relevance of those outcomes by designing the schooling process to foster different (ostensibly superior) outcomes, or contribute to other than academic and instructional outcomes. One of the more recent attempts to improve the school enterprise is team teaching; another attempt has been nongraded schooling, and a third the extension of the educational process out of the schoolhouse into the wider community. I discuss these three schemes for changing social arrangements for their variety, not their exhaustiveness.

To call team teaching a movement, as some observers have done, would be an exaggeration.[28] Essentially, it

> is a type of instructional organization, involving teaching personnel and the students assigned to them, in which two or more teachers are given responsibility, working together, for all or a significant part of the instruction of the same group of students.[29]

Oddly enough, the instructional elements found in the definition are given a subsidiary place in Judson Shaplin's elaboration of a scheme in which joint planning by team members, curriculum development, flexibility in grouping pupils within classrooms, teacher training, supervision and evaluation, and hierarchical differentiation in the teaching career receive far greater emphasis. In short, team teaching as an administrative innovation in which opportunities to exploit teacher specialization and to involve them more directly (than in conventional schools) in educational planning appears far more central in Shaplin's thinking than does the improvement of instruction.[30] Shaplin, in fact, sidesteps the question of instructional efficacy by disclaiming that improved instruction necessarily follows from the purported changes involved in team teaching: independent study, small-group interaction, large-group instruction, and diverse forms of grouping.[31]

Several technological issues are involved in the establishment of team teaching; some issues pertain to school operation (Shaplin's concern), others to outcomes produced in children. Lortie, for example, sees at least two possible directions in which con-

ventional classroom arrangements can change under team teaching, each with different implications for learning outcomes. Starting from an analysis of conventional, self-contained classrooms
in which he finds an "autonomy-equality" pattern predominant
among teachers,[32] he argues that teams with teachers as instructional agents are likely to take one of two forms: (1) a "vertical-
bureaucratic" form where the team leader (in a stratified team)
becomes part of the administrative hierarchy and holds both control and coordinative powers over teacher-subordinates; or (2) a
"horizontal-collegial" form in which team members constitute a
relatively egalitarian, self-regulating instructional group.[33]

Lortie then speculates about the likely instructional outcomes
of each team arrangement. The vertical-bureaucratic case, he
anticipates, is more compatible with teaching specific skills and
established bodies of information than with arousing initiative,
questioning attitudes, and egalitarian values among pupils.[34] The
latter set of outcomes, by implication, would be more likely to
appear under horizontal-collegial conditions. He considers as
well the problems likely to arise under each arrangement: how
will instructional and disciplinary responsiblilties be allocated;
how will the team deal with situations where pupils show deference
to one team member but not to others; will pupils become confused by the airing of controversy among the members or will
they thrive on it; and will the expression of a homogeneous point
of view stultify the thinking of pupils? All these are questions because we simply don't know the answers.

The technological issues in team teaching are manifold; at
the minimum they include the establishment of such programs
in schools,[35] and the impact, if any, of established team arrangements on what pupils learn, as well as others. According to Glen
Heathers, the instructional effects on pupils are scarcely dramatic,
and I limit my concern here to the single question of whether
team teaching makes a difference in learning outcomes, one among
many legitimate criteria for assessment.[36] In general, Heathers
finds the research on instructional outcomes unsatisfactory on
several counts. Most if not all the assessment research done to
date is either inadequately and inappropriately designed or un-
controlled; studies have failed to take into account the extent to
which team teaching programs have actually been implemented,
how well they work once implemented, and the conditions unrelated to the programs themselves that affect their impact. Given
these limitations, he finds few large differences between what
pupils learn under team teaching and conventional programs.
There are nonconsistent differences where a program has modest
effects in one area of learning but not in another, and findings

that indicate the superiority of team teaching in some schools or classrooms and the superiority of conventional arrangements in others, within the same schools and in different schools. More sophisticated types of research designed to identify which aspects of team teaching are most effective have not been undertaken. Overall, Heathers finds no evidence that team teaching harms pupils, but the research completed so far provides few if any guidelines to administrators in formulating school policy.

Although Heathers reports that parents and pupils who have been exposed to team teaching are reasonably happy with it, the evidence so far indicates a technological nullity in the area of instruction. Certainly the advent of team teaching has led to no marked changes in the occupational career line of teachers (as envisioned), and according to the testimony of Joseph Grannis, the implementation of team teaching programs leans somewhat to the chaotic side. These judgments, of course, may well be premature given the recency of the innovation itself; but at present, little or no evidence suggests that this particular change in the social arrangements of schools has had much systematic impact, either organizational or instructional, on educational outcomes of any kind.

I do not argue, however, that organizational change is inherently ineffectual in general (or with team teaching in particular); nor can one decide whether the current weaknesses of team teaching are inherent or whether they are products of the lack of time, experience, and knowledge in putting the program into effect.

The nongraded school, characteristically found at the elementary level, represents a second mode of altering social arrangements to change the impact of the schooling process. John Goodlad and Robert Anderson, two exponents of nongraded schooling, contend "that abolition of grade barriers frees each child, whatever his ability, to move forward in his learnings as rapidly and smoothly as possible. But we also believe that such structure is in harmony with his social and emotional well-being."[37] By grades, they refer to the conventional organization of schools into sequential, one-year time intervals at the end of which pupils are either promoted or left back, and to pupil placement in classrooms largely on the basis of age. Barriers refer to the socially and psychologically deleterious effects they attribute to the wide variations in children placed in a single grade.

Their argument rests on an empirical description of the types and extent of pupil variation found in several conventional classrooms (and probably characteristic of a large number of them), as shown in Table 4.1.

TABLE 4.1   *Variations in School Performance Measures, Within Grades.*

	Within-Grade Difference	
	First Grade	*Third Grade*
Chronological age	1 yr. 7 mos.	1 yr. 9 mos.
Mental age	4 yrs. 6 mos.	4 yrs. 0 mos.
I.Q.	61	56
Paragraph meaning	1.9 grade intervals	4.4 grade intervals
Word meaning	1.4 grade intervals	4.3 grade intervals
Spelling	2.0 grade intervals	2.7 grade intervals
Arithmetic reasoning	2.1 grade intervals	2.7 grade intervals
Arithmetic composition	1.3 grade intervals	1.5 grade intervals

Adapted from Goodlad and Anderson, *The Nongraded Elementary School*, table 2, p. 7, and table 4, p. 12.

Although the spread in chronological age in these particular classrooms is not especially large, the mental age and I.Q. spreads are considerable; moreover, the data (only some of which I have included here) indicate that within-grade achievement scores increase in range over the course of time. Other types of variation also appear; individual pupils differ in their achievement levels from one skill to another (one fifth grader, for example, achieved at the 9.4 grade level in paragraph meaning and at the 5.1 grade level in arithmetic computation, a difference of over four years). Within a given classroom, children vary in learning pace (the pace of a particular child may even vary from year to year), and indications of general potentiality are not always commensurate with actual performance. Goodlad and Anderson argue accordingly that the usual graded school does grave injustice to the real variation within classrooms and "within" children, and that some different arrangement of grouping would be better than lumping pupils of roughly the same age in the same grade.

Unfortunately, they do not present a shred of evidence documenting the harmfulness of the consequences; there is only their assertion to go on. However, they find within-class variation problematic in two ways: it is large (i.e., too large), and it is various (i.e., there are many different types of it). Having proclaimed the problem, they propose a remedy of two parts: a nongraded elementary school, and a longitudinal perspective on schooling.

> Concepts, skills, and values do not lend themselves to grade packaging any more than pupil realities [such as the achievement and mental age scores described earlier] do. But these organizing threads of the curriculum lend themselves very well to the concept of the nongraded school. . . . A longitudinal view of pupil development, a longitudinal view of curriculum, and an organizational structure unbroken by grade-to-grade divisions go hand in hand.[38]

It is not at all clear how far Goodlad and Anderson propose taking the nongraded idea; how far beyond his age peers should the intellectually precocious child proceed at his own rate, and how large a discrepancy between the achievement rates of one child in different intellectual areas should the nongraded school accommodate? Several nongraded plans are described containing conventional single, double, and triple grades. One proposes covering the six elementary years in eleven two- and three-grade stages (although it does not seem likely that each child will proceed through all eleven; he might well finish the six years in fewer). The point is, however, that the plan recognizes that some children need more than six years and some fewer to complete elementary school, and that the school should cater to these variations by creating broader grade groupings that blur the boundaries between conventional grades in the hope that the stigma of being left back or failing will be mitigated, and by designing the program to give the slower and the faster pupil some leeway in the appropriate direction according to how well he does.

It seems fairly clear that the schemes described are best adapted to classrooms where differences among children are modest to begin with; the wider the spread among pupils, the more the strain placed on the nongraded school will be comparable to that placed on the graded school—though perhaps somewhat less—and for precisely the same reasons. The logic of my demurrer rests partly on the material Goodlad and Anderson present in stating their case. When many considerations are taken into account as relevant to a pupil's progress through school, it is highly unlikely that one organizational remedy can cope satisfactorily with the variety of problems involved. In one program the following ten were considered: ability, achievement, desirability of friends, emotional stability, number of years in school, parental attitudes, physical maturity, pupils' attitudes, social development, teacher-pupil rapport.[39]

Interesting as the Goodlad-Anderson proposal is, their description of the graded school is something of a straw man; the strategy of argument is to compare the loftiest promises of the nongraded with the harshest realities of graded schools. Although the nongraded school dispenses with the six (or eight) traditional grade boundaries of the elementary school, it does not dispense with boundaries. If not being promoted constitues failure in the conventional school, doesn't the delayed crossing of the boundary separating a two- or three-year grade sequence also constitute failure (acknowledging, of course, that the longer time interval provides teachers with a longer and more flexible period of time before the pupil is confronted with a day of reckoning), perhaps even a greater sense of failure when the pupil is unable to make it in two or three years? In fact, the nongraded school does not dispense with grades and boundaries; it only rearranges them in ways likely to be helpful to children in the middle ability and achievement ranges. The plan is not likely to be much more helpful for the exceptionally bright and dull children than the graded school; and although Goodlad and Anderson do not push their plan to the *reductio ad absurdum* of Mark Hopkins, the student, and the log, they don't really say where the plan properly stops in terms of the appropriateness of a learning situation and of legitimate administrative realities.

Aside from the fact that Goodlad and Anderson present only the scantiest research findings (and without any satisfactory evaluation of the adequacy of research design),[40] their advocacy of the nongraded school and their assertion of its benefits take insufficient account of the external constraints impinging on the schools. The research includes far too little from which to draw even the most tentative conclusions about efficacy and administrative guidelines, or to make claims for the harmfulness of graded schools.[41] On moral and humanitarian grounds, with perspective restricted to events internal to the school, one can justify evaluating performance according to individual improvement and minimizing the impact of failure by reducing invidious comparisons between pupils; but on more realistic grounds, social standards (particularly where college and occupational requirements are concerned) tend to be more absolute than relative with respect to individuals. Employers, for example, are more interested in what a person can do and how well he can do it than in how much he has improved. There is much to be said for mitigating the personally destructive effects of failure at all stages of a person's life but one of the most demanding tasks confronting the schools is how to cope with pupils whose level of performance is poor, whose aptitudes give little hope of promise; it is among these pupils that the later demands of adult life will likely take their greatest psychological toll. Whereas a nongraded program may make the school lives of these pupils more palatable, it does not necessarily deal with the larger problem of poor performance any better than a graded program.

Viewed as an educational strategy in technological terms, nongraded schooling may contribute to the educational welfare of pupils depending on how the organizational arrangements are used; but the same contention holds for the graded school. In the interest of promoting individualized modes of instruction that take account of individual variations, an enlightened teacher (alone or with assistants) can care for diverse needs and interests by varying method and curriculum content within graded, self-contained classrooms; and if the school is large enough to contain several classrooms at each grade, a flexible tracking system with adequate mechanisms enabling pupils to change tracks depending on their performance might accomplish the same ends claimed for nongraded schools. But these claims, like the proposals for nongraded schools, are merely assertions; each can be made to sound convincing. Perhaps the nongraded school provides an advantage in individualizing instruction, in mitigating the effects of failure, in easing the task of teachers who confront a substantial variety of aptitudes and levels of performance in each curricular area; but until this plan is compared with a variety of strategies designed to accomplish the same ends within graded settings, there is no basis for asserting the superiority of one over the other.

Finally, I turn to a proposal expounded by Fred Newmann and Donald Oliver for extending the educational process beyond the confines of the school and out into the larger community.[42] Once finished with their critique of the contemporary educational enterprise and of other putative evils, they enumerate specific problems—the failure to employ "the rich educational potential" available in institutions not specifically devoted to instruction, the neglect of educational contributions that "diverse public and private associations" can make, and the organization of schools designed according to the models of "corporate industry and bureaucratic civil service"[43]—for which they prescribe new remedies involving changes in conventional arrangements.

Newmann and Oliver propose that education should occur in three distinct settings, only one of which resembles formal schooling; the others they call the "laboratory-studio-work context" and the "community seminar context." Schools, they believe, should be designed (as they are now) for systematic instruction in basic skills and for accomplishing prescribed learning outcomes. Although their agendas can be formalized and planned in advance, the modes of instruction need not be restricted to formal classroom training but should employ, in addition, tutorials, programmed and computerized instruction, audio-visual techniques, and recent advances in measurement and testing; moreover, teaching can be carried out in a variety of in-school settings including small groups and large assemblages. Schools, according to Newmann and Oliver, are best adapted organizationally to those portions of the educational process that lend themselves to preplanning and the formulation of discrete outcomes; hence, schools should be restricted to what they can do best and not be saddled with legitimate educational tasks that strain their resources to the detriment both of the school and of the broader educational agenda.

The laboratory-studio-work context is designed for a very different task: to provide a setting for people to deal with problems of personal concern, to let the modes of approaching these problems lead where they may (i.e., with no preestablished outcomes), and to utilize the institutional resources of the community such as factories, hospitals, libraries, political organizations, government agencies, and the like, as educational settings. Learning experiences are expected to derive from participation in the usual activities of these outside agencies; the "teachers" are simply people who go about their daily work (not employed instructors), and the learners are those who do it with them, not as apprentices training to become adult members of occupations. The hope is that the outcomes will not necessarily be specific skills, but that the setting will provide opportunities for participants to pursue "broader humanistic and aesthetic goals." The question of how these goals, nonspecific in character, will emerge receives no answer (nor, as a matter of fact, do the writers raise the question). Yet the educational purpose of these nonschool agencies is to provide settings where people can involve themselves in a wide range of occupational, political, service, and aesthetic activities, and grapple with the problems inherent in them as they arise. Whether broad humanistic and aesthetic outcomes emerge will depend on people's capacities to formulate and generalize from their experiences.

Finally, Newmann and Oliver consider the community seminar as the appropriate context for exploring "community issues and ultimate meanings in human experience."[44] By community, they refer to a group in which membership is valued for its own sake, a group concerned with important aspects of its members' lives. The members of a community have a common purpose, agree on methods for dealing with conflict, share responsibility for group action, and have long-range and extensive personal contact. What real social entities this definition pertains to is not in the least clear; but in any case, the seminar is designed as a setting in which the youth and adults of a community gather to discuss the major issues of the community with an eye toward social action. As in the case of the laboratory-studio-work setting, the outcomes of the seminar are not laid out in advance; rather a forum is provided for working out the major value issues confronting the community.

The Newmann-Oliver plan for extending the educational process outside the boundaries of the school hovers even closer to the proposal stage than either team teaching or nongraded schooling; and whether the three contexts comprising their scheme will contribute to the outcomes they desire remains a matter of conjecture given the vagueness of their concept of community, the weakness of the connections linking context with outcome, and the failure to distinguish—at least for the laboratories and the community seminars—the educational from the customary working aspects of these institutions. Clearly they cannot be identical. A hospital, for example, as an organization designed for patient care, the training of medical personnel, and research, is not the same thing as a hospital designed in part as an institution for community education. Newmann and Oliver do not concern themselves at all with how the latter component gets built in and how the hospital adapts itself to take on the new function assigned to it. If team teaching and nongraded schooling represent relatively crude and undeveloped forms of educational technology, the Newmann-Oliver proposal, however intriguing, is proto-technological. Yet all of these plans advocate direct changes in social arrangements both within and without the school as ways of forging linkages between educational institutions and outcomes.

ADDITIONAL TECHNOLOGICAL ISSUES

This discussion of teaching technology remains far from complete both because the issues are too numerous and because substantial knowledge about them is too limited. I have not, for example, discussed the diagnosis and treatment of the many types of learning disability; and more than likely, there is probably not one but a variety of technologies pertinent to problems of diagnosis. Likewise, I have given no consideration here to the technological questions implicit in the recent work on school desegregation.[45] This issue is usually viewed from one or both of the following perspectives: (1) as a question of public morals—is it right to keep schools segregated whether or not educational gains follow from integration? and (2) as a question of public policy—should units of government, at any level, effect the integration of schools, and if so, how? The policy question is in substantial part a technological one: Given the moral assumption that it is right to assure every child a decent education, what must teachers do and how should schools be designed to assure the outcome? There is some evidence to support the efficacy of school desegregation, but with the currently inadequate state of our knowledge about how schools work, it would be premature to call school desegregation a technology. We know very little about what particular racial compositions are most efficacious and for which children; we know little about critical points (the ages at which desegregation is likely to work and those at which it may not make any difference); and we know appallingly little about whether desegregation can stand alone as a remedy or whether it must be combined with one or another mode of instruction, size of classroom, type of curriculum, and so on.[46]

In the field of reading, Jeanne Chall has written perhaps the most thoroughgoing assessment (compared to other areas) of the state of our knowledge in that central area of the educational enterprise. Her investigation is clearly technological in intent: "My major concern," she writes, "was with studies investigating method—the *how* of beginning reading instruction. . .";[47] and although at times she deplores the inconclusiveness of available research and the gaps in our knowledge, two facts about her study stand out clearly. First, she located the research and found it in such condition and quantity that she could bring it directly to bear on some of the major issues in the teaching of reading (i.e., she was able to write the book in the first place); and second, she formulated the central issue: "Do children learn to read better with a beginning method that stresses reading for meaning or with one that concentrates on teaching them how to break the code?"[48] She examined this question not as the exponent of an ideological position but primarily as an outside inquirer concerned with the efficacy of methods and the conditions (e.g., pupil age, teaching method, format of reading materials, type of classroom setting, and so on) under which they work. Despite her disclaimers about her own work, it is difficult to find any other part of the educational enterprise sufficiently developed technologically to permit a book of this type to be written.

Although much remains to be known and formulated about the teaching and learning of reading, other areas of the schooling process are not nearly so well understood; some interesting and provocative beginnings, however, have been made. One is the recent volume of Louis Smith and William Geoffrey—the former a nonparticipant observer, the latter the teacher whose daily activities were observed (by Smith) over an extended period in one classroom.[49] This is one of the few studies charting the events of a classroom at the level of first-order description, with the aim of formulating the elements of the teaching process. Although the formulation is crude in many respects, it represents an important effort to break out of the traditional and sterile modes of studying schools in which one or more styles of teaching (usually democratic vs. authoritarian, *ad nauseam*) are related to one or another learning outcome (e.g., levels of achievement, self-initiated work, and the like), approaches that largely ignore the social organization of classrooms.

Implicit in their approach are the indisputable facts that classrooms are collective entities containing both individuals and fluid, informal cliques, and that teachers, in addition to following some instructional plan of their own, cope both with this social reality and with the predictable and unpredictable contingencies that arise out of it. The teacher, according to Smith and Geoffrey,

> presents cues to the children which indicate he is aware of the latent meaning of events outside the give-and-take of recitation. In the vernacular he *knows what is going on.* . . . Our process conception suggests also that the *tentativeness in teaching gambits, the provisional try,* is a dimension of teacher behavior. . . . The oft mentioned analogy that the elementary school classroom is a "three-ring circus" found concrete substance in our data . . . the *handling of multiple simultaneous facets of the classroom system* [ringmaster-ship] . . . *Continuity* seems almost a variant of ringmaster-ship and refers to the degree to which the teacher relates the present events with those that have gone before and those which are likely to follow. . . . *Sequential smoothness,* the easy flow of event upon event, and *pacing,* the number of events per unit of time, add further specification to a broad model of teaching. . . . *Autonomy, skirmishing, banter, and getting off the hook* . . .—all these are imaginative methods that highlight the children and teachers as separate entities.[50]

Implicit in this rough-and-ready classification of teaching activities is the idea of the teacher as strategist and tactician whose perspective encompasses a substantial period of time and an awareness of his pupils' capacities. His actions include attempts not only to do the instructional job, but also to avoid getting trapped by pupils' attempts to test the limits, to try new procedures while avoiding such strong commitments that they cannot be revised, to establish routines and standards of acceptable conduct through both enforcement and maintenance of goodwill, and so on. Throughout, Smith and Geoffrey attempt to formalize their conception of teaching by illustrating sequences of classroom events: for example, given some remark or action by a pupil, they indicate the range of responses the teacher might make, speculate on the possible outcomes (for pupils both individually and collectively, in terms of achievement, classroom control, pupils' perceptions of what is going on, new problems arising that may not have been inherent in the original event), and set the whole sequence in the context of classroom and school-wide conditions.

SUMMARY

Having begun this chapter with an extremely general formulation of teaching technology—the linkages between means and ends in the performance of some task—I have taken a long excursion in surveying some of the components of the teacher's work. But this has been a critique as well as an excursion, a questioning of whether teaching need be an occupation that Lortie has described—I believe correctly—as composed of Robinson Crusoes.

> As with Defoe's hero, the beginning teacher may find that prior experience supplies him with some alternatives for action, but his crucial learning comes from his personal errors; he fits together specific solutions and specific problems *into some kind of whole* and at times finds leeway for the expression of personal tastes. Working largely alone, he cannot make the specifics of his working knowledge base explicit, nor need he, as his victories are private.[51]

And what is true of the beginning teacher also happens to be true of the experienced one. The crucial point is the view of the job *as a whole*, as an entity without parts, a perspective maintained by the scant opportunities available in schools and in classrooms for teachers to analyze the content of their work, to identify its parts.

The "unity of the job" perspective is shored up and maintained by the particular style of teachers' language. As Jackson sees it:

> When a student makes a sudden leap of progress or when an apathetic youngster undergoes a dramatic reversal of attitude, the teacher's response, quite naturally, is apt to

be one of delight and thankfulness. But this response is unlikely to be followed by an analytic scrutiny of what has taken place. When good fortune strikes, the teachers seem to be saying, it is best not to ask too many questions. The unquestioning acceptance of classroom miracles is part of a broader tendency that reveals itself in several ways in the talk of teachers. This is the tendency to approach educational affairs intuitively rather than rationally . . . In other words, they were more likely to [justify their professional decisions] by pointing out that a particular course of action *felt* like the right thing to do, rather than by claiming that they *knew* it to be right.[52]

I have argued, in effect, that existing evidence indicates that teaching contains reasonably distinct tasks classifiable under familiar rubrics; instruction, motivation, and classroom control. That is to say, teaching comprises specifiable activities that can be mastered separately once they are properly identified. (One need not assume that instruction, motivation, and control are the best formulations; but given the crude state of current knowledge, they remain plausible.) To observe that teaching has parts and to identify them, however tentatively, does not add up to a stunning intellectual accomplishment; but having made the observation, it is possible to release teachers from the trap of discovering that their work is overwhelmingly complex. It also means that once the elements of teaching are identified, it becomes possible for a new teacher to master each component of the job, task by task.

Interestingly, the experience of medical training provides support for the notion that jobs can be learned a piece at a time; and if we reflect on it, there is something absurd about becoming a doctor by learning "medicine" as if medicine were a unity. Yet this is precisely what we expect of prospective teachers: that they "learn to teach," and in a short time.

Occupationally, teaching is a late arrival in the field of training its members to perform the elemental skills of the trade. Work in the area of "microteaching" is a case in point. According to Allen and Ryan:

> The basic structure of microteaching and its built-in flexibility make it a natural setting in which to develop instructional methods of *various teaching skills and techniques.* Teaching skills can be isolated and their performance highlighted so that the viewer can more easily identify *the behaviors that make up the skill.*[53]

The heart of the scheme is to identify component skills (such as

stimulus variation, set induction, silence and nonverbal cues, flu-
ency in asking questions, among others); analyze them further
into specific acts; and create small-scale teaching situations in which
one act is performed with a small number of pupils, over a brief
time span, under supervision, and with almost immediate feedback from students and supervisors.

Consider the case of stimulus variation: The problem is to
reduce boredom among pupils by expanding the teacher's repertoire of skills for gaining their attention. Accordingly, teachers
are shown that they can move freely in the classroom; that they
can gesture with their head, hands, and body; employ devices for
focusing the pupils' attention to specific messages; and use a variety
of ways to communicate with students. Not only are they shown
these things, they do them repeatedly by teaching small portions
of material under supervisors whose task is to call their attention
to what they are doing and not doing—not to rate them for promotion. The rationale is clear:

> [Microteaching] makes [the] task much less complex and
> mystifying. If the training program can isolate specific
> skills and describe and demonstrate them to the teacher,
> the teacher is more likely to acquire these skills. For one
> thing, the teacher can discriminate these activities from
> what was previously a more general teaching-learning pro-
> cess. If the teacher recognizes the teaching skill to be learned,
> he begins to recognize the behaviors that make up the skill
> and the situational factors that dictate when it can be used.[54]

The implications of the microteaching technique go considerably
beyond the definition and acquisition of specific skills, but there
is little question that it addresses itself to one of the most recalcitrant problems of the occupation. The problems have by no
means been completely resolved if for no other reason than that
the technique has been formulated primarily in terms of teaching
activities—no mean accomplishment—but not yet in terms of
what pupils learn and of the connection between the two. However, it clearly represents an important start in creating a technology of teaching.

There remains the question of why I have included team
teaching, nongraded schooling, and the extension of education
outside the confines of school buildings as aspects of teaching
technology. It is easy to understand microteaching in a technological context because it deals specifically with the things teachers
do in the course of their work. Yet teaching does not occur in a
social vacuum, and it would be shortsighted to assume that the

only elements of teaching technology are the activities of teachers, however important they are. We implicitly accept the idea that the natural setting for teaching activities is the classroom, probably because we have frozen classrooms into our thinking architecturally. Some alternatives we reject because they are ridiculous on their face, and we never even raise them as possibility (for good reasons); teachers do not hold classes on crowded buses. Scrapping the schools and substituting televised courses at home strikes us as misguided, but not as ridiculous. We do accept field trips of various kinds, movies, and homework, all of which employ either nonschool settings or unconventional ones (considering the age-homogeneous, self-contained classroom as the model).

The point is, however, that technology includes all aspects of the environment that we can harness in the service of creating desired outcomes in children. To the extent that we learn how to use the social environment by creating new social arrangements —larger or smaller aggregates of pupils and teachers of varying degrees of homogeneity and heterogeneity, time units of varying duration, social settings outside the conventional boundaries of the school, and the like—we thereby expand technological resources beyond the activities of teachers to the extent that these changes can be directly related to learning outcomes. Jackson, for one, contends that: "The job of managing the activities of 25 or 30 children for 5 or 6 hours a day, 5 days a week, 40 weeks a year, is quite a bit different from what abstract consideration of the learning process might lead us to believe."[55] However, the abstract consideration permits an expansion of the imagination and can lead to an enrichment of our thinking about what we can achieve and how we can achieve it technologically.

•

CHAPTER FIVE

Settings

for Teacher Training

•

TEACHER COMPETENCE

Over the last two decades, schools of education have been targets of steady criticism, some pertinent, some wide of the mark. Most striking are not the indictments themselves—much of what passes for teacher training warrants indictment—but their origin outside the occupation rather than within it, and the assumptions on which they are often based, leading critics away from the crucial problems. The question I raise here is not whether teachers as individuals or in the aggregate are competent or adequately trained, but rather what is the nature and setting of the training experience that shapes the working lives of teachers. I am not indifferent to the problem of teacher competence, but it is part of a larger constellation of problems.

Consider Conant's major concerns in his book on teacher training: what are the basic skills of teaching, how can they be taught to others, and how can they be mastered?[1] And consider his perspective on them. Basically, he proposes juggling the content and distribution of the training curriculum to create an appropriate balance between general and specialized skills (adapted to the respective requirements of elementary and secondary schools), setting a minimum standard for hours of supervised practice teaching,[2] and establishing the clinical professorship as a university faculty position to provide a link between the academic community, the source of professionally relevant knowledge, and the schools. (The clinical professor by definition has training and experience in both settings.)

Although he makes the proper qualifications about the state of knowledge in teaching and teacher training and asserts correctly that we do not know enough to prescribe what methods to teach, Conant views the school of education almost wholly in terms of its curriculum (and those training experiences directly tied to it) and of its personnel—a narrow perspective indeed. The same can be said of James Koerner's book, *The Miseducation of American Teachers,* one of the better balanced and less shrill critiques of teacher training.[3]

Koerner's argument rests on the premise that schooling should present pupils with:

> the principal areas of human knowledge: *English and foreign languages, history, mathematics, and the natural sciences.* These subjects are not arbitrary divisions of knowledge, as they are so often alleged to be by educationists, but are the divisions, each with its own techniques of research and advancement, that men over long periods have found to produce the most fruitful results.[4]

A short and reasonable step from this premise leads to the conclusion that teachers should know their subject content and present it competently. One may or may not accept Koerner's ideas about what should be taught and still agree that competence is a central issue and that the way to instil it is to design "a reliable method . . . for connecting the training programs with the on-the-job performance of teachers."[5]

The villains of Koerner's piece are methods courses and educational research. The former, he argues, should be curtailed; the latter he finds harmful in that it turns teachers away from "the necessarily imprecise, intuitional, frustrating means that must be used in any effort to solve the really important problems of education,"[6] in the mistaken belief that teaching has some "exact or scientific" foundation. Teacher competence, he continues, should be gauged not by the number of education courses taken but by discovering how well pupils do under the tutelage of a particular teacher; and before taking the first job, teachers should take examinations indicating their mastery of the subject matter they plan to teach[7] in the same way that doctors become certified by taking National and Specialty Boards.

There can be little quarrel with Koerner's concern over competence; but although one can safely claim that a teacher ignorant of his subject matter lacks competence, the question of competence is not settled even if we know a teacher has mastered his subject. Undoubtedly many courses in teaching methods are vacuous; but a stronger case can be made for making them substantial (a task that will depend heavily on research) than for curtailing them. If Koerner wants to draw from the medical experience, he should take his argument the rest of the way; after all, doing research and applying it to practice have greatly reduced the elements of imprecision and intuition in that field (which was euphemistically called an "art" not so many years ago).

Both Conant and Koerner find distressing amounts of mediocrity in teaching and teacher education; and though their remedies differ, they both direct their attention to the individual teacher and the improvement of his performance. There is nothing wrong with making teachers better, but have Conant and Koerner concerned themselves with a broad enough range of issues? I think not. Although there is much to be said for showing concern about the competence of teachers,[8] the question of competence may be more fully understood in terms of the occupational characteristics of teaching rather than in terms of the curriculum of teacher training institutions. It is to this latter question that I address myself in the belief that problems of competence grow out of the relationships among schools of education, universities, and school systems; between training institutions and prevailing career patterns; and from the way these institutions shape the occupation and its members.[9]

THE CASE FOR AN OCCUPATIONAL PERSPECTIVE

In his paper on the histories of those occupations conventionally called professions, Harold Wilensky presents some revealing observations. He maintains that:

> any occupation wishing to exercise professional authority *must find a technical base for it,* assert an exclusive jurisdiction, *link both skill and jurisdiction to standards of training,* and convince the public that its services are uniquely trustworthy.[10]

This statement refers to occupations whose members have a technical, circumscribed competence based on abstract principles learned through academic *and* practical training. Although these occupations are also known as professions, the associated considerations of status and invidious distinction are beside the point here. Wilensky continues by arguing that this cluster of characteristics emerges over time, and that occupations so characterized develop in patterned stages. By implication, the characteristics of teaching can be understood in a developmental context.

The first stage, he contends, consists of transforming areas of work into full-time occupations; for example, provision has usually been made to care for the sick, but nursing emerged as an occupation concerned with and restricted to the tasks of doing so. Second, training schools for practitioners are established and affiliated with universities where occupationally relevant training and research become formalized. Third, the members of occupations develop associations to establish distinctions between the competent and the incompetent, between members and non-members, and to define those essential occupational tasks that only members should perform. Fourth, codes of ethics are developed to define and control incompetence, reduce internal competition, and protect clients.

Other observers of the occupational scene have attempted to formulate occupational changes in terms of stages; all such attempts, including Wilensky's, so far have been vulnerable to the criticism that the history of one or another occupation "failed" to follow the scheme.[11] Yet even with these qualifications, stage formulations are not without utility. One facet of occupational development is particularly relevant to teaching: the temporal order in which university training schools (explicitly dedicated to advancing knowledge) and national occupational associations (primarily protective in nature) are established.

> In the recent history of professionalism, the organization push often comes before a solid technical and institutional base is formed; the professional association, for instance, typically precedes university-based training schools, and the whole effort seems more an opportunistic struggle for the rewards of monopoly than a "natural history" of professionalism.[12]

The historical record yields much the same picture, as Table 5.1 indicates. Of the first six occupations listed (those generally conceded to be organized around a substantial technological base), four had established university schools prior to forming a national association, a sequence suggesting early recognition of the importance of creating and disseminating knowledge for the competent performance of work. In all the remaining seven occupations, associations for the advancement and protection of occu-

TABLE 5.1   *Critical Stages in the History of American Occupations*

Occupation	Date of First University School	Date of First National Professional Association	University School Antedates National Association	
			Yes	No
Accounting (CPA)	1881	1887	x	
Architecture	1868	1857		x
Civil engineering	1847	1852	x	
Dentistry	1867	1840		x
Law	1817	1878	x	
Medicine	1779	1847	x	
Librarianship	1897	1876		x
Nursing	1909	1896		x
Optometry	1910	1897		x
Pharmacy	1868	1852		x
School teaching	1879	1857		x
Social work	1904	1874		x
Veterinary medicine	1879	1863		x

Adapted from Harold L. Wilensky, "The Professionalization of Everyone?" *American Journal of Sociology*, LXX, No. 2 (1964), table 1, p. 143.

pational members preceded the founding of university schools, a sequence suggesting greater concern with the welfare of members than with the intellectual basis of their work.

In the second list of seven occupations, one finds the so-called human relations occupations of teaching, social work, and nursing —all of which find their claim to special competence in the relatively new and undeveloped social sciences. According to Wilensky:

> The search of social work for a technical base illustrates the dilemma of most "human-relations" professions—knowledge which is at once too broad and too vague. *Paradoxically, knowledge at the other extreme—narrowly restricted, very precise —is also a poor foundation for professional jurisdiction,*[13]

and the same problem prevails in teaching.

Wilensky's data indicate the importance of the connection between occupations and universities in several ways: first, the existence of the connection itself; second, the temporal order in which it is established; and third, the extent to which the apposite university-based knowledge is developed. These considerations, however, do not exhaust the problem because they refer only globally to occupations and to institutions that generate knowledge. Particularly since the temporal order of events in the history of occupations is inherently problematic, the *nature* of the connection between universities and occupations, particularly the connection between the experiences of workers-in-training and full-fledged occupational members, needs to be examined.

THE TRAINING EXPERIENCE IN SCHOOLS OF EDUCATION

Wilensky's work suggests that occupations differ in the way their sources of knowledge are related to patterns of training, self-protection, and self-advancement. What, then, are the peculiar characteristics of institutions that produce teachers? Some are familiar but warrant description here to put the discussion in context. First, two types of training institutions prevail: four-year undergraduate bachelor of science programs comprising liberal arts and job preparation courses (the latter primarily devoted to curriculum and methods); and various graduate programs. Compared to medical, law, and architecture students, teacher trainees usually either start and finish young (like nurses), or spend a very limited amount of time as graduate students.

Second, teaching is one of the largest occupations (along with engineering), and it has a high drop-out rate, especially among new teachers. Schools of education, therefore, must turn out large numbers of fresh recruits simply to supply the market.

Third, schools of education are staffed mostly by faculty who do not teach in the public schools, by people who have never taught or who have taught and stopped to become full- or part-time academicians.

Fourth, with the exception of a few graduate schools connected with large universities, schools of education are not major producers of research on educational practice or on its disciplinary underpinnings. And as for the former graduate schools, one can raise legitimate questions about the relevance of their research activities for the work of teachers and for the technological development of the occupation. Moreover, academics have long shown coolness toward undertaking the difficult tasks of disseminating their research.

Finally, many schools of education carry substantial numbers of students who obtain degrees by studying part-time during the academic year and in the summer only.

THE PRETRAINING EXPERIENCE

Evidence indicates that events preceding formal training influence the shape of the occupation. Traditional approaches to understanding the effect of early events on subsequent occupational outcomes usually include discussions of social origins (these investigations are so readily accessible that I omit discussion of them), types of credentials, and prior training. Ward Mason, for example, finds that most first-year teachers graduated from four-year training institutions or from graduate schools of education hold teaching certificates rather than some less advanced credential (a larger proportion than those who come from liberal arts and junior colleges). They are substantially more likely to have had seven or more semester hours of practice teaching, but anticipate leaving the occupation within five years at the same rate as graduates of other kinds of schools (about twenty-five percent in both groups).[14] Although this kind of information tells us something about the background of teachers, it says nothing about the *nature* of the training experience.

Gordon McIntosh, however, speculates that students entering professional schools from liberal arts colleges may indeed face problems of transition; he maintains that they may tend to organize their teaching around academic disciplines (as presented in college), rather than in some other way, and may gravitate toward teaching levels (mainly secondary) and types of schools (probably middle-class suburban) in which an academic disciplinary approach to teaching appears appropriate.[15] McIntosh continues to pursue a neglected question: the extent that training institutions must get students to discard perspectives acquired previously so that recruits to the occupation can better meet actual job requirements. Graduate training programs, he finds, are likely to adopt a didactic strategy in dealing with this problem: instructing students about what to do, opening the resources of the university to them, insulating them from those actively engaged as teachers, and failing to provide experiences discontinuous with the undergraduate years and organized around tasks they will confront later at work. In short, graduate schools of education resemble liberal, undergraduate colleges in several important ways,[16] and to that extent may fail to provide the resources teachers need to cope with the demands of teaching that differ so markedly from those required to get through college.

Studies of the undergraduate training of teachers indicate that in the aggregate those students heading toward careers in education score lower on tests of intellectual ability than those choosing other occupations. As an estimate of the calibre of education students, this comparison is somewhat misleading because it is contaminated by differences in the market for recruits to various occupations. If, for example, the base for comparison were the top intellectual quarter of undergraduates, it may be that education draws its proportionate share from this elite group; but since the occupation is so large and provides so many openings for first-year teachers, school systems must draw increasingly from the less intellectually gifted simply to fill empty positions, a predicament that smaller occupations need not face if the supply of bright students suffices to fill the openings for new recruits. The more important question here, however, is what happens to the occupational choices of freshman *cohorts*, distinguished by occupational plans, over the four undergraduate years.

James Davis, in his study of the career choices of undergraduates, speaks directly to the questions of loyalty to and defection from occupational-choice cohorts in terms of occupational retentiveness and attractiveness.[17] A retentive cohort consists largely of loyalists, individuals who as seniors hold to their freshman occupational choice; an attractive cohort consists of individuals who by their senior year have switched from their freshman choice to some new one. Retentive occupations have few defectors; attractive ones, many recruits (see Table 5.2). Since retentiveness and attractiveness are independent measures, one can identify types of occupational cohorts: (1) retentive-attractive (education and business); (2) nonretentive-unattractive (medicine and engineering); (3) nonretentive-attractive (social work and religion); and (4) retentive-unattractive (nursing).

The contrast between education and business, on the one hand, and medicine and engineering, on the other, proves illuminating. For the latter pair, many freshmen initially choosing medicine and engineering change their minds and head elsewhere as seniors for reasons probably related to the nature of undergraduate training in these fields and to "mismatches" between the demands of the work (and training for it) and personality characteristics. Undergraduate programs in both fields are demanding in time, number of requirements, and in the difficulty of advanced science courses (and mathematics for engineers). Many premedical students very likely choose medicine for humanitarian reasons but find they spent much of their time in college in the relative isolation of laboratories. These same characteristics of undergraduate programs that drive many initial recruits out probably discourage other students, unhappy with their own initial choices, from coming in. In addition, the greater the number of difficult required courses, the less likely that other students will be able to transfer into the field late in their college careers. Both fields, then, will appeal most to those with a strong initial commitment and with realistic ideas about what will be expected.[18] The college experience, in effect, winnows the cohort out and leaves a com-

TABLE 5.2 *Changes in Occupational Plans During Four Undergraduate Years*

Retentive[1]		Attractive[2]	
	Percent Defectors		*Percent Recruits*
Education	15	Education	16
Business	27	Business	10
Nursing	30	Social work	10
		Religion	7

Nonretentive		Unattractive	
	Percent Defectors		*Percent Recruits*
Law	44	Journalism	5
Religion	45	Architecture	2
Architecture	48	Law	2
Engineering	49	Librarianship	2
Medicine	56	Nursing	2
Journalism	64	Engineering	1
Librarianship	64	Medicine	1
Social work	68		

Adapted from Davis, *Undergraduate Career Decisions*, table 2.5, p. 20; and from data collected by NORC but not published in this volume.
[1]Retentive occupations: few transfers out between freshman and senior year. Index of retentiveness: number of defectors from an occupation (as planned), divided by the number of freshmen choosing that occupation.
[2]Attractive occupations: many recruits between freshman and senior year. Index of attractiveness: number of recruits to an occupation (as planned), divided by the number of freshmen choosing some other occupation.

mitted core prepared to move on to graduate training. In medicine, by implication, it is not surprising to find few dropouts from medical school, and, among physicians, a strong tendency to remain in the occupation for the duration of working life; the potential occupational defectors have already left during their undergraduate years.

In education and business the undergraduate cohort undergoes a different experience (and here I restrict myself only to education). Of the eleven occupations listed in Table 5.2 education is the most retentive; only 15 percent of the freshmen planning to enter the field leave for some other one. It is also the most attractive; 16 percent of all freshmen who select a field other than education plan educational careers as seniors. The senior cohort, then, consists of both loyalists and recruits.[19]

Education, moreover, is widely recognized as an "insurance" occupation; students not sure about what they want to do can pick up the credits necessary to become teachers with relatively little effort, saying, in effect: "Since I don't really know what I want to do, and don't know exactly when I'll find out, at least I can teach until I do or remain a teacher if I like the work." This is hardly the language of strong commitment, though undoubtedly many education students are in fact deeply committed. By the time the education cohort has reached the senior year, its ranks swell to include those with strong and weak commitments to teaching, and refugees from other undergraduate programs who have yet to make up their minds about their life's work. In short, the expanded cohort is marked by great diversity in both interest and commitment.

Education students completing undergraduate programs usually enter the job market directly; those students graduated from liberal arts programs customarily enter graduate school for one or two years before starting the first job. In both cases the extent of formal training is minimal, and the time spent in apprenticeship to learn the skills of the trade through direct experience is scandalously brief. The beginning teacher, woefully unprepared, then starts the first job, one that characteristically entails the same responsibilities that the veteran of many years assumes.

Both folklore and reality testify to the demandingness of the first job. The teacher's isolation (with minimal help from colleagues and superiors), the weakness of the technology in both instructional methods and classroom management, and the difficulties that some pupils create in the classroom all conspire to make the initial experience intensely demanding (one that provides few guidelines for distinguishing personal inadequacy from difficulties inherent in the work). Of course, the first job in many high level occupations is likely to be difficult, but teachers begin work with special disadvantages that derive from their undergraduate experiences. The cohort of beginning teachers, in the light of Davis' data, is typically heterogeneous in its composition rather than honed down to meet the trials of the first job; the demands of the work would be more easily met by a strongly motivated, highly skilled group trained to cope with its stringent demands. In the preoccupational undergraduate experience, then, one finds the seeds of an unstable occupation plagued by high rates of defection and a low degree of commitment.

THE TRAINING EXPERIENCE

Any social institution can be described in terms of its manifest characteristics and by the picture it presents of itself publicly. Institutions of higher education do this by means of a catalogue describing the academic experiences available to students. Although some schools of education serve undergraduates, and others serve just graduate students, the educational experiences they provide are similar (aside from the organizational differences between them). Quite naturally, schools of education differ among themselves over what areas of knowledge are central to the field: emphasis on research, service for school systems, training teachers, or influencing educational policy at various levels of government. But in the training of teachers one finds the staples of the educational curriculum: courses in subject-matter content, in teaching methods, in the social-scientific bases of instruction and classroom management, and in supervised practice teaching. With minor variations from place to place, this set of experiences constitutes the core of teaching training conceived in terms of *curriculum*.

Teacher training programs are not at all unique; new members of most occupations are trained in the principles underlying their work, in the content of the tasks, and in the methods of performing them. Despite these similarities, the social organization of different occupations and of their training institutions varies enormously; and this fact requires consideration of more than just curriculum.

Although one never finds explicit advertisements to this effect, training schools differ in the extent to which they afford students opportunities to develop occupational commitment. Medicine and engineering offer clear cases in point, even during the undergraduate years prior to formal training. Students are exposed to highly concentrated programs taken largely with others with the same occupational destination. The courses are demanding and take up a lot of time, and perhaps most important, the investment is gaining competence in one field means closing options in others.[20] Medical training, accordingly, constrains recruits to remain in the occupation because it exacts large personal investments. It is similar to legal training but not to the same extent; many students attend law school intending to become accountants, businessmen, and politicians—as well as lawyers—because legal training is relevant to those fields. Correlatively, undergraduate prelaw programs lack specificity, and do not exist in many colleges.

Teacher training does not require comparable personal investments, nor are the skills so specific that they preclude other job options; perhaps even the reverse is true: the skills are so nonspecific that they scarcely prepare one to become a teacher. To a greater extent than law schools, schools of education provide occupational insurance: a time to wait before deciding on some other occupation, preparation for a short-term job before getting married, an occupation to fall back on after finding another one unsatisfactory, a small investment of time and money to gain passable credentials, a set of soft, human relations skills useful in many service and business occupations. In short, the training of teachers doesn't contain the elements that retain people in an occupation for a long time. For some it may actually open up non-teaching alternatives both within and without the educational field; for others, of course, the training does what it is supposed to do.

Like the workplace, the training schools separate prospective teachers in ways that militate against the formation of a unified occupation. Elementary and secondary teachers are trained as if they belonged to different occupations. In addition to the invidious status distinctions between the two levels of teaching (distinctions that have remained unaffected by the single salary schedules used in most school systems), the courses of study are so different that a single core of training experiences is nearly unavailable. Many schools provide separate programs in different subject-matter areas, another source of divisiveness within the occupation. The heart of the problem is that no widely agreed-upon core of general principles, courses, and training experiences exists around which to create occupational coherence and unity. Finally, practice teaching is primarily built around a dyadic relationship between apprentice and cooperating teacher rather than around a cohort of apprentices working under experienced practitioners and supervisors.[21]

Some evidence suggests that practice teaching, however brief, constitutes the crucial training experience. Laurence Iannaccone and Warren Button, in one of the few systematic investigations of practice teaching, argue that this phase of training contributes not to the development of occupational norms but to reducing anxiety about teaching and to learning classroom techniques "that work" even when those techniques violate apprentices' idealistic conceptions of good teaching.[22] In moving from the position of classroom observer to operative, the practice teacher discovers that the perspective imported from college:

> does not work to solve the problematic situation she faces in the teaching set. A new perspective which she develops with the combined help of the flow of information, evaluation and advice in the dyad, and the example of her cooperating teacher does work to solve the problematic situation she faces in the teaching set.[23]

That is, practice teaching, in addition to reducing anxiety, seems to contribute most to discovering workable conduct where "workable" becomes characteristically defined as classroom management: following fixed schedules of instruction, simplifying lesson plans, getting through the material, and cutting back on the breadth and richness of the material presented. These skills are picked up by watching the cooperating teachers at work, listening to their advice, and trying out their methods.[24] Practice teaching, however, being primarily dyadic in character, tends to restrict the apprentice's scope of vision and experience to events occurring under the jurisdiction of one cooperating teacher.

SCHOOLS OF EDUCATION AND OTHER TRAINING INSTITUTIONS

Since occupations differ, there is little surprise in finding that training schools do also. Occupations, however, differ in ways not readily explained by variations in the training curriculum: to what extent do members form a cohesive occupational community? How much faith does the public have in the members' capacity to fulfill their mandate, to cope with the contingencies and uncertainties of the job? Finally, training institutions themselves differ in social organization from one occupation to another. Consider teaching, medicine, law, college "teaching," and social work.

Teacher training tends to be short in duration (even in four-year undergraduate programs where time must be divided between professional training and liberal arts education). Many students attend part-time or acquire degrees and credits by studying summers; some, in fact, obtain their formal credentials *after* starting the first job. Education school faculties almost always have at least a few members trained in disciplinary fields (psychology, history, philosophy, languages, science, and mathematics), but many if not most are nonteachers or ex-teachers rather than persons currently employed in the occupation for which they train others, hardly a good advertisement for the field. The so-called cooperating teachers are full-time employees of school systems but do not hold faculty positions in schools of education—hence a split into professional and academic contingents among those responsible for training teachers.

Research, theoretical and applied, does not constitute one of the central activities in schools of education except at a few institutions. Prospective teachers, consequently, fail to become engaged in it—perhaps remain unexposed to it—as part of their training; and once on the job, they do not become consumers of it. Immediately following graduation (or even before), students embark on the first job, one entailing full classroom responsibilities, ecologically isolated from experienced colleagues, but subject to sporadic supervision by school administrators, supervision that even if helpful cannot be based on prolonged observation. Hence the portrait of the beginning teacher: cut off from the sources of knowledge underlying his work, isolated from colleagues and superiors, left alone to figure out the job—discover, correct, or repeat his own errors—through his own experience.

MEDICAL SCHOOLS

The medical case differs sharply. Medical education is strictly graduate training though many students are products of undergraduate premedical programs consisting of courses in the medically related sciences, but without training in the practice of medicine. A medical degree takes four years to acquire; at the outset, medical students encounter some faculty with Ph.D.'s in scientific disciplines and some who are physicians; later, all their instructors are physicians engaged in medical practice—either full-time house staff members of a teaching hospital or part-time (with the remainder spent in private practice or research).

Medical schools are always affiliated with hospitals; that is, training takes place where the full range of medical work is done. Even nonclinical courses are offered by members of the medical faculty, not by the chemistry and biology departments of the universities to which medical schools are affiliated. Clinical training takes place in small groups with students, members of the house and attending hospital staff participating. Students' activities are closely supervised and usually consist of some small part of a total medical procedure; responsibilities are doled out in small quantities and increase in scope over time. Unlike schools of education, didactic training and actual job performance are closely joined; and although medical students read books and listen to lectures, the basic training consists of actual practice with medical men of varying degrees of experience. To a large extent, then, work and training coincide in an apprenticeship system.

Medical schools and their associated hospitals are typically research centers. Although schools vary in how much they emphasize research and promote scientific and clinical careers, medical students, because of their proximity to research and its infusion into their training, tend to become consumers of and participants in it. The training of a doctor, that is, brings him into close contact with the process of producing and advancing the technical knowledge that forms the scientific basis of his work.

Finally, medical education does not end with the completion of medical school. The new M.D. is unqualified to begin practice, and his training continues through a year of internship and at least one or more—and many more with certain specialties—years of residency. Although interns and residents assume both training and treatment responsibilities, they still remain students while their responsibility for making unsupervised decisions increases.

The training of academicians resembles that of physicians in many ways. Although students enter separate graduate departments they do so as a cohort and usually remain with their peers until the completion of residence requirements or doctoral examinations. At the thesis writing stage, the original cohort often disperses; but graduate students, at least through the second year, usually attend school together and share many academic experiences, particularly the ritual crises of general exams. In time, interests become specialized, often along lines that follow faculty research projects or the availability of fellowship and assistantship money. Graduate training, just prior to and during the thesis stage, has the characteristics of an apprenticeship in research and scholarship. A variety of options open up for students, each with advantages and costs: they may do research on their own with faculty supervision, work *with* some faculty member on a part of his research and maintain considerable control over it, or do research *for* a faculty member under his close direction, an arrangement that comes very close to employment.

However much apprenticeship is involved, it is an apprenticeship in scholarly activity and not in college *teaching*, even though many students completing graduate school enter careers in college teaching. Most universities, in fact, hire teachers even though they really expect research output from their faculty. The teaching component of the academician's job receives little formal emphasis, although that varies with the institution, and graduate schools provide little preparation for it.

In addition to apprenticeship, graduate schools resemble medical schools in forging a sense of unity around scholarly disciplines. A discipline is in part a public arena for the circulation of ideas within an area of knowledge, public at least for those affiliated with it. Publication is the circulating medium for ideas; and whereas individuals establish an attachment to the discipline in graduate school, formal manifestations of it are found in the "learned societies" and in university and college departments. Reputations are made and lost in the eyes of one's colleagues through publication wherever they happen to be located; and careers are advanced or broken in the same way. It is largely collegial esteem for scholarly output (with some petty irrelevancies mixed in) that determines where an academician will "teach," a judgment of performance having little to do with teaching.

The crucial difference between university teaching and medicine, on the one hand, and public (or private) school teaching, on the other, is that in the latter, the employer—the school system through its administrative decision—controls one's occupational fate; and in the former, the community of disciplinary colleagues exercises more control than the employing university. The school teacher, in other words, is an employee; the college teacher is an employee as far as his teaching obligations are concerned, but his research activities are patronized, and their quality reflects on both the university's and the faculty member's reputation.

Whatever the gains and costs of each system of training, clearly the training experiences of prospective teachers do not include situations conducive to the production and public dissemination of knowledge about their work so characteristic of medical and academic training. The absence of a research tradition in schools of education is one of the prime reasons for the relative absence of a viable technology and an occupational community among teachers; for without research *or its equivalents* (precedent and statute for lawyers, theology for clergymen), there is little impetus to establish public communication among members of the occupation.

LAW SCHOOLS

Legal training represents still a different pattern. Two types of law schools predominate: the university school, which is really a professional school attached to a large university (this type is usually accorded the most prestige and sends many of its graduates to large, prestigious firms that in turn serve wealthy, corporate clients in the higher level courts); and the proprietary school, usually privately owned and staffed by lawyers with small, private practices who teach part-time, which attracts students (many of whom study part-time and at night) who generally lack the financial resources to attend university schools, and who are likely to practice in small firms serving poorer clients in the lower level courts. Obviously this is an oversimplification, but as a broad generalization it contains the major distinctions.[25] Law schools—although the distinction appears most clearly in the university schools—when compared with medical and education schools illustrate some of the fundamental connections between preparation for an occupation and practice in it. On their face, law and medical schools appear to be analogous institutions for preparing practitioners; in fact, the direct analogy is misleading. The law school graduate—particularly of a university-affiliated school—knows little about the day-to-day practice of law. As Lortie puts it:

> For three years the young attorney, studying in a special school, is isolated from the marketplace of legal services,

and he often graduates without any contact with real legal work. His school environment provides small opportunity to witness the varieties and subtleties of lawyer roles, and although his knowledge of legal principles probably exceeds that of his nineteenth century predecessor, he graduates with minimal knowledge of the procedures and institutions of practice.[26]

In effect, law schools train their students largely in the *principles* of the law; the appropriate analogy must be drawn, then, not with medical schools but with their preclinical years where the bulk of the curriculum is devoted to the scientific principles of medicine. The *practice* of medicine and the treatment of patients is reserved mainly for the clinical years.

Where, then, does the young lawyer learn his trade if not in law school? Characteristically, on the first job with a firm or as a clerk for a judge; that is, where law is practiced, not in academic institutions. In fact, the same situation prevails in medicine; medical students learn to practice in hospitals, but medical schools and hospitals occupy the same premises, while law schools are not attached to courts or firms. In both cases, however, learning the trade by doing it, task by task and under close supervision, is preceded by a period of learning the underlying principles. As Erwin Smigel, in his study of large Wall Street law firms contends, the reason that law school graduates, especially from the large university law schools, take their first jobs in the large firms is because these firms provide a post-graduate education in the practice of law.[27] The price they pay is getting caught in the conflicting demands of being both employees and free professionals, a conflict that the medical man, at the same stage in his training, does not face to the same degree because the internship and the early years of residency are still considered student statuses. The young lawyer is not formally a student, but he is treated like one by partners of the firm.

Legal training, at least at the university schools, creates conditions conducive to forming a sense of unity among students. All students take required courses in the first and sometimes the second year. They experience common demands, reflecting, in good part, substantial agreement within the profession on a common core of knowledge. In addition, methods of instruction require that a student know his material thoroughly; he may be called on at random and asked to explain a point of law publicly and have his answer challenged or torn apart in front of his peers, a situation ingeniously designed to make all those present feel they are in the same boat.

The law does not have a research tradition in the same sense that medicine, engineering, academic life, and, to a lesser extent, architecture do. Although a law student must learn how to look up the law (far from a simple procedure), his work does not consist of the advancement or creation of new knowledge. The intellectual underpinnings of the profession lie not in scientific knowledge and principles, as in medicine and engineering, but in the cumulative body of court decisions, statute law, rules of evidence, and courtroom procedure. This body of knowledge supports the lawyer's technology as used in the courtroom, but not only there. According to Paul Freund, the practice of law outside the courtroom contains perhaps the most interesting challenges:

> Consensual arrangements contrived through negotiation and formulated in legal documents are less subject to these constraints and represent a form of law making in which the legal imagination is called upon to devise a viable framework that will provide a modicum of order while respecting the disorder, complexity, and spontaneity of men's aspirations. It is this aspect of legal practice that most nearly resembles the enterprise of the artist.[28]

Law schools, then, provide the rudiments of later practice (although proprietary law schools probably come closer to being vocational schools than do the university schools); the *practice* of law is learned more on the job than in school.

Teachers also learn their craft on the job, but the difference between their experiences and those of young lawyers is striking since the teacher lacks prior, rigorous training in the principles of his work. He learns to practice his occupation as a nearly solitary employee, largely cut off from older and contemporary colleagues and from administrators (the analogues of employers), who simply cannot get around to enough classrooms or spend enough time in them to teach teachers their jobs. The teacher learns largely on his own, from his classroom experiences and from his pupils; and he is hard put to find out whether his experiences are unique or typical.

SCHOOLS OF SOCIAL WORK

Preparation for social work has many of the problems found in teacher training; foremost is the haziness of underlying technology. Both teaching and social work fall into that group of human welfare occupations whose technology depends on the state of the social and psychological sciences, which currently do not provide adequate guidelines for practice. Just as many people out-side teaching claim expertise in education, others beside social workers claim knowledge in the humane care of people in adversity. Neither teachers nor social workers can claim an exclusive mandate having broad public acknowledgement. Both accordingly suffer from the softness of their technologies and from the inability to establish monopolies over them. Social workers have perhaps moved farther, however, in trying to define their core activities, but in neither occupation does the state of the art provide clear criteria for defining a training program.

Although social work is a variegated occupation that includes different kinds of individual case work, group work, and the management of welfare agencies, the recent trend has been to professionalize the occupation around the skills of psychiatric case work. Training, at least over the past several decades, according to Harold Wilensky and Charles Lebeaux, has drawn increasingly on the contributions of psychoanalytic theory with an admixture of research in the social sciences.[29] Social workers, in other words, while moving in the direction of individual case work, continue an older belief that people's misfortunes are partly a product of their social and economic circumstances. In their search for a central area of competence they have put particular emphasis on training in interviewing, counseling, obtaining information about clients' backgrounds, distinguishing surface from underlying problems, and gaining knowledge about available community resources for referrals;[30] around this core of skills they have established two-year graduate training programs. The more rigorous training requirements, such as taking the academic and field-work components simultaneously, are part of a self-conscious attempt to professionalize the occupation. Thus they have made preparation more demanding than teachers have, making it longer in duration and discouraging the acquisition of degrees through part-time study. At the same time, they have put themselves at a competitive disadvantage in gaining recruits. Teachers, by comparison, can earn roughly the same salaries with a smaller and easier investment in preparation, and both occupations draw from similar segments of the female population.

Social workers have drawn more than their technology from psychiatry; their training, unlike that of teachers, is heavily supervised, and supervision continues once social workers become employed—in hospitals, family service, and welfare agencies. The great emphasis on supervision perhaps reflects an attempt to compensate for the softness of the technology and to preserve a sense of autonomy in an occupation whose jurisdictional boundaries with psychiatry and clinical psychology are indistinct (and where psychiatrists, however low their status within the medical fraternity, hold the advantage in status).[31]

Schools of education, medical schools, law schools, schools of social work, architecture, divinity, and engineering belong to a class of social settings whose primary mission is to bring about psychological changes in people. To fill out the category more, one should include families, colleges, prisons, mental hospitals, and churches; also various contrived arrangements such as psychotherapy, brainwashing, religious conversion, and mass-media exposure. Despite their variety, they have certain social properties in common even though these properties vary in manifestation. In addition, some are more successful in their mission than others. Some changes are modest, like the small accretions of skill and information that training schools for business machine operators (described earlier) produce; others are more profound, like the shaping of children's basic personality characteristics during their years as dependent members of families. Prisons and mental hospitals are noted for their failures to rehabilitate; medical schools are known for their success in creating physicians out of college graduates. And most, if not all, of these settings produce both intended and unanticipated changes. To understand how schools of education (and other occupational training institutions) work, they must be viewed in this broader context. Although a full discussion of the common and variant properties of "person-changing" institutions is far beyond the scope of this book, two properties are of central importance: first, those aspects of the setting that exert pressure of leverage on their members to change; and second, those aspects that provide social linkage with both previous and subsequent situations in which trainees find themselves.

Leverage. Consider first the *pressures* that medical schools exert on their students, particularly during the preclinical years. According to Howard Becker and his colleagues in their study of the University of Kansas Medical School, first-year students are confronted with an unmanageably heavy work load.[32] They discover early that even if they spend nearly all their time studying, the task remains insurmountable, and that their initial strategy for coping with the task—"learn everything"—proves unworkable. Learning the material proves problematic in another way. The failure of their initial strategy provokes them to find a viable alternative; for example, to discover what the faculty deems important and learn, or to devote time to learning those things that appear most useful for later practice. While these criteria seem appropriate in principle, in reality they do not provide students with adequate guidelines simply because the faculty offers no explicit clues about what they want nor about what will be useful later. The students' situation, then, is scarcely improved, and they remain individually confronted with the uncertainty of their predicament.

The work load problem confronts students individually and collectively. Because they spend so much time together and work jointly on the same laboratory tasks, they have opportunities to talk about their work and about the problems of studying posed by it. Their engagement in common tasks, the shared uncertainty, the intensive and extensive social contact, and the isolation from upper classmen in the medical school and from the faculty (at least in the sense that the faculty will not "spoonfeed" them) and from conventional social contacts because there is so much work to do collectively provide the impetus to work out a *collective* solution to the work load problem.

Dealing with their situation collectively rather than individually makes a crucial difference. They still try to figure out what the faculty wants and learn techniques for doing so mainly from those of their number who were fraternity members as undergraduates (i.e., those already possessing some experience in discovering what a faculty wants, at least on examinations).[33] They continue to study hard, and "try to find out, in every way . . . short of cheating, what questions will be on the examinations and how they should be answered and *share this information with other members of the class.*"[34] The willingness to share is extremely important. One would not expect to find it in highly competitive situations, but medical students know that medical school mortality rates are low. They carry out much of their laboratory work in small groups whose members have equal and joint responsibility for doing it; in effect, they teach each other. There is little reason not to share because no one jeopardizes his own chances of success by making public what he knows, by contributing to the commonweal.

Properties of the medical school environment (not just the curriculum) affect the character of medical education. First, medical school presents a clear discontinuity with the preceding undergraduate years in that it is homogenizing in its impact: all students study the same subjects, it is relatively noncompetitive (certainly less so than in premedical programs where the competition to get into medical schools, particularly into good ones, can be ferocious), it presents students with an academic work load larger than any they have encountered previously, and it creates a condition of social isolation and of being "in the same boat" by virtue of both

the work load (leaving little time for other activities beside studying) and the single purpose that brings only medical students
together and excludes others preparing for different occupations.
Second, the situation generates pressures that prove personally problematic to each individual and sufficiently intense
to call for an adaptive solution, for a new way of thinking about
and coping with the immediate environment. As I have indicated,
medical school provides social resources for students to develop
a workable collective solution, one in which they can find safety
in numbers, and form a cohesive unit attributable to individually
felt threat in a situation that moderates competitiveness. The first
year at Kansas Medical School produces conditions not unlike
those found in industrial work groups where collectively determined rates of production protect workers against the competitive
threat of rate-busters and the indolence of goldbrickers.

Similar work load problems confront students of law and
architecture. Law students also must master formidable amounts
of material and defend their understanding and interpretation
of it publicly under personally threatening conditions. With students of architecture the problem is not so much one of absorbing
vast amounts of knowledge as one of putting time into preparing
projects that represent solutions to problems of design and
construction to be submitted for faculty evaluation. In both cases
the training situation creates pressures that drive students together for mutual support and protection. Similarly, among graduate students in academic disciplines, the impending crisis of
general examinations, particularly when members of a cohort
take them together, provides an incentive to form study groups
where they pool their knowledge and work out strategies for answering a broad range of questions likely to appear on the exam.

It would be incorrect to regard these collective responses to
the crises of occupational training solely as defensive maneuvers.
Equally important, they provide conditions for shaping an occupational perspective. Externally imposed academic demands provide students with opportunities to think like doctors, lawyers,
architects, academicians, or whatever, and to press each other
to contribute out of a sense of mutual obligation. The collective
nature of these settings, in which students seek each other out to
cope with individual crises, becomes one condition for developing
an occupational point of view.[35] In the vicissitudes of training,
therefore, one finds social forces that later identify those occupations resembling occupational communities and those that do
not.[36]

Schools of education generate few of the pressures on their
students that medical schools, law schools, and others impose; the

TABLE 5.3   *Teachers' Sentiments About Teaching Again, by Academic Attainment and Years of Teaching Experience*

Highest Degree Held and Years of College Completed	Number of teachers reporting	Willingness to Teach Again	
		Certainly would %	Certainly or probably would not %
No degree	274	63.0	5.5
Bachelor's degree and less than 5 years	893	49.7	9.6
Bachelor's degree and 5 or more years	271	45.7	13.1
Master's or higher	443	44.7	14.6
Years of Experience in Teaching			
Less than 3 years	265	51.5	7.2
3–9 years	604	45.1	12.3
10–19 years	471	51.3	9.1
20 years or more	512	53.1	12.4

Adapted from *The American Public-School Teacher*, table 43, p. 63; copyright 1965. Reprinted by permission of The National Education Association. Two categories of "Willingness to teach again" are omitted in the NEA data: "Probably would teach again," and "Chances about even." For the total sample of teachers the responses to these alternatives amount to 26.9 percent and 12.5 percent respectively.

reason lies partly in the social organization of the schools. A symptom of one problem in teacher training is illustrated by the NEA figures indicating an inverse relationship between occupational commitment and the amount of academic training, as shown in Table 5.3. The evidence indicates that the higher the degree of the teachers' academic attainment, the *less* their willingness to teach again if they had the choice to make over (among those with at least a B.A., half or fewer would become teachers again). The number of years employed in teaching has no clear relationship to the likelihood of reentering the occupation.

The strength of the first relationship is not dramatic; what is dramatic is that increased schooling—the NEA does not specify whether the advanced training is in education or in some other field—is associated with decreasing commitment to the occupation. Why this is so is not immediately apparent. Perhaps men undertake advanced training to become administrators, or teachers take advanced work in fields outside education to prepare for other occupations, or advanced training produces disenchantment because teachers cannot readily connect what they learn academically to the problems they face in the classroom. Whatever the reason, greater academic preparation does not signify greater occupational allegiance among substantial numbers of teachers.

Additional evidence on the character of schools of education relates to the financial support of graduate students. A student who doesn't need to support himself through his own efforts can devote a more substantial portion of his time to academic activities; and to the extent that he also involves himself in the social life of the school—those social relationships centering around the training process itself—the more he subjects himself to the inculcating influences of the school. (Whether he accepts or rejects the school's agenda is a separate question, but social involvement provides more opportunities for academic involvement than does isolation.) By contrast, the student who earns his own living must commit more of his time (and perhaps also more of his interest and loyalty) to his employment. One can argue, then, that the more time and energy a student devotes to earning a livelihood, the less accessible he will be to those social forces that deepen his involvement in the training institution.[37] Davis reports some fragmentary findings on this point, as shown in Table 5.4.

TABLE 5.4 *The Financing of Graduate Training, by Occupation*

| | **Expected Modes of Support** | | | |
Occupations	*Full-time Job[a]*	*Part-time Job[a]*	*Support Other than Work[b]*	*Number Planning Grad School*
	%	%	%	
Nursing	53	4	43	76
Education	52	19	29	3377
Engineering	45	19	36	1315
Business	41	26	33	1334
Law	15	35	50	1645
Social work	15	29	56	239
Medicine	3	32	65	1261

Adapted from James A. Davis, *Great Aspirations*, table 4.24, p. 212.
[a]Includes some students who anticipate receiving support from sources other than work: savings, loans, parents and other relatives, income from spouses, etc.
[b]Estimate of support from sources other than employment, although some students included here are also employed.

Seniors planning careers in education rank second to prospective nurses (52 percent and 53 percent respectively) on the
likelihood of intending to hold full-time jobs while putting themselves through school, a finding consistent with the fact that many
students in education attend school part-time and that many
teachers, particularly men, moonlight for financial reasons. Although lack of money is probably the main contributing cause
(note that a very small proportion of medical and law students
plan to work full-time—it must be virtually impossible to go through
medical school while doing so—most likely because they come
from wealthier families), the likely effects of full-time employment are apposite. Particularly at the graduate level, the distinction between outside employment and employment as part of
training (such as assistantships) must be distinguished. The latter
is one good way to increase students' involvement in their own
occupational development. Outside employment, at least when
time consuming, can partially negate the advantages of undertaking graduate work as a member of a cohort whose members
can exert lateral pressures on each other (as at Kansas Medical
School).[38]

If faculty members exemplify conventional professional values
and perspectives and also stand as figures of authority within training institutions, their influence on students in passing on an occupational tradition probably works as follows:

> Common values of the group of subordinates [students]
> legitimate the superior's expanded control over them. If
> the performance of a supervisor [faculty member] furthers
> the collective interests of subordinates and commands their
> common respect and loyalty, social agreement is likely to
> develop among them that they owe a *collective* obligation
> to him. To repay their joint obligation and maintain the
> supervisor's good will, the group of subordinates is under
> pressure to make compliance with his directives part of
> the common norms. . . .[39]

That is, lateral pressure generated within the cohort abets the
process of occupational transmission by legitimizing faculty influence.

The employed graduate student often finds himself tied ten-
uously to a network of peers and superiors; his outside obligations
remove him partially from the social context that can bind him
into occupational life. Jerome Carlin provides an interesting example of this process among lawyers. In accounting for varying
rates of ethical violation, a sign of weak community control over

members, he indicates that: "fifty-one per cent of the disciplined lawyers and forty-six per cent of the violators were graduates of lower-quality law schools, compared to twenty-three per cent of the high conformers."[40] One important characteristic of poor law schools (usually proprietary night schools) is that they serve large numbers of part-time students who because of their part-time involvement are least likely to become subject to and absorbed into the more conventional culture of legal practice, and are most likely to practice highly competitive types of law that encourage the most dubious methods for attracting clients, in the lowest level courts where the sanctions against unethical conduct are least stringent.

In comparing two academic occupations, public school and college teaching, Lortie contends that a collectively experienced ordeal *built into the formal pattern of training* contributes to the development of occupational commitment and of individual enhancement defined in terms of self-identification as a full-fledged practitioner.[41] To support his argument he cites a study of M.I.T. graduate students taking general examinations for the doctorate. Summarizing the findings "in the rhetoric of puberty rites," he states:

> Those who endured and passed the tests imposed by the elders [professors] changed subjectively—the gap they had felt between themselves and adults narrowed appreciably. Candidates who *shared the trial with others* changed more than those who went it alone; sharing added to the impact of the experience. All who participated in the experience gained something from it; the general exams, in short, accelerated a sense of manhood [professionalism].[42]

It is well known, as Lortie indicates, that graduate training for an academic career includes a sequence of hurdles, some routine, others demanding in their own right and in the intense anxiety they generate. Students view them not only as tests of what they know but also as proof of occupational commitment; having passed them, they see themselves as having moved that much closer to being professors, as having gained in competence. Clearly they don't *know* more after the examination than they did immediately before it, but by bearing up under the ordeal they have apparently proved something to themselves and about themselves: that they more closely resemble their mentors in competence and stature.

Passage through graduate schools of education differs conspicuously. Entrance is easy, an advance indication that students will not confront serious obstacles along the way. Courses, or perhaps more correctly credit for courses, can be accumulated over time; and when amassed in sufficient quantity, they become negotiable for credentials to teach (not infrequently *after* the individual has already begun teaching). In his own research Lortie asked teachers if in the course of their training they experienced "turning points" indicating to them that they had become "pros."

> Some respondents refused to grant the premise of the question, alleging that teachers never become sure of their competence. Those who did cite a turning point mentioned a wide variety of occasions when it occurred; few turning points mentioned can be classified as *institutionalized recognitions of performance.*[43]

Practice teaching *is* commonly considered an ordeal; and even more so, the first job. Both, moreover, are experienced individually; if the interpretation of the M.I.T. findings is correct (that the collective character of the ordeal is important for establishing both commitment and a sense of enhanced occupational competence), teacher preparation is conspicuously lacking in that ingredient. An individually confronted crisis certainly can have more than one outcome. Some teachers undoubtedly experience it as a test of their mettle and emerge with a sense of newly discovered strength; others are carried out feet first. Both outcomes occur in the training of teachers, in graduate school, and on the job; but the point is that the standard training process *contains no formal provision* for the creation and management of such crises. On the assumption that this argument is correct, the high drop-out rate among teachers comes as no surprise.[44]

Schools of education, then, mobilize few of the resources apparently necessary to form an occupational community among teachers. They do not subject students to the intense pressures and crises that contribute to the creation of solidarity among them, a solidarity that can produce unanticipated benefits in occupational learning. Part-time—and by implication partly committed—participation characterizes these schools. Unlike medical schools where training in both general principles and practice fall under the jurisdiction of a single faculty, and unlike law schools where these two components of training follow sequentially, schools of education (through practice teaching arrangements with public schools) foster a potential conflict between these components by assigning them to separate jurisdictions simultaneously. This arrangement can be most pernicious in its effect; the academic component is characteristically condemned by students as impractical and irrelevant; the practice teaching component, although acknowledged to be the most valuable part of inadequate training, is based primarily on a dyadic relationship between cooperating and practice teachers, sealing students from colleagues and making them dependent on the example of one person's experience in finding out "what works" in the classroom. This situation narrows the scope of students' training, inhibits the circulation of knowledge and experience among them, and restricts opportunities to work out general formulations of the teaching experience by those engaged in it.

The continuity between undergraduate and graduate training —the latter strongly resembling a liberal arts curriculum, however much watered down—obstructs the formation of a distinctively occupational culture. Wherein lies the teacher's claim to a peculiar identity if his occupational training scarcely distinguishes him from common garden-variety liberal arts college graduates? Unlike the medical school, law school, religious seminary, or military officers' candidate school, the school of education fails to isolate its students sufficiently from conventional obligations, nor does it restrict social contacts to their own kind in order to propagate a characteristic occupational "party line." These social limitations, taken together with a poorly delineated technology and a period of training perhaps too brief for a cohesive cohort to develop, cannot readily support a strong occupational training institution. Of course, the cynic might argue: better a weak institution than a strong one that creates durable commitments to an occupation with an ineffective technology. The educational establishment can ill afford to follow the route of psychoanalytic institutes and the colleges of chiropractic.

To state the main issue in general terms, an organization that aims to change people—their styles of thinking, repertoire of skills, patterns of conduct, attitudes, and beliefs—must have certain capacities: to induce, to punish, to reward, to create goodwill, to support—that is, to exert leverage.

Leverage takes many forms depending on the setting. In families, parents attempting to shape the conduct and thinking of their young children, consciously and unconsciously establish and exploit relationships of dependency and affection; that is, they employ the deepest and most elemental emotional resources available. Psychotherapists, following the familial model, use the relationships of transference and countertransference to achieve similar results with adults. Brainwashing relies on terror; military relocation centers on deracination; school classrooms on public assaults on self-respect; peer groups on the tyranny of majorities. And as I have argued earlier, professional schools create anxiety-provoking tasks and unmanageable work situations that create individual crises and responses of collective defense. All have in common some means of arousing emotion of sufficient intensity that individuals seek a way out of a psychologically problematic, often intolerable, situation. But seldom, if ever, is it a matter of indifference *which* way out an individual selects; and particularly where an agency, such as a professional school, is involved, one finds attempts to shape the outcome, to direct the way out. Emotional leverage is not usually generated for its own sake, but rather in the service of some desired outcome. When the school of education is viewed in these terms, its resources for exerting leverage appear exceedingly limited; and in those situations where teacher training does produce individual crises, the school is poorly placed to channel the emotional energy released because the crises usually occur within some other jurisdiction.

Linkage. The second major property of "person-changing" institutions are arrangements that provide linkage between people's previous and subsequent social situations. The institutional forms of linkage bear directly on the problem of directing individuals whose situation during training subjects them to psychological stress.

To understand the problem of linkage and to distinguish it from that of leverage, consider the case of schools of education (primarily at the graduate level) in contrast to other training settings. The school typically admits a cohort of students whose members have recently completed college. The education student's transition into graduate school requires no substantial departure from his undergraduate liberal arts preparation. With the exception of courses in teaching methods and experience in practice teaching, the change consists largely of engaging in a similar type of *academic* activity but with some differences in curriculum content. That is, the transition from undergraduate to graduate school demands no fundamental change in style of thinking or academic conduct.

On completing his formal graduate training the ex-student (now a teacher) begins his first job almost immediately, and this transition from school to work makes substantial demands. First, and most obvious, the change from student to employee is abrupt. Practice teaching, because of its brevity, inadequacy of supervision, lack of focus on specific job-relevant skills (as opposed to its broad orientation to the whole job of teaching), and its reliance on a two-person apprenticeship cannot adequately bridge the gap between job requirements and undergraduate preparation. Medicine, law, and architecture, in contrast, create abrupt transitions between college and graduate school, but prolong and blur the transition between training and full occupational engagement. Schools of education ease the student in; other training schools ease him out. Second, the beginning teacher undertakes employment without command over a viable technology and without close contact with and support by peers similarly situated. Third, fresh out of school and often bringing new ideas with him, the new recruit often confronts the skepticism of older "experienced" colleagues who "have tried all those new things and know they don't work." As Lortie describes it:

> There is a subtle but pervasive mistrust between older and beginning teachers. Eased entry into teaching [i.e., through nondemanding preparation] means that some beginners are, in fact, merely "putting in time" or "looking around" while performing as teachers. Older teachers generalize observations of such beginners to the entire category and hesitate to support younger colleagues against the administrative hierarchy.[45]

That is, the public schools, as work settings, provide a weak connection between experienced and inexperienced teachers, a particularly acute liability in an occupation where the circulation of lore must compensate for the near absence of codified technology.

The problem of linkage is to create capacities, job-related competencies which trainees lack. This statement, however, construes the problem psychologically, in terms of what happens to people. There is also an organizational side to the question: what properties of an organization, agency, or social setting make it possible for personal changes to occur in one direction or another?

Consider nursing schools. According to Ida Simpson, first-year students enter with a strong commitment to help the sick and the suffering. Their training begins, however, with a strong dose of academic work and training in technical skills and routines.

> This technical orientation was evident in the teaching of simple basic nursing tasks, which were defined as standardized procedures to be performed in precise sequences of steps. Making a bed, for instance, called for twenty-one consecutive steps. In both teaching and grading the faculty emphasized the accuracy with which these routines were mastered, not the welfare of the patients on whom the students practiced their nursing skills.[46]

Learning to follow orders from both physicians and nursing supervisors also comprised a significant component of their training. True, many of the skills and the orders pertain directly to the proper care of patients, but this could scarcely be called training in nurturance.

The character of general nursing preparation appears in bold relief when students undertake training in psychiatric nursing. According to JoAnne Medalie and Daniel Levinson:

> A common goal in nursing training is to condition students to accept negative criticism and benefit from it; giving the student a "hard time" is part of the culture of general hospital nursing training. The rather militaristic kind of discipline is thought to prepare a student for the exigencies of being a nurse.[47]

This represents the traditional model; the psychiatric setting calls for something strikingly different:

> An individual member is expected to immerse himself [sic] in the milieu, to learn for himself, and eventually to define his mode of operation in terms that best suit him as an individual. The emphasis on psychodynamics leads to a wide tolerance in individual job performance—work difficulties tend to be understood in terms of the individual's emotional adjustment and are dealt with in a somewhat clinical manner. The very nature of the work—dealing with emotionally disturbed people—demands that wider limits be allowed for personnel to develop themselves as therapeutic agents.[48]

The rule, then, is "be yourself," an injunction difficult to translate into specific procedures around which to design a training program.

The training of general hospital nurses is not designed to create a cadre of cold-hearted technicians—undoubtedly some turn out that way—but rather to impose a set of specific skills and habits of mind on an existing base of nurturant impulses, which if allowed to run free, might actually make the nurse's job psychologically punishing.

In most occupational training programs the basic mechanism for establishing linkage between the position of student and "adult" practitioner is his active involvement in performing activities that will occupy him in the future. For nurses, that responsibility is carrying out tasks properly *and* doing so when they are told; hence, the considerable emphasis on obedience.[49] As already indicated, the same principle holds for medical, legal, architectural, and social work students, and to a lesser extent for prospective teachers. In essence, a prime element in establishing linkage is a system of apprenticeship: supervised participation in each facet of the job, controlled either by the training institution, an employer, or both. Another aspect of linkage is the composition of work groups in which training occurs (with particular reference to the association between more- and less-experienced trainees, and between trainees and practicing members of the occupation). Stanton Wheeler discusses four types of settings designed for changing people: according to whether new members enter individually or collectively; and according to whether members, alone or in cohorts, establish contact with their immediate predecessors (serial), or enter as if they were unpreceded (disjunctive).[50]

The serial-disjunctive dimension pertains to generations: Does the setting provide opportunities for social contact between veterans and neophytes? A serial arrangement allows the new generation to gather knowledge about the setting, activities, problems, and workable modes of adaptation from those who came just before them; it forms a basis of vertical solidarity. There is no guarantee that the knowledge communicated vertically will be salutary or destructive for the new recruits, the old hands, or the setting itself. Nevertheless, serial arrangements open up opportunities not provided by disjunctive ones. But like the second child in a family, the second and subsequent cohorts in training institutions find the ground broken for them, battles already fought and won; they need not start from scratch.

The individual-collective dimension pertains to peer solidarity: does the setting provide opportunities for members of a cohort to form social relationships with each other?[51] Again, the existence of an arrangement only makes opportunities available for cohesive groups to form among peers; it does not guarantee their formation. (Wheeler's scheme is restricted to the "clients" of socializing organizations—patients, inmates, students, etc.—and does not include functionaries—socializing agents—whose presence and conduct are equally important in shaping the training process.)

Wheeler treats occupational training institutions as collective-serial settings; the preparation of surgeons, for example, indicates the utility of his formulation. One observer describes the setting for surgical training as follows:

> The ward includes a manageable number of patients, placed under the care of a group of young physicians and surgeons of *graded seniority*. This group of doctors is a stable one, with the same individuals working together as a team for at least *some months at a time*. They are *closely supervised* by senior

men of much wider experience who are constantly available for consultation, and who act as guarantors of the quality of the over-all care of the patient. *Consultants* representing a wide range of specialities are freely available. The ward thus becomes the scene of *enlightening discussion* and *debate.* New *evidence from the literature* is constantly being brought forward.[52]

If allowance is made for the overidealization in this portrait, what remains is a cluster of social properties constituting the linking mechanisms of a training institution. First, the writer refers to a training group consisting of medical men differing in experience. By implication, the least experienced student associates with master craftsmen and with physicians whose knowledge and experience exceeds his own only slightly. In a sense, the neophyte can view himself as standing on a lower rung of a ladder, but not gazing across a chasm. It is far easier to establish social connections and communicate with people who differ slightly than with those whose knowledge and experience make them remote and awesome. In other words, surgical training (and medical training as well) includes both collective and serial components; it brings together students at various stages in their training, and practitioners with varying degrees of experience.

Second, these groups endure long enough that members learn to know each other, develop a sense of solidarity that comes from working together at the same task, and divide up the work among themselves. (There is no denying that conflict and disruption arise for a variety of reasons; but the arrangement is at least conducive for cohesiveness to emerge.) Although senior members hold ultimate responsibility for what transpires (particularly regarding patient welfare), all members assume some responsibility. The arrangement, in other words, promotes active and reflective engagement in the work.

Third, because teaching hospitals bring treatment, training, and research into proximity, new knowledge, both theoretical and practical, finds an easy port of entry into the training process; moreover, because a hospital houses a wide variety of medical specialists, knowledge filters into training through the use of consultants. Calling on consultants has several functions; most obviously, the consultant provides knowledge at points where members of a medical team become stymied by their own ignorance. Perhaps more important, the neophyte learns the limits of the most experienced man's knowledge, and that ignorance can either be dispelled by what another man knows or simply transformed into controversy or uncertainty. As Renee Fox puts it:

> When [the advanced medical student] meets clinical prob-
> lems that "even stump the experts," [he] is confronted with
> uncertainty that derives from the limitations of medical
> science. . . . Uncertainty over how to distinguish his own
> inadequacies from those which are general to the field con-
> tinues to pose a problem for the student.[53]

And finally, the student learns how to find and use the resources
he needs to cope with particularly demanding problems.

This last point raises an important and neglected area in the
study of socializing institutions. Most attention has been paid to
discovering how trainees learn the skills and norms of an occupation. Equally important is how they learn to get along in the organizations in which they practice: acting appropriately *vis-à-vis* peers,
administrators, senior colleagues, clients, and so on; learning
what resources the organization possesses, where they are, and
how to get them. Although he attends medical school to learn the
medical aspects of being a doctor and not to become an "operator"
within the hospital, the student soon finds that he must learn his
way around and how to deal with people variously located within
it because his success in treating patients depends on both what
he knows medically and his success in locating and using available resources.

Fourth, the structure of the hospital ward as well as the nature of medical activities make it possible to serve the interests
of both student training and patient care. The tasks of medical
treatment can be divided into parts, permitting differentiation in
responsibility and the assignment of the simpler, less critical parts
to trainees with the least experience. In addition, the arrangement of wards and the availability of large numbers of patients
who collectively present a large number of different illnesses and
variations of the same illness make observation and both concentrated and extensive exposure easy to arrange. Clinical rounds,
where medical students, interns, residents, and senior men circu-
late from bed to bed, are daily occurrences in hospitals and provide opportunities to perform whatever procedures are necessary,
to talk about patients and their responses to treatment, and to
discuss the general medical issues involved.[54]

ISSUES CONFRONTING SCHOOLS OF EDUCATION

According to Israel Scheffler:

> Recent educational reforms have largely addressed them-
> selves to the proper structuring of subject-matter and its ar-

ticulation in the teaching process. Discussion of the teacher's
education has tended accordingly to concern itself, not with
the general strengthening of his powers through scholarly
studies, but with improving his grasp of the particular subject to be taught and providing him with practical experience in its classroom presentation.[55]

Scheffler's concern with the strengthening of powers through
"scholarly studies" is the nub of the problem in teacher training.
His statement asks for no cutting back in practical training or
in mastering subject-matter, the preoccupations of Conant and
Koerner; rather, he claims that something is missing—a provision
for infusing scholarship into the occupation.

A look at the history of occupations, and particularly those
conventionally recognized as professions, indicates the crucial
importance of establishing a connection between training institutions and universities. Although Scheffler is primarily concerned
with the kind of contribution a university can make to teacher
training, the prior question of what the relationship between university and training institution should be remains open. Medicine
and law have come up with their solutions; although no one would
claim perfection for them, undoubtedly they have each worked
out ways—however different—to bring knowledge and apprenticeship viably if not flawlessly together. Education has not been as
fortunate; in fact, only the faintest glimmerings give any indication that the issue has been identified, let alone joined.

The idea of a scientific discipline of education (or teaching)
has little if anything to recommend it. Teaching, like a variety of
other occupations, draws from a range of scientific disciplines
that provide general principles, however crude (that is, theoretical
bases of technology). A search for the educational analogues of
anatomy, physiology, biochemistry, jurisprudence, rules of evidence, structural design, physics, pharmacology, and the like
leads mainly to the psychology departments of universities where
much of the work on learning, cognition, and motivation is done,
and secondarily to some of the larger, university-affiliated schools
of education that harbor programs in the social sciences. The
same search will also indicate that much of the research in the
psychology of learning (broadly conceived), has no earthly relevance to what happens in classrooms—what is true for rats, pi-
geons, apes, and individual people under experimental conditions does not necessarily hold for an aggregate of thirty children
and a teacher over the course of a school year—and that much that
is relevant never finds its way into teacher training programs.

The social, as distinct from the psychological, sciences have not developed sufficiently to support a workable technology. In addition to this latter problem, for which there is no easy short-range solution, schools of education have neither become indigenous producers of their own research nor have they tapped the disciplinary departments of universities sufficiently or appropriately for the basic knowledge they need. Until one or both of these events occurs, the infusion of knowledge into teacher training necessary to support a viable technology will itself remain an intractable problem. Teacher training institutions, in other words, have yet to incorporate or ally with knowledge-producing institutions in a way that will support relevant job preparation.

The prevailing pattern of apprenticeship—practice teaching—raises a number of issues; its brief duration—however important—being the least of them. As currently organized, practice teaching usually consists of a period of classroom observation, some experience instructing small groups of students, and the assumption of major responsibility for preparing and teaching a piece of the existing curriculum,[56] under the general supervision of a cooperating teacher and the occasional supervision of education school faculty. This system is implicitly predicated on the assumption that teaching is a unitary occupation, that if one acts like a teacher by taking a teacher's responsibilities (under supervision), one thereby learns the job.

If the experience of other occupations has any relevance, it is more than likely that teaching consists of a variety of skills each of which must be mastered. For example, an apprentice should perhaps spend a substantial block of time learning the various skills—most of which have yet to be identified—required to motivate pupils to like school and to do their work, to diagnose learning difficulties, to impart information, to cope with the spread of interests and capacities represented in classrooms, and the like, or even specialize in some. This list of skills represents a common-sense and conventional inventory and may be a poor one. But the fact is that there is no widely accepted formulation of what the several components of teaching are, and without such a formulation it is not possible to identify the core activities of teaching or design a program of training directed toward their mastery. It is in this light that Allen and Ryan's work on microteaching takes on particular importance. They state:

> our discussions of teaching rarely get close to what a teacher *actually does* in the classroom. . . . It would be valuable for teachers to have a *more precise means of describing their activities* and recently some new ways of conceptualizing teach-

> ing are leading us toward this means: A more precise vocab-
> ulary for the specifics of teaching. . . .   When teachers work
> within this new frame of reference and refine . . . [the]
> categories of teaching activities, . . . they can *isolate the be-
> haviors involved in certain teaching skills and make them the focus
> of training.*[57]

As the occupation is currently constituted, specialization follows the distinctions between school levels and subject matter; and
although these distinctions may well be basic, there is little reason
to assume that they are exhaustive. If they are not basic, or if additional distinctions are, then it appears incumbent upon schools
of education to arrive at a more sensitive delineation of what the
core skills of teaching are and to develop specific forms of training around them. Such a strategy may well portend a vast reorgani-
zation of schools of education and particularly their relationships
with school systems.

The fact that teaching lacks a job description reduces the
perennial quest for more supervision, both in training and on
the job, to pious cant. If one cannot properly identify the parts
of the job and the activities required to perform them, what should
the supervisor supervise? If this question cannot be answered—
and I don't think it can be at the present time—then supervisors
will continue doing what they always have: deciding vacuously
whether a teacher is "good" or "effective" with only the crudest
rules of thumb (at best) or biases (at worst) to go by, suggesting
how to get pupils to participate more, gathering instructional
materials, making the classroom more democratic, setting up small
instructional groups, and on through the catalogue of helpful
advice whose items have not been put to any systematic test of
efficacy.

Finally, teacher training institutions have yet to identify and
establish those settings that serve the interests of *both* teaching
pupils and training new teachers. Premature commitment to the
medical, legal, architectural, academic, social work, or nursing
models may ill serve the interests of teaching. But the classroom,
as currently constituted, appears notably ill-suited to accomplish
both tasks, particularly since the basic components of the job remain undefined. Two people, a teacher and an apprentice, cannot
instruct simultaneously from the front of a class; in fact, if one
person is directing the activities of a class, the other is restricted
mainly to watching and listening. If both simultaneously instruct
small groups within the classroom, the cooperating teacher is in
no position to supervise the apprentice. One way to avoid the
problems of training that arise *because* the classroom is the ap-

prenticeship site is to identify those components of the teacher's work that can be carried on outside that setting (such as diagnosing learning difficulties through pupils' written materials) and to design training activities that can be carried on elsewhere. Clearly, though, this will not solve the whole problem because schools are now organized around classrooms as the primary instructional setting; and as long as this is so, it will have to serve as the locus for substantial parts of training.

The self-contained classroom with one teacher and from twenty to fifty pupils is thoroughly embedded in the educational tradition; yet there is no defensible reason for not contemplating and experimenting with alternative arrangements, particularly ones better adapted to the requirements of both instruction and training. We do not yet know what kind of arrangements best serve the interests of instructing both pupils and new teachers, nor do we know what spatial arrangements are best adapted to performing the various component skills of teaching—if for no other reason than that the latter have only begun to be identified. The point, however, is that to advance the technologies of teaching and teacher training, we need to think about the design of space. If the conventional classroom proves to be an obstacle to the adequate training of teachers, there is no logic that demands subordinating the interests of training to the preservation of the classroom, as currently designed, as the main instructional unit. If the effective instruction of pupils is the first order of priority, the next question is what *variety* of settings is most conducive to learning what *kinds* of skills. Stated in this way, the issue of maintaining the classroom becomes problematic; it may be useful for some activities, inhibiting for others. But, there is no reason to assume that arrangements designed to cope with the various tasks of teaching and training will be completely consistent; they aren't in any other occupation.

In recent years, teaching machines and language laboratories have appeared on the educational scene; although they cannot stand as instructional panaceas, neither one inherently presumes the prior existence of classrooms even though they have been used predominantly within the classroom format. And as I have noted earlier, Newmann and Oliver, while acknowledging the usefulness of classrooms for some kinds of instruction, have argued for the employment of "laboratory" and "community" settings (as they define them) as more suitable for other kinds of learning. The efficacy of their proposals remains to be tested, but they do join the issue.

Teachers for a long time have agitated for small classes; and perhaps they are right in believing that pupils learn better in groups of five to ten (although they haven't asked for classes that small) than in larger ones. In any case, we don't know. But if one can question the value of large classes, why not also question the premise that teaching is a one-man job? Team teaching, of course, has been tried; its results, indeterminate. Proponents of team teaching arrangements, however, assume that two or more heads are better than one, that advantages will accrue from group planning and evaluation, and that pupils will benefit (particularly at the elementary level) if a teacher who is strong in a given area replaces one who is weak. In effect, team teaching has amounted to little more than extending secondary school departmentalization into the elementary grades while retaining the self-contained classroom as the main instructional unit: the *status quo ante* with minor variations. Other multi-teacher arrangements, however, have not been tried; but to experiment with them intelligently requires the analysis of teaching into its component activities. Were this to be done, we might find that teaching is best carried out by a group of specialists and para-professionals whose work requires different sizes and types of pupil groupings, one of which *may* be classrooms.

Schools of education have manifest weaknesses in the generation of research and in the development of technology as well as in the nature of their relationship to universities. The same sentence could have been written decades ago; and in response to rumblings about inadequate teacher training, one heard about the need to "professionalize" teaching—a "good thing," except that nobody knew what it meant other than that it was something like medicine—and to "upgrade" it generally, about the need to stiffen up the academic requirements for entering the occupation (in the face of a teacher shortage), and about the urgent necessity to throw out courses in teaching methods and let teachers ply their trade armed with a good liberal education and their wits. In a way, the situation was, and is, comical what with the guardians of public education prescribing remedies of unknown constituents for symptoms of unknown ills, all the while waiting for another Abraham Flexner to descend and clean up the whole mess.

We have not suddenly come upon good times in teacher training; but the last few years have witnessed the emergence of more penetrating and realistic analyses of the problems and some early attempts to design specific activities for training teachers to perform some of the discrete skills of teaching. Schaefer, for example, has identified two pressing needs: the creation of colleagueship among teachers; and the establishment of an intellectually rich climate in schools, a source of enduring intellectual excitement about the work—this rather than the traditional in-service courses.

The precise mechanisms for satisfying the needs are not identified as clearly as the needs themselves, but most important in Schaefer's statement is the identification of problems relevant to the work and careers of teachers. The absence of colleagueship is strongly linked to the failure of work-relevant knowledge to flow freely among teachers, to the absence of a tradition of occupational self-criticism, and to the maintenance of a broad occupational community of teachers across schools.

The Master of Arts in Teaching Program, the brainchild of the 1950's, has perhaps run its course. While it was clearly an imaginative attempt to bring provocative ideas into teaching, it did so, perhaps, at the wrong point in the occupational career and used the wrong vehicle in the wrong place. With hindsight, it is not too difficult to realize that one doesn't infuse an enormous and geographically dispersed occupation with fresh ideas by re-cruiting novices from the elite liberal arts colleges. They are few in number, are unlikely to make durable commitments to the occupation, and most likely to win the resentment of experienced teachers who have learned their trade, however competently, through experience. What experienced worker is going to listen to a brash, young kid who, fresh out of a fancy college with his head full of "advanced" ideas, tells him how to do his job, or is going to follow such an "enlightened" example? But whatever the success or failure of M.A.T. programs, they did reveal a concern with the intellectual and imaginative facets of the work—with the infusion of ideas into an occupation that was widely believed to be nearing stagnancy.

The 1966 Report of the Harvard Graduate School of Education, *The Graduate Study of Education,* again reveals a concern with knowledge. Both the focus and the strategy are markedly different from those of M.A.T. programs. Implicit in the Report is the idea that the occupation needs a substantial base of knowledge to support a developing technology. The strategy, then, is to turn not to "bright" new recruits, but to those institutions in society that assume a large responsibility for generating and dis-seminating abstract knowledge: the universities. Hence the Re-port enjoins the school of education to exploit the full resources of the university and to modify its priorities from training teachers to producing scholars with doctorates.

Finally, there have recently been direct attempts to formulate the specific activities comprising the technology of teaching as manifest in the work of Smith and Geoffrey and in Allen and Ryan's work on microteaching; and interest in "hardware"—com-puters, teaching machines, and the like—has continued.

In short, there is growing evidence that a variety of observers are beginning to identify, in specific terms, what the problems of the occupation are, foremost among them being teacher training. At this point, one can clearly identify concern with the intellectual climate of schools, the technological base of the work as derived from abstract knowledge, the performance of classroom activities, and the development of colleagueship among teachers. Little, however, has been said about how these parts shall fit together, what new arrangements between school systems and universities shall be formed and in what manner, how the work of teachers can be rearranged so that collegial relationships become possible, how a spirit of intellectual excitement can enter the schools, and the like. But after many years there are glimmerings that some observers of the educational scene have discovered elements of teaching that have long been recognized as integral parts of other occupations.[58]

•

CHAPTER SIX

Occupational Careers

in Teaching

•

The concept *career* has at least three meanings. It refers, first, to the phases of individual life histories considered as job sequences. In this sense, career is a category of the individual in that we can understand something about a person's working life by cataloguing the jobs he has held, where he has held them, for how long, and how often he changed them. Second, it refers to occupations independently of individuals. A given type of work, for example, may attract and hold substantial numbers of people who as individuals have similar work histories; other types attract people with dissimilar histories. Medicine is a case of the first kind; most physicians follow a standard sequence of training, entry into practice, and continuation in the occupation for the duration of their working lives. Political occupations, by contrast, and especially those that involve elective office-holding, draw people from a variety of callings—law, journalism, business, and academic life, for example —and hold them for varying lengths of time before they return to their previous occupations or enter new ones. Career in this sense is a category of occupations. Third, organizations are characterized by more or less typical career lines. In hospitals, for example, nurses can advance through the nursing hierarchy but cannot become physicians—at least not without leaving nursing and completing medical school. Similarly, in industrial establishments, blue collar workers can become foremen in a particular factory but cannot readily move into the white collar contingent of the same establishment, while lower ranked white collar workers can more readily advance into the higher managerial echelons. Here, career is a category of organizations.[1] In this chapter I am primarily concerned with the second two types of careers: the dominant career patterns found in the occupation of teaching (a question that requires some consideration of educational and nonteaching occupations), and the dominant career patterns characteristic of schools and school systems.

The idea of career should not be confused with vertical mobility, although the latter can be subsumed under the former. At the minimum, career entails the notion of *sequence* whether the motion implied is up, down, or lateral; into or out of the labor force; between one or another type of occupation, industry, or individual practice; involving already established positions or ones newly created. Although occupational and organizational careers entail personal sequences, they can be better understood with some knowledge of the aggregate characteristics of occupational members, particularly when some of these characteristics turn out to be important career contingencies.

CHARACTERISTICS OF TEACHERS

Prospective teachers, while undergraduates, are predominantly female, are more likely to come from smaller than larger cities, and are likely to hold values indicating concern for people rather than for making money or for doing creative and original things. In their small-city origins they resemble students of nursing, librarianship, and religion, and differ from those planning careers in architecture, communications, medicine, law, and business. In values, prospective teachers roughly resemble members of other predominantly female occupations who have small-city origins but differ most sharply from potential engineers, lawyers, and architects. In socio-economic status, those planning to enter teaching resemble future engineers and businessmen in that they originate somewhat more from the lower than from the higher end of the socio-economic scale.[2] There are no surprises here.

Beginning teachers are more likely to come from white collar than from blue collar or farm families but less likely to have white collar origins than medical students, college faculties in the social sciences, independent attorneys, and dental students. There are marked differences, however, between men and women teachers, the latter originating more from white collar and farm families than the former. Both the fathers and mothers of beginning teachers are better educated than men and women in the population at large, and the women are more likely to have better educated fathers and mothers than the men. Beginning teachers come from the whole spectrum of residential communities, from the largest cities to the smallest rural areas.[3]

The NEA describes the background characteristics of a broader sample of teachers (i.e., excluding prospective teachers and not limited to first-year teachers). The findings, however, are similar to those just described. About one-quarter of the teachers came from farm families, another quarter from families where the father was a skilled or semiskilled worker, and a third from families with a managerial or self-employed father. Almost 15 percent came from professional or semiprofessional families, and another 7 percent had fathers who were clerical or sales workers.[4] This pattern is roughly the same for men and women and for primary and secondary school teachers, though more women and elementary teachers have farm backgrounds than men, and more women than men come from upper middle class families. In general, teaching recruits from the whole range of the socio-economic spectrum, though more from the center than from the extremes; and the distribution of family occupational backgrounds of teachers resembles that of occupations in the current labor force. Although these are at best rough socio-economic distinctions, they provide only modest support for the contention that teaching *now*—it might have been so earlier—is a major avenue for social mobility (though it probably is for teachers with working class or farm backgrounds) since many teachers remain roughly at the same socio-economic level as their fathers, and some move downward. There is no indication that the phases of becoming a full-time teacher, from undergraduate prospect to veteran, are associated with any marked selection process based on social class.

Since 1947 to 1948, according to the NEA, the educational preparation of teachers has increased, at least as indicated by degree-holding. The proportion of teachers with bachelor's degrees has increased from that time to 1965 from 44.3 percent to 67.3 percent, and the proportion with master's and higher degrees has risen from 15.1 percent to 24.1 percent (though that change occurred from about 1947 to 1955 and has since remained about constant). Teachers with less than a bachelor's degree have declined in proportion from 40.6 percent to 8.6 percent (1947 to 1965), and those with emergency certificates (unqualified in terms of standard credentials) dropped from 13.6 percent to 5.1 percent, a trend consistent with the increasing tendency of states to enforce minimum standards of preparation.[5] Although the trends are clear, their interpretation remains equivocal since we know that substantial numbers of teachers simply collect credentials negotiable for cash, that degrees in education can be obtained by accumulating credits in courses unimbedded in any programmatic design, and that a substantial though unknown number of these courses make minimal intellectual demands and have only questionable relevance to the actual work of teaching. A face-value interpretation, then, would indicate the growth of a more academically qualified teaching force, while a more cynical one would indicate an increase in credential-gathering (with some of the credentials being collected to pave the road out of teaching and into administration).

Teaching is not an occupation for gaining public renown or amassing wealth. In their well-known 1947 study of occupational status in which a national sample of the American public was asked to judge the "general standing" of ninety occupations, North and Hatt found that 28 percent rated the standing of "instructor in the public school" excellent, 45 percent rated it good, 24 percent average, 2 percent somewhat below average, and 1 percent poor; another 1 percent did not know how highly to judge it. (Members of the sample rated "public school teacher," an alternative wording, almost exactly the same way.) Instructors and teachers ranked 34th and 36th, respectively, among the ninety occupations, and their position was close to army captain, building contractor, economist, county agricultural agent, railroad engineer, and farm owner and operator. They ranked substantially lower than lawyers, dentists, ministers, and college professors, and substantially higher than trained machinists, undertakers, newspaper reporters, and insurance agents. A 1963 replication of the original North-Hatt study showed the same patterns.[6]

The highest ranked cluster of jobs in 1947 was government officials; the second highest, consisting of thirty occupations, was the professions and semiprofessions ranging from second to seventy-fourth in ranking; teaching ranked very close to the mean within that occupational grouping. Its position is also consistent with the criteria people use in rating occupations; 18 percent of the sample (the largest proportion) judge them according to how well they pay, and 16 percent (the second largest proportion) judge according to their service to humanity. Teaching loses by the first criterion and gains by the second.

Economically, the position of teachers is strained, although in recent years the growth of the union movement and the increased militancy of the NEA have brought about both direct and indirect financial gains. Beardsley Ruml and Sidney Tickton, in their report on salary trends (adjusted to reflect purchasing power) in education and in other occupations, covering the period from 1904 to 1953, state:

> Between 1904 and 1933, the "real" purchasing power of the salaries and wages of most people in industry and education rose substantially, but the rise in the field of education was less, generally, than in industry, and the rate of increase was slower. Between 1933 and 1947, the real purchasing power of many people in industry rose further . . . but in the field of education, the real purchasing power of people in all types of teaching declined.[7]

In a later report on 1959 salaries and wages, Tickton compares the income of teachers with that of people working in other occupations. For example: starting salaries of teachers with a B.A. (in New York, Albany, Buffalo, Washington, D.C., Chicago, and Los Angeles ranged from $4000 to $5000, while starting salaries for general business trainees, salesmen, accountants, chemists, engineers, and research and development personnel with the same academic training ranged from $5000 to slightly over $6000. He finds the same general pattern for jobs requiring an M.A.; teachers in high-paying school systems in the New York area receive less than chemists, physicists, pharmacists, and engineers (with the salary gap between teachers and the others becoming wider at the M.A. rather than at the B.A. level). He also finds that clerical workers (tabulating machine operators, private secretaries, accounting clerks, and switchboard operators with high school diplomas and two to three years of job experience make slightly more than elementary school teachers (in New York, Albany, and Buffalo).[8] More recent statistics gathered by the NEA indicate (according to the U.S. Census classification) that the salaries of "craftsmen, foremen, and kindred workers" and occupations lower on the scale fall short of those earned by teachers, and that occupations (with a few exceptions) above the upper level of the blue collar stratum are better paid than teachers.[9] Within the category of professional workers the NEA reports the following mean annual salary comparisons: public school classroom teachers, $6298; accountants and auditors, $8890; attorneys, $14,499; chemists, $11,024; engineers, $11,575; nonsupervisory scientists without a doctorate, $11,652.[10]

The income picture for teachers is hardly sanguine, but the point is not to make their financial situation look disadvantageous by documenting its similarity to lower level occupations and its economic disadvantage to occupations requiring roughly similar training. In work-life terms, teaching is not an occupation that rewards service and experience with money. According to NEA figures, based on its 1961 sample, teachers with less than three years' experience earned an average annual salary of $4328, and those spending twenty or more years on the job earned an average of $5714.[11] Even if one views the economic picture from the most optimistic perspective, it is clear that remaining in the classroom is not the way to get rich. If a teacher wants to remain in the field of education and also wishes to earn more money, he must either leave the classroom and enter school administration, or take on an additional job.

The NEA finds that administrative salaries vary directly with school system size (measured by pupil enrollment). Thus the teacher-administrator salary contrast is sharpest when we consider the smallest systems (those enrolling between 600 and 11,999 pupils); that is, those that pay their administrators *least* well. To make administrators' salaries most comparable with those of classroom teachers ($6298, reported above), I consider salaries for the 1964–65 academic year: superintendents, $17,726; assistant superintendents, $15,483; directors, $13,173; coordinators, $12,440; and supervisors, $10,341.[12] It should come as no surprise, then, that substantial numbers of teachers, and for obvious reasons more men than women, hold additional jobs. The NEA reports that 20.4 percent of all teachers hold outside jobs during the school year (1960–61), and 33.8 percent hold one or more jobs either during the summer or during the school year. Among married men, this last figure rises to 76.5 percent. Some 27.3 percent of all teachers hold summer jobs either inside or outside their school system,[13] but summer employment must be understood as a way of supplementing income during vacation, not as moonlighting. The male teacher closely resembles Wilensky's portrait of the moonlighter as a man with "a disorderly worklife, blocked mobility, life-cycle squeeze, and related feelings of deprivation, as well as the kinds of deviant schedules conducive to moonlighting. . . ."[14] And if either the magnitude of earnings or the amount of time devoted to work is taken as the criterion defining one's major occupation, teaching itself can sometimes—though not typically— be considered moonlighting from some other occupation.

The intellectual calibre of teachers has often been subject to derision and ridicule; the occupation, one hears, simply does not attract and hold talented people. The evidence most frequently cited comes from Wolfle's work, *America's Resources of Specialized Talent* (1954), and indicates that among students graduated with a bachelor's degree, those specializing in education rank seventeenth (on the Army General Classification Test) on a list of twenty fields led by students in the physical sciences, chemistry, engineering, and law. Education students exceed only students in the social sciences (other than economics and history, who rank higher), home economics, and physical education, and in turn are outranked by students in nursing, agriculture, and business. Although there is substantial overlap in AGCT scores among all fields, the mean score in education is lower than the mean for all twenty occupations combined, though not substantially so. There are similar findings for graduate students in nineteen fields among which education ranks fifteenth.[15]

It is important to understand what questions these figures do and do not answer. Usually, they have been used to document the alleged intellectual inferiority of teachers compared to people entering other professions. In fact, they do not speak directly to that point even though it may be true. The figures as they stand fail to account for occupational size and market conditions. If there is a yearly contingent of intellectually talented college graduates and graduate students, the first question is what occupations they select. If, for example, they spread themselves about equally over the professions, a segment of the talented cohort will fill up the vacancies in a small occupation but not in a large one. Large occupations, simply to fill the available openings, have to fish deeper in the intellectual pool to fill its positions. Teaching is one such large occupation; it comes under particular pressure to find warm bodies to fill classrooms particularly during times of an expanding youth population.

Evidence bearing on this point is found in Davis' work on the graduate school plans of college seniors from which it is possible to calculate (1) the intended occupational destination of graduate students in the top fifth in academic performance (an index based on each student's grade point average and the quality of his college based on the intellectual abilities of its freshmen), and (2) the proportion of students with different occupational destinations found in the top fifth in academic performance, as shown in Table 6.1.

Consider the college seniors planning careers in medicine: 42.1 percent of them, the highest proportion for any of the occupations listed, are in the top fifth academically. This proportion corresponds to the Wolfle data. But of the college seniors in the top fifth academically, medicine draws only 7.2 percent, a proportion probably large enough on a national basis to fill *numerically* a substantial portion of the open positions in medical schools. Education, in contrast, attracts the highest proportion, 18.8 percent of the academically able seniors, while only 13.6 percent of the seniors heading for careers in education fall within the top fifth academically, the second lowest proportion. Clearly

TABLE 6.1   *Undergraduate Academic Performance and Anticipated Field of Graduate Study*

	Number in Top Fifth	Percent of Top Fifth in Each Field	Percent of Each Field in Top Fifth
Social Sciences			
Political science, psychology, history, economics, and sociology.	1035	12.4	28.8
Physical, Biological Sciences			
Physics, mathematics, biology, microbiology, chemistry, biochemistry, zoology, physiology, earth sciences, botany, and biology.	1196	14.3	28.5
Arts and Humanities			
English, philosophy, language, and fine arts.	1276	15.3	34.5
Professions			
Business	594	7.1	13.2
Education	1567	18.8	13.6
Engineering	744	8.9	24.6
Law	571	6.8	23.5
Medicine	599	7.2	42.1
Nursing	118	1.4	27.6
Social work	120	1.4	16.9
Other	532	6.4	17.8
Total	8352	100.0	

Adapted from James A. Davis, *Great Aspirations* (Chicago: Aldine Publishing Co., 1964), table 4.2, p. 145. For the measurement of academic performance, see pp. 26–31.

education draws its share of able college students—it is possible, of course, that grading standards for these students are lower than for students in other fields, especially for undergraduate education majors—but that share is not enough to fill the vacancies in teaching. The figures, of course, do not tell us whether these students actually arrive in classrooms to teach, and if they do, how long they stay. Teaching, as we know, is a large occupation as well as one that loses many members; and both conditions conspire to increase the demand for manpower, both talented and untalented. Medicine, in contrast, holds most of its recruits for the duration of their working lives.

In terms of characteristics related to the life cycle, Mason finds that most beginning teachers are women (63.6 percent), that more men than women are married, and that the proportion of married teachers increases with age among both men and women.[16] These findings are clearly consistent with the fact that women leave teaching permanently or temporarily to raise their own children instead of other people's, and that men leave to support families.

The NEA's national survey of teachers reports that 17.3 percent of all male teachers are single and 80.5 percent are married, while 24.6 percent of the women are single, and 62.4 percent married,[17] indicating an increase in the proportion of married persons and a decline in the proportion of single persons when compared with Mason's sample of first-year teachers. Sharp differences in age distinguish the 31.4 percent male and 68.6 percent female contingents. Among those twenty-five and younger, 70.2 percent are women; but in the decade (twenty-six to thirty-five years), that proportion drops to 42.8 percent, only to increase again to 79.8 percent among teachers thirty-six and older.[18] For women, these findings are consistent with those on marital status, suggesting that women leave the work force to raise families. The exodus of older men suggests that they are either leaving the ranks of teachers for noneducational employment or for careers in school administration or higher education.

Finally, government statistics document the well-known association between sex and school level. Among elementary teachers, 13.4 percent are men and 86.6 percent are women; among secondary teachers, 52.3 percent are men and 47.7 percent are women.[19] Although most of these findings are familiar, they have important implications for the nature of teaching careers. Except for the fact that men and women engage in the same work at each school level, their careers, as I shall indicate later, are different enough that one can almost talk about two distinct teaching careers, one for men, another for women; symptomatically, one finds this distinction in a median age difference of more than a decade between men and women: 33.6 years and 45.5 years, respectively.[20]

In summary, the nature of occupational careers in teaching is affected by the characteristics of teachers considered in the aggregate. Teaching draws its membership from the whole range of the socio-economic spectrum (though more from the middle than from the edges); its members are modestly trained before they begin their first jobs; they are not highly paid either in absolute terms or in comparison to members of other occupations with similar or even less training, and long tenure in the classroom does not bring very large increases in salary; most teachers are women (overwhelmingly at the elementary level, slightly less than half

at the secondary level); the occupation attracts a substantial proportion of academically able college graduates, but its manpower
needs are so large that it must also recruit large numbers of less
talented people simply to fill positions that cannot remain empty.
Given only this amount of information, we have a set of precon-
ditions for an occupation characterized by fairly high rates of
turnover and multiple job-holding, one that elicits only modest
commitment to work-life tenure on the job.

RECRUITMENT TO THE OCCUPATION

School systems vary greatly in how they locate, attract, and
hire new teachers. In some, responsibility for these activities lies
in the central office where they may be carried out more or less
actively. In the more active case, recruiters beat the bushes for
prospective teachers by interviewing college and graduate students and by "raiding" other school systems for able and experienced teachers. They may restrict their efforts to the surrounding
geographical area or spread themselves out regionally or even
nationally. In more passive school systems they may count more
on the efforts of local schools of education and municipal colleges
to steer their graduates toward the local system. Some systems
allow recruiters to offer contracts on the spot; others require candidates to appear at the central office for interviews and examinations.[21]

Systems also vary in the extent to which recruitment is centralized and in how much principals participate in selection and
assignment. Where recruiting is highly centralized, the assignment of teachers to individual schools is determined by the central administration with or without regard for the particular conditions prevailing in each school or the appropriateness of teachers
to those conditions. With less centralization the participation of
principals becomes greater. They may have veto power over central assignments, may ask for particular teachers to work at their
schools after interviewing a number of them, or may actively do
the recruiting themselves (needing only final rubber-stamp approval by the administration). Legally, of course, the school board
as a unit hires teachers; the board is the contractual agent.

Several issues relate to the question of who appoints and assigns. First, who is closest to the school scene, who knows at first-
hand what the problems are, and who is in the best position to
judge what kinds of teachers should be hired in a particular school
in light of its character? In terms of proximity (and assuming that
hiring is an administrative function), the principal has the best
vantage point, and on that basis should have a great deal to say

about who is hired. Although this argument is logically and practically defensible, it also presents problems of a political nature within the school system. Particularly in large systems, many schools have both problems to solve and teaching positions to fill; seldom is there a large enough pool of talent among new teachers to fill all positions in the light of each school's most pressing problems. With competing demands on the pool originating in different schools, the recruitment and assignment functions tend to be decided at levels higher than the individual school so that there is some possibility of achieving equity in the distribution of new recruits.

The superintendent's office, in contrast, is farthest removed from particular school situations; consequently, unilateral or random assignments—or worse, political ones—from that level appear least defensible. It is necessary, most importantly, to view hiring and assigning as real problems of competing priorities that lend themselves to several solutions, some better than others, depending on conditions. Perhaps the strongest case can be made for establishing machinery designed to allocate new teachers in a way that optimizes both local and system-wide considerations, within the limits set by available human resources.

Second, there are problems of equity, reward, and punishment both within schools and school systems. Some schools are known as "difficult"—or are labeled or libeled as such—a contemporary euphemism for ghetto schools or those located in tough neighborhoods; in fact, there are schools, euphemism or not, whose pupils present teachers with demanding problems in instruction, motivation, and classroom management. It is not tortured logic that leads to the belief that the most competent and talented teachers should be working at these schools (to the extent that competence in teachers can be adequately judged). However, it is often the most recent recruits, the least knowledgeable and experienced, who are given their first assignments in such schools; and the reasons are not hard to find. They are often schools with high rates of teacher turnover, hence the steady need for replacements. Teachers who have worked in them for substantial periods of time often wish to transfer out to find situations that are less demanding on their energies and ingenuity; this is not to deny that many able and dedicated teachers do remain. Under the circumstances it is reasonable for some to want transfers to "more desirable" schools, and school administrators are not blind to these desires. But one can question the wisdom of assigning the least experienced recruits to these teaching positions under present conditions where the resources for helping new teachers learn their jobs under adequate supervision are in painfully short supply;

for where the task is most demanding and teaching capacities are least well-suited to the demands, the pressures to leave rise accordingly. The result is often the perpetuation of high rates of turnover for the school and loss to the occupation of young teachers with promise who have been initially assigned "over their heads."

Daniel Griffiths and his colleagues describe a broad range of issues concerning the appointment of inexperienced teachers in the New York City system, the so-called substitute teachers, who in 1962 comprised about 75 percent of those entering secondary and about 33 percent of those entering elementary school positions. The remainder of the teachers at each level were regular licensed teachers.[22] A substitute can choose both the area of the city and the school in which to work, can agree or refuse to work on a particular day, and can decide whether that school is desirable for regular employment (after obtaining a regular license). A principal, likewise, can choose among substitutes to fill a vacancy, can assign them to undesirable classes and duties, can screen them for future regular employment, and can get rid of a substitute more easily than a regular teacher. On the debit side, substitute teachers get no salary increments after the sixth year, may have to teach in fields in which they do not hold a license, and may have to spend considerable time shopping around to get a job. Principals, by hiring substitutes rather than licensed teachers, are more likely to get inexperienced and less motivated teachers, whose commitment to the school is temporary.[23]

Although substitute teaching has advantages both for the teacher and the school, the advantages are based on calculations of short-run gain and militate against the development of a firm match between person and job conducive to learning some of the basic skills of teaching on the first job and establishing the groundwork for a stable occupational career. The absence of a stable working experience in the earliest years on the job takes on critical importance, at least in the New York City system where Griffiths and his colleagues report that 47.5 percent of the elementary teachers, 73.1 percent of the junior high teachers, and 46.8 percent of the senior high teachers have had *no* practice teaching experience before starting the first job.[24] Although neither Mason nor the NEA report specifically on the proportion of teachers, new and experienced, who have never done practice teaching, Mason indicates that 22 percent of all beginning teachers in his sample are uncertificated (12 percent with a bachelor's degree, 10 percent without), that is, have substandard qualifications,[25] and it is reasonable to assume that one explanation for these teachers not being fully certificated is that they have never had practice teaching experience or other kinds of pre-occupational training.

Although I have described recruitment into the occupation primarily in terms of the New York situation, the general principles involved are not limited to New York nor are they limited to schools. In any occupation where competent performance is required, the question of qualifications becomes important; but qualifications are never and cannot be the whole story. Naturally, an organization will want the most competent people it can get; but it will also want people who are not personally disruptive (however good they are at doing their work), who will bring a sense of commitment to their work, and who will show evidence of loyalty to the organization in times of adversity. Of course there are always scarcities of each qualification in any labor market. The problem of recruitment is to get the best people available with respect to *each* of these considerations, and there is no reason to believe that a person who is strong on one is strong on the rest. Accordingly, it may be more important for the welfare of a school and its pupils for a principal to have a new teacher who will stick with him in the face of difficult problems rather than to have one who scores high on some qualifying examination.

I have used the New York case to illustrate the methods one school system uses to discover the balance of relevant considerations in selecting teachers; other systems use different means, but in so doing they attempt to learn the same things. The means, at times, look suspiciously like "politics," favoritism, and nepotism; and sometimes they are. But sometimes they are also straightforward ways of obtaining an assortment of information about people that is exceedingly difficult to come by particularly because school systems want teachers who "show promise" now and will develop over time and not simply remain flashes in the pan; and this kind of information is the hardest to get.

STAGES OF THE WORK CAREER

In the case of teaching, the topic of this section nicely begs the question: are there career stages? Raising the question, however, does not set up a straw man when teaching is compared with other occupations. Psychiatric social workers, for example, who, like teachers, are predominantly women and are not highly paid, can advance in the supervisory hierarchy of a case work agency while maintaining a case load of clients; that is, they continue to ply their trade even when they achieve positions of greater responsibility and remuneration. Both physicians and lawyers have several career options; each can continue to practice individually (or in the case of lawyers, in partnership or in a firm) with a reasonable expectation of making a substantial amount of money if they have some talent (and in some cases, even if they do not). Alternatively, each can pursue an academic career or combine academic life with private practice. Although academic life is likely to be less remunerative than private practice (unless combined with consulting), in both occupations it brings high esteem within the occupation and high prestige in the public eye. In both medicine and law, then, an individual can trade off money against prestige, or have both in some cases. Medicine, to a far greater extent than law, also provides careers in research which may or may not be combined with consulting and teaching; again, research is a highly prestigious form of professional activity that may or may not be lucrative. The important point, however, is that in both occupations the practitioner can spend his full working life engaged in the activities to which he is dedicated; and while so doing, he can advance in terms of wealth, prestige, responsibility, or some combination of each.

Where work is carried on in large, stratified, bureaucratic organizations, such as in the military, the civil service, and large industrial or commercial organizations, paths of advancement are reasonably clear—at least the array of positions is clear if not always how to make one's way up the ladder. This is not to suggest that everyone someday arrives at the top or, if they do arrive there, that they did so by the conventional route. The point is that some occupations present their members with a demarcated scale of positions along which many, not all, can rise and reap the rewards of having risen. The politics of advancement, of course, is another matter.

The presence of hierarchically arranged positions in organizations is no guarantee that a career line exists any more than the absence of such organizations precludes a career line (as in the case of the physician in private practice). I have already mentioned blue collar workers in industrial establishments; their avenues of mobility within the plant or even in the industry are limited in terms of increments of responsibility, although they may improve their financial position through pay increases and salary schedule increases with or without the participation of unions. Nurses and teachers find themselves in much the same position: Their occupations are characterized by restricted opportunities to advance.

Blocked mobility does not simply refer to a situation in which people are unable to advance; certain occupations have low rates of promotion. But slow and blocked mobility should not be confused; the crucial question is whether people can advance in an occupation *while continuing to do the work to which they have dedicated themselves*. To state the issue somewhat differently: does an occupation provide a career line in which people can continue to do their work yet gain substantially in income, prestige, responsibility, or some combination of these? In medicine and law the answer is clearly affirmative. In other occupations, particularly in the industrial and commercial sectors of the economy, some workers are primarily interested in attaining managerial positions; although their work lives may not begin at that level, they are willing to spend time in accounting, merchandising, selling, and the like, without any commitment to those occupations, but with an eye to the future. In these cases, lack of commitment to the initial occupation is not especially problematic; it may become so if the individual does not like the work, and if opportunities for a managerial position become closed off.

Undoubtedly, a substantial number of teachers—how many we don't know—and particularly men, do not want to teach but do so temporarily in order to become administrators. Here one expects little commitment to teaching; and although its absence may be problematic to the school and to the occupation, it is not so to the individual. But the teacher who plans to spend his working life in the classroom because he likes the work and thinks it is important not infrequently finds his situation untenable. His opportunities for advancement *as a teacher* are limited. Salary, of course, rises with time on the job, and the salary schedule itself rises from time to time. Some school systems have merit pay arrangements, though many teachers oppose this basis of remuneration.[26] The larger secondary schools have department chairmanships that provide a limited number of positions in which teachers can increase their salaries and responsibilities, *and* continue teaching. But as the Ruml and Tickton data indicate (even though the financial status of classroom teachers has improved considerably since the publication of their first work, especially in the large cities), the economic outlook for teachers remains unpromising when compared to other occupations that require as much and sometimes less academic preparation. There is no evidence, moreover, that the public prestige of classroom teaching has increased despite the fact that the teacher's financial position has improved, that his economic bargaining position has become stronger with the growing strength of teachers' unions and the increased militancy of the NEA, and that an increasing proportion of men have entered the occupation, at least at the secondary level. The stability of teacher prestige partially answers those critics of the occupation who claim that the relatively low prestige of teaching can be attributed to the presence of large numbers of women since, as the proportion of men increases, the prestige of the occupation stays about the same.

Although the person who spends his working life as a classroom teacher stands to gain financially and in responsibility (and
occasionally in power and influence within a particular school),
on the whole his opportunities are fewer than those accruing to
members of other occupations. Perhaps the financial disadvantages are most acute in terms of commitment to the occupation
because the unlikelihood of amassing some wealth as a teacher
is a direct inducement to moonlight or to look for employment
elsewhere. The unions, dedicated as they are to improving the
economic lot of teachers, must extract their gains directly from
municipal governments and indirectly from state governments,
both of which turn out to be formidable foes because public monies
come from taxes, and in many municipalities primarily from real
estate taxes. It is not altogether surprising, then, to find that union
strength rests to a considerable extent on success in gaining fringe
benefits (pension rights and medical benefits, and perhaps in future funds for the college education of teachers' children), which
make it financially difficult, especially for the older and more experienced teachers, to leave the occupation. Although supporting
data are not available, it may turn out that the effect of unionism
is to stabilize membership in the occupation—to cut down on the
teacher dropout rate—particularly among those teachers who
cannot afford to leave because they have so much invested in
fringe benefits.

The occupational irony of teaching, because the career line
is truncated, is that teachers must renounce their occupation in
order to advance; they must either enter noneducational work
or leave teaching for school administration, which is far more
remunerative. The NEA's traditional contention that teachers
and administrators are all members of the same occupational
fraternity—brothers under the skin—and dedicated to the same
enterprise of educating children is at best wishful thinking and
at worst myth. Even if we ignore the trade union rhetoric of labor
and management, the fact remains that teachers and administrators perform different kinds of work. True enough, they both
labor in the educational vineyard, but administrators have entirely
different jurisdictions than teachers: they occupy managerial
positions in school systems, and most importantly, they do not
teach (even though they once did). Oddly enough, teaching is an
occupation that seems to extrude its own members.

One of the most conspicuous occupational properties of teaching, then, is that it lacks both the hierarchical array of positions
forming the basis of career stages (characteristic of the army, the
civil service, and to some extent social case work agencies and
universities), and the opportunities for substantial gains in finan-

cial and status rewards. With the exceptions of the department chairmanship and informal opportunities to gain political power within a school, the careers of classroom teachers remain constricted to the extent that they—men in particular—must make difficult calculations in weighing the relative importance of security, dedication, and standard of living in deciding how to spend their working lives. The difficulty of making this calculation manifests itself in an occupational portrait characterized by substantial rates of remaining *and* of leaving.

Fred Goldner and R. R. Ritti provide some interesting speculations about this phenomenon as it applies to engineers who resemble teachers in certain respects, not least of which is that both consist of largely professionalized workers in bureaucratized organizations with limited opportunities for career advancement. They state that:

> Organizations require the continued productive efforts of experienced specialists *who will remain in their specialties.* Management thus attempts to impose professionalism as a definition of success within the organization in order to maintain commitment on the part of those specialists who would ordinarily be considered failures for not having moved into management. Identification as professional has become a way to redefine failure as success.[27]

It might be gratuitous to assume that school administrators "impose" the definition of professionalism on teachers who remain in the classroom for the duration of their working lives since substantial numbers of teachers already consider themselves professional (where the concept, for both engineers and teachers, contains elements of technical expertise and honorific status). But perhaps this is a phenomenon characteristic of technical workers whose careers are associated largely with organizations having both strong bureaucratic elements and few opportunities for advancement from technical to managerial levels. The worker who enters the occupation with hopes (subsequently unrequited) of advancement must either leave, suffer his lot, or remain a dedicated worker (where advancement either is not that important initially or becomes less so as the pleasures of the work become visible and dominant). Perhaps the Goldner-Ritti formulation above provides some insight into both the NEA "we're all professionals together" mentality, and the union "bread, butter, and fringe benefits" mentality; both of which provide alternative solutions to the same problem—constraints on members of an occupation which prevent commitment to the job for their full, working lives.

PROBLEMS OF PROMOTION

Teachers who wish to advance yet stay within the educational enterprise must, for the most part, leave teaching and move into school administration.[28] Advancement from teaching into administration is a process of many parts, involving both increased emoluments and a broadening of responsibility and jurisdiction (in addition to changes in the nature of the work itself). These parts are found in other occupations as well. Sponsorship by superiors (and the seeking of sponsorship by subordinates) is one of them, as Oswald Hall states, in describing physicians within a community.

> One of the major stages of a medical career involves acceptance by the inner fraternity. . . . The mechanisms include such phenomena as the institutional investigation of the newcomer, informal discussion and advice by high-ranking medical personnel, casual neglect in granting promotion in the hospital system, specific acts of encouragement and reward by the established practitioners, and direct sponsorship of a new recruit by one of the inner fraternity . . . the sponsored protégé must be assisted and vouched for at each step in his career.[29]

And the process of sponsorship may appear more subtly in the medical schools when students decide to enter general practice or to specialize. As Patricia Kendall and Hanan Selvin report:

> In some cases, members of the staff express their values [in urging a student to specialize] in the judgment that a rotating internship is less desirable than a specialized one, and they may respond in terms of these values when they learn of the plans of a high-ranking student to apply for a rotating internship. In contrast, the high-ranking student who expresses a preference for a specialized internship will, on occasion, receive support and encouragement from the faculty.[30]

Although medical advancement, or at least gaining acceptance within a local group of practitioners with all that implies for necessary hospital affiliations, occurs within a community (occupational and geographical), and not within an organizational setting, the processes involved are much the same as those found in school systems.

As in medicine, sponsorship within school systems has its subordinate and superordinate components. In their description of the New York City system, Griffiths and his colleagues comment:

> Once a teacher begins seeking vertical mobility (i.e., promotion) another kind of personalistic behavior is vital. This the research team has termed "GASing"—Gaining the Attention of Superiors. In essence GASing is doing a particular job to the satisfaction of one's superiors. That job may not be difficult to do, but it is either one that few can do successfully or one that only a few persons will undertake. It is a non-teaching job and time-consuming. It is ratable by the superior and important to him.[31]

When the initiative arises from below, it may represent a form of bootlicking motivated by the desire for future gain, requiring administrative sponsorship (which is not to deny the possibility of genuine helpfulness). Similarly, when the initiative comes from the top, subtle and not so subtle blackmail may occur, in which onerous or dirty jobs are assigned and undertaken as prepayment for later sponsorship.

Again, I have drawn my examples from the New York scene solely for purposes of illustration. Other school systems have their equivalents of GASing, known under different names, and often unaccompanied by the heavy examining apparatus characteristic of New York. There are numerous informal ways to recruit people into administrative positions, and the strategies (perhaps tactics), are not always lofty nor immediately relevant to the nature of the job: whom one entertains for dinner or plays poker with (to win or to lose); how one stays sober at parties, or keeps one's wife sober. Whyte's *The Organization Man* is the standard handbook for these events.[32] If the discussion sounds cynical and the process appears nefarious, one should consider the dimensions of the problem: finding people to fill a small number of top level jobs (jobs whose requirements are exceedingly difficult to define and whose component tasks depend on unknown future contingencies); people who have some political sophistication, who can get along with each other as well as with members of the diverse publics that make up the constituency of a school system, and who can make their way through the bureaucratic labyrinth of most school systems. Under these circumstances, one expects to find strong reliance on informal, social modes of recruitment. It is also important to recognize that I refer to widespread organizational events, not just school system events.

However, the world is not a totally evil place, as some of the principals interviewed in the National Principalship Study revealed. They found that as teachers, often much to their surprise, they were approached by an administrator wanting to discover whether they were interested in being considered for an administrative position; that is, the possibility of promotion was presented. Such teachers, later to become principals, had only to undertake the required and conventional preparation without doing personal favors.

Although school systems vary in the length, difficulty, and formality of the promotional obstacle course, New York's is one of the most strenuous. Sponsorship is important in New York and elsewhere, but there are other systematized mechanisms for promotion beside those involved in the exchange of favors characteristic of the sponsorship system. Every stage of advancement in the New York system requires a heavy dose of testing, testing in which, apparently, there are some "right" answers; and any situation that involves testing, right answers, and a seller's market for promotion is ideally suited to the flourishing of "cram schools" and "coaching." According to Griffiths' study:

> The importance of being coached and attending association meetings must not be underrated. As one principal-interviewee succinctly put it, "Coaching is all!" To be coached by one's principal or chairman, especially if that person has been an assistant examiner, is an advantage usually available to the person filling an acting role. Also, attendance at association meetings brings one into contact with those who have passed the examination and who have assisted and are assisting in writing the examinations.[33]

Coaching, or "prepping," as it is sometimes called, is designed for the benefit of the coach as well as the teacher preparing to become a principal or assistant principal. According to David Rogers:

> The [coaching] courses are recognized by people inside the system as "really a big business." "People really make money with coaching," a school official said. "They have coaching schools that charge $300 to $500, taught by principals or department heads who have been examiners before," reported an NYU researcher.[34]

There is no reason to suspect that considerations of competence and merit slip through the promotional net, either in New York or elsewhere; but clearly, a promotional mechanism that consists of testing, sponsorship, cramming, establishing personal contacts, and the like permits other considerations in addition to competence to become weighty parts of the assessment. As Rogers contends:

> Particular ethnic groups have been the historical gate-keepers of the system at different historical periods, reflecting an ethnic politics that existed throughout New York City government.[35]

Although the promotional system in New York (undoubtedly in other cities as well) appears vulnerable to the charge that the prevailing mechanisms are too open to favoritism of various kinds, the problems of promotion run deeper. Just as no method currently exists for judging the competence of teachers, neither does one exist for establishing the competence of administrators, especially when there is no necessary reason why a prolonged or "successful" career as a teacher constitutes appropriate preparation for becoming an administrator. *In the absence of valid criteria for predicting satisfactory administrative performance,* it is reasonable to approach the problem on the basis of plausibility—testing programs and the observation of teachers performing low level administrative tasks at least provide plausible conjectures about what it takes to be an administrator—and on the basis of personal connections, providing the latter are not simply manifestations of back-scratching. One might even make a defensible case for the tacit use of ethnic or religious criteria based on the social composition of the administrator's constituency, provided he *also* shows a capacity for using good judgment and tact, has some knowledge of how schools and school systems work, and understands the problems confronting schools, teachers, children, and school communities. Moreover, the legitimate political component of the school administrator's job should not remain unrecognized; whereas competence in specific tasks (as yet only vaguely identified) are likely to be important, administrators, and particularly principals, are executive officers in organizations where the support and allegiance of diverse constituencies must be gained: teachers, pupils, parents, unions, and community organizations among them. Thus, *beyond* identifying certain basic competencies and establishing a pool of persons possessing them, perhaps election is an appropriate way to select administrators, although identifying the appropriate electorate for administrative elections is not likely to prove a simple task.

It is easy to look at the seamy side of promotion in school systems, or in any organization, for there is nothing unique about school systems in this respect. But a preoccupation with atrocity stories takes one's eye away from some of the real problems. Anyone will agree in principle that promotion from teaching to administrative positions should rest on considerations of competence and impartiality, but this contention is based on prior suppositions: that competence can be gauged (a question to which I have alluded earlier), that performance at work is visible, and that those who judge do so legitimately.

Who sees the teacher at work, and who should have the right to judge the quality of performance? Pupils, obviously, see teachers considerably more than anyone else, but their observational familiarity does not necessarily mean that they can formulate the nature of the teacher's work or judge its adequacy. This is not to suggest that pupils hold no opinions about teachers or that they should not; rather, they are not in a good position to take enough considerations about teaching into account, nor are they located appropriately to gauge the needs and priorities of schools and school systems which figure into decisions about promotion. Pupils, particularly in the upper high school grades, can make intelligent observations about the work of particular teachers that may prove useful in decisions about promotion, but clearly it would be inappropriate to assign legitimate promoting *authority* to pupils because their competence in the matter is questionable, their position provides only limited perspective, and they possess no sanction from the community to influence directly the allocation of tax money. Pupils, in other words, can see but lack a legitimate basis to judge, and in most cases are incompetent to judge.

There is no reason *in principle* why teachers cannot judge each other in matters of promotion; collegial arrangements (though usually with formal or informal modifications based on status, rank, seniority, or experience *within* the occupational group) are common in medicine, law, and university teaching. The assumption underlying collegial promotion is that members of an occupation are sufficiently steeped in the nature of the work that they can claim the legitimate right to judge the work of others on the basis of competence. But while there is nothing in principle that precludes this type of arrangement among teachers, the ecology of schools is such that teachers seldom if ever observe each other at work. Schools are so organized that teachers work simultaneously in different places; and though they have opportunities to talk about work when they are not engaged in it, they lack the opportunities that doctors, lawyers, and architects have for *direct* observation of the work process itself and of the finished product. The situation in academic life is somewhat different; the public medium of "observation" and the judgment of competence derive mainly from publication, not through the direct observation of teaching even though the ecology of universities and the flexibility of time schedules makes such observation possible. Normative proscriptions related to academic freedom and equality among colleagues militate against such observation occurring. Teachers, then, *can* be legitimate judges of each other's competence, but in fact do not judge because they do not see each other at work.

Parents and other members of the municipality or of the school community have some claim to a legitimate place in the promotional process because they are taxpayers and because the schools are public agencies. This claim is currently being pressed in many urban ghetto areas and extends well beyond the issue of promotion. As one would expect, it meets opposition from some teachers and teachers' organizations. The ensuing conflict develops, at bottom, out of contrasting principles of legitimacy: teacher competence versus the taxpayers' claim for a voice in the expenditure of public funds, particularly when the prevailing sentiment is that the schools are not doing their job. The public controversy rages not over the principles of legitimacy in an explicit sense but rather over a variety of ideological questions and statements of the group interests related to those principles. It also feeds on the inability of teachers to claim convincingly that they command an esoteric technology and expertness not available to laymen. But aside from the issues in the present controversy, parents are located disadvantageously for participating in the process of promotion. At best, their knowledge of teaching competence is learned only indirectly from their children (and not without some distortion), and accordingly they have no practical way of assessing a teacher's qualifications to become an administrator; in short, their vision is impaired. They can, of course, attempt to create more localized school boards and administrative structures; but in *organizational* terms—as distinct from ideological ones—this strategy simply duplicates the existing mechanisms on a smaller scale and continues the same problems of legitimacy and visibility.

Given the prevailing organization of schools and school systems, administrators (those based in schools and in the central office of the system) have the strongest claim to deciding about promotion on the basis of what they can see and have a right to judge. Their position affords them the opportunity to observe teachers at work —they don't always make use of it—since they have direct access to classrooms and presumably can formulate their observations for deciding about promotion. Moreover, they can legitimately claim a right to decide by virtue of their position in the system hierarchy and their knowledge of teaching and administrative competence. Even though both types of competence are difficult to define, the administrators' capacity to identify them is as good as or better than anyone else's; and, of course, their location in the system provides them with a reasonably broad perspective on system-wide requirements.

In sum, the conventional mechanisms of promotion, at least from teacher to school administrator, tend to follow bureaucratic principles in that they are based on an assessment of competence (valid or not), and on a principle of legitimacy consisting of rules that establish the hierarchical arrangement of positions in the school system. Under these circumstances, it is not surprising to find (as shown in Chapter 3), that teachers favor the idea of principals reviewing their work and supervising them. At least for those who plan to leave the classroom for careers in administration, it is important that their superiors see them at work and become aware of their talents. Moreover, when administrative positions are scarce relative to the number of applicants, and when there are sharp salary differences between teaching and administrative positions, it is hardly surprising to find teachers moving outside the conventional avenues of promotion (testing and recommendations) to enroll in cram schools, find sponsors, and seek personal associations with those whose word might carry some weight in gaining a promotion.

COMMITMENT TO TEACHING CAREERS

To inquire into all the psychological components of commitment would lead into a quagmire of definitional problems. By commitment, from the teacher's point of view, I refer simply to spending the better part or all of one's working life as a classroom teacher, to a conception of teaching as one's life work. From the viewpoint of schools, school systems, and the occupation, teacher commitment becomes a question of holding power: is teaching an occupation that retains its members over a substantial period of their working lives? The main issue is not the moral one of whether individuals should or should not stay at their work, but rather the factual ones of whether the occupation can maintain a stable labor force and whether its collective membership contains "such traits as cohesion, commitment to norms of service, [a substantial] percentage of members remaining in the profession throughout their lifetime, control over professional violations, . . ."[36] and a codified body of theoretical knowledge that informs practice. This is not an arbitrary catalogue of traits, but one whose existence has important implications for the development of high level occupations, as I shall explain later. First, however, there is the empirical question of how strongly classroom teachers are committed to their occupation (teaching), and obversely, to what extent the occupation holds its members.

One indication of prior commitment is the extent to which undergraduates, such as those questioned by Davis during the spring of their senior year, plan to start their occupational career activities right after graduation, at some later time, or never. One can argue plausibly that occupational planning that begins soon after college graduation provides one sign of a mind made up and of the availability of necessary resources. (Although Davis reported that his data were collected during the spring of 1961, a specific time designation in one sense but vague in another, it is likely that some students had already been accepted at graduate schools and at other training institutions so that their statement of plans had some realism.)

The occupations in Table 6.2 are ranked in order of the percentage of college seniors who expected to begin their occupational training "next year" (presumably the following fall); several rough inferences can be made from the ranking. The list is headed by four occupations widely acknowledged by the public to be "professions." Occupational fields that usually have substantial representation in academia (not shown in the table) also rank high.[37] There is, then, a clear association between professionalism in the traditional sense and the tendency to begin occupational training shortly after college graduation.

One limitation on Davis' data, as they pertain to prospective teachers, is that most members of the occupation receive their training in undergraduate rather than in graduate programs. Insofar as occupational commitment is the issue, Mason provides data bearing indirectly on it. Among the male beginning teachers in his sample, 25 percent of those trained in four-year teachers colleges planned definitely or probably to leave teaching within the next five years, while 26 percent of those trained in a teacher preparation unit of a university so planned. The corresponding figures for women are 63 percent and 71 percent. As for planning to teach until retirement, another index of commitment, 29 percent of the men with undergraduate teacher training and 30 percent with graduate school training expected to remain until retirement; for women, the comparable figures are 16 percent and 13 percent.[38] Sex, in other words, and not type of training, appears to affect occupational commitment. For the minority of prospective teachers who trained at the graduate level, Davis' data can be taken at face value.

TABLE 6.2   *Percent of College Seniors Expecting to Begin Occupational Training at Various Times after Graduation*

Occupational Field	Next Year	Later	Never
Medicine	89	11	0
Dentistry	79	20	1
Law	76	23	1
Theology, Religion	72	22	6
Library	53	27	20
Engineering	32	45	23
Social Work	27	53	20
Education	25	60	15
Secondary languages	44	41	15
Secondary science	38	55	8
Exceptional children	36	59	5
Secondary history	33	57	10
Vocational	28	50	22
Secondary English	27	59	14
Secondary mathematics	23	70	7
Physical education	19	75	6
Elementary	17	67	16
Art, music	15	72	13
Housewife, teaching	14	46	40
Other	10	75	15
Architecture, City Planning	22	35	43
Business	17	41	42
Journalism	14	42	44
Accounting	13	47	40
Nursing	9	45	46
Pharmacy	5	32	63
Military	5	70	25

Adapted from James A. Davis, *Great Aspirations* (Chicago: Aldine Publishing Company, 1964), table 2.3, pp. 50–52; copyright © 1964 by National Opinion Research Center. Reprinted by permission.

Also from data collected by NORC but not published in this volume. The figures for medicine (those planning to start "next year") are probably inflated. Some men heading for other occupations probably try to get their military obligations out of the way before starting graduate schools; doctors all do two years of military service anyway, and there are advantages to doing them as physicians rather than as draftees or enlistees.

Among the occupations listed in Table 6.2, the percentage of college seniors who planned immediate training drops precipitously following librarianship, with occupations varying in the proportion of prospective members who planned later training and who planned no training. Among these is education (actually, teaching),[39] whose conspicuous characteristics are substantial *in-*

ternal variation according to subject matter and school level, and, among women, indications of the dilemma between working and raising a family. The predominant trend among prospective teachers was to delay occupational training (60 percent planned to begin preparation "later"), and with the exception of secondary mathematics, the percentage of those who planned early training appears related to the extent to which undergraduate education itself provides much of the substantive preparation for the subject field: the more subject matter that can be mastered during the undergraduate years, the greater the likelihood of delay in obtaining more advanced training. Note, however, that many states consider a bachelor's degree a sufficient academic credential to teach; for those states, plans to begin graduate training do not represent a good index of commitment.

Thus, Table 6.2 offers only a rough indication of prospective commitment; the ranking does, however, have an understandable plausibility. Occupations that characteristically hold their members for the duration of their working lives exact early decisions to begin training. Architecture apparently is an exception to this generalization, but it is combined in these data with city planning, a new and somewhat amorphously defined occupation that requires of prospective recruits some sense of artistic, engineering, and political aptitude, hardly a commonplace combination. Occupations through which people can readily move—business, journalism, accounting, nursing, some of which do not necessarily require academic training in addition to apprenticeship—rank low. Teaching is certainly one of the latter type whose members, particularly young ones, can readily enter and leave. Those occupations, moreover, that frequently represent second-choice jobs also rank low; this is true not only of teaching generally, but especially of its branches in which women predominate (elementary, art, and music) and of those women who plan both teaching and homemaking careers.[40]

If early entrance into training is a defensible index of occupational commitment, then graduate schools of education, in contrast to medical and law schools, train a substantial number of students who have not yet made up their minds about what work they want to do; and an entering student may well sense the climate of a teacher training institution as one whose members are still in the process of deciding. If so, this is hardly the kind of atmosphere where students will have their lingering doubts dispelled by the lateral pressure of student colleagues who know where they are going. Thus, if a liberal arts college keeps students' occupational options open, or even opens up new ones not previously contemplated—I exclude here those prevocational undergraduate programs that reinforce or destroy previously made choices—a school of education, by virtue of its composition, also continues to keep options open for many students, and in effect extends the liberal arts experience.[41]

Among the first-year teachers in his study, Mason discovered that 79 percent considered teaching their first occupational choice and 88 percent thought that if they had the choice to make over, they probably or definitely would enter teaching again. He then cross-classified the responses to these two questions and obtained four types of beginning teachers in the following proportions:

(1) contented—first choice, would enter again, 74 percent;

(2) converted—not first choice, would enter again, 14 percent;

(3) disappointed—first choice, would not enter again, 5 percent; and

(4) unconvinced—not first choice, would not enter again, 7 percent.

Having established these four types, he determined the proportion within each type "stating definitely or probably [that] they could achieve their long-run life goals by continuing in classroom teaching as a career. . . ."[42] The findings appear in Table 6.3.

Among teachers, substantial differences in the expectation of achieving life goals through teaching distinguish the contented from the disappointed, and the converted from the unconvinced. These differences of more than 40 percent and 30 percent, respectively, are more strongly related to favorable and unfavorable sentiments about entering the occupation again if the choice could be remade than they are to original priority of choice. This suggests that the actual experiences of teachers in the classroom exert a major influence on this early estimate of commitment. Of course,

TABLE 6.3   *Percent Stating They Could Achieve Long-run Life Goals As Classroom Teachers*

		Would definitely or probably choose teaching if the choice could be made again	
		Yes	No
Teaching was first choice	Yes	*Contented* 72	*Disappointed* 28
	No	*Converted* 54	*Unconvinced* 21

Adapted from Mason, *The Beginning Teacher*, p. 98; table 69, p. 99.

this finding must be considered in the light of the prior evidence that 88 percent of all beginning teachers sampled said they would make the same occupational choice again, and that 74 percent were contented. But for nascent disaffection, something in the actual teaching or school experience appears to have the major impact.

In the aggregate, Mason's reentry findings for beginning teachers hold with remarkable consistency for teachers at all stages of their careers, for both sexes, and at the elementary and secondary levels—as indicated by the NEA survey done four years later (see Table 6.4). Not surprisingly, those who remained in the occupation are also the ones who would enter again if they had it to do over, and except for teachers in the three-to-nine-year experience range whose enthusiasm wavers a bit, length of tenure in the occupation has virtually no effect on commitment (as indicated by rechoosing). Teachers who were experienced enough to become convinced that they disliked teaching had probably left the occupation already; to the extent this is so, the NEA findings are somewhat tautologous.

The potentiality for attrition in the cohort of beginning teachers has both short- and long-term manifestations. Mason reported that 14 percent of the men in his sample had occupational plans *for the next year* outside education, and that an additional 3 percent had educational plans that did not involve teaching; that is, 17 percent did not plan to return to the classroom. The corresponding figures for women are 12 percent and 3 percent, a total of 15 percent planning to leave the classroom.[43] It is fair to assume, however, that some of these teachers will not follow their plans to leave, that others who do not plan to leave teaching will actually do so, and that some of the men who do leave for the military and some of the women who do leave for homemaking will return at some later time. Although in the aggregate, men and women do not differ substantially in their short-run plans to leave teaching, they differ considerably when marital status is taken into account. Among single men, 27 percent planned to leave the classroom the following year while only 12 percent of the married men so planned. Among single women, 9 percent planned to leave; of the married women, 21 percent planned to leave.[44]

With a longer time span taken into account, the proportion of teachers planning to leave the classroom increases. Accordingly, in response to the question: "What is the likelihood of your leaving classroom teaching WITHIN THE NEXT 5 YEARS?" Mason found that 18 percent of the beginning teachers said they would definitely leave within that time; 33 percent probably; 30

TABLE 6.4 *Commitment to Teaching, by Sex, Level, and Years of Experience*

Suppose you could go back to your college days and start over again; in view of your present knowledge, would you become a teacher?	All teachers	Sex		School Level		Total Years of Teaching Experience			
		Men	Women	Elementary	Secondary	Less than 3 years	3–9 years	10–19 years	20 or more years
	%	%	%	%	%	%	%	%	%
Certainly would become a teacher	49.9	35.2	56.6	57.3	40.0	51.5	45.1	51.3	53.1
Probably would become a teacher	26.9	26.8	26.9	25.7	28.5	28.4	28.3	27.7	23.7
Chances about even for and against	12.5	19.3	9.5	9.9	16.1	12.9	14.3	11.9	10.8
Probably would not become a teacher	7.9	12.7	5.7	5.3	11.3	4.5	9.3	6.8	9.3
Certainly would not become a teacher	2.8	6.0	1.3	1.8	4.1	2.7	3.0	2.3	3.1
Number	1863	585	1278	1060	803	264	601	470	507

National Education Association, *The American Public-School Teacher, 1960–61*, Appendix A, No. 61, p. 101.

percent might but considered it unlikely; and 19 percent thought it extremely unlikely.[45] When teachers are asked to consider their working lives from the present until retirement, the prospects for occupational attrition become even more marked. Among men, though 80 percent intended to devote their working lives to educational pursuits, only 29 percent planned to teach until retirement; 51 percent contemplated nonteaching jobs in education, which for most of them probably means administration. Among women, 82 percent planned educational careers, but only 16 percent intended to teach until retirement; 9 percent planned nonteaching jobs in education; and 58 percent intended to become homemakers with the intention of returning to the classroom. Almost as many women wanted to leave and not return (12 percent) as wanted to teach until retirement (16 percent).[46]

If we look at these findings not in terms of the occupational aspirations of beginning teachers but in terms of the character of teaching as an occupation, several points appear very striking. It is important to remember that Mason polled these teachers before they had completed one full year on the job; yet in that fraction of a year, about half expected to be out of the classroom within five years, and only 21 percent expected to remain until retirement. Teaching, then, is an occupation containing only a small contingent of new recruits who claim a strong initial commitment. For men, one can attribute greater realism to the plans of the 20 percent who intended to enter another occupation than to the 51 percent who intended to enter nonteaching (administrative) jobs.[47] Even if the contingent with administrative aspirations amounts to only 40 percent in a given year, these occupational aspirations are clearly unrealistic in terms of the number of administrative positions available. Among those who will fail to become administrators, three reactions are likely: (1) leaving teaching out of discontent; (2) remaining in teaching with discontent; and (3) changing sentiments about teaching and continuing as satisfied teachers. The proportions of each are unknown, but if the first two occur with any substantial frequency, additional sentiments militate against strong occupational commitment.

For women, the fact that 58 percent intended to leave teaching for homemaking with the intention of returning (presumably when their youngest children are old enough) indicates some substantial degree of commitment; but that they *can* return, and usually without much difficulty, implies that the technology of teaching will not have changed very much in ten years or more. For if it changes appreciably, the problem of reentry would become severe indeed; women (or men) returning after a long lapse of time, accordingly, would need to devote substantial time and energy to becoming up to date. Perhaps it is important to draw a distinction here between commitment to a craft (or a type of work), and commitment to an occupation; for if mastery of the craft requires only a small personal investment, then the occupation subsuming the craft is not likely to inspire commitment by virtue of dedication *to the work itself.* The desire of many women to return, then, perhaps indicates more of a commitment to the occupation for reasons other than the nature of the work: the supplementary income, the desire to help children and to help the community, and the like (which is not to deny some commitment to the craft).

Several characteristics of teachers and of their jobs contribute to understanding the patterns of short- and long-run commitment to teaching, as summarized in Table 6.5. For both men and women, age has a strong association in the moderately short run (five years), but more so among women than men. Once a person reaches thirty, the chances of leaving the classroom within the next five years are modest (about 20 percent), but the youngest women are substantially more likely to leave within five years than the youngest men. Among men, lifetime commitment is affected only moderately by age; while among women, the chances of the young making teaching a lifetime commitment are negligible, and the chances of a woman over thirty doing so are considerable. Age among teachers, then, appears to be an index of options open and options foreclosed, and these options are apparently tied to contingencies of the life cycles peculiar to men and women.[48]

Most striking is the modesty of the impact of formal training (credentials, actually) on both short- and long-term commitment. This is true for both men and women, although women plan to leave teaching within five years to a substantially greater extent than men. Among men, holding a Master's degree or higher (rather than a B.A.) appears to make only a minor difference in five-year commitment, the relationship being positive; among women the pattern is indeterminate. The most important generalization from these findings is that the amount of formal training has a negligible impact on first-year teachers' intentions to remain in the classroom until retirement. The overall long-term commitment is small, as already noted; and there is roughly a 10 percent difference, on the average, between men and women. Apparently, teachers do not consider their academic preparation as an investment in a *teaching* career spanning a lifetime. There is some indication that men regard such training as preparation for an *educational* career outside the classroom. Between 49 percent and 54 percent holding some academic degree short of a Master's had nonteaching educational plans (probably in administration), while 59 percent with a Master's degree or higher had such educational plans.[49] These findings

Table 6.5 *Correlates of Short- and Long-run Commitment to Teach*

	Short-run Commitment		Long-run Commitment
	Definitely or probably leave within 5 years	*Teach next year**	*Teach until retirement*
	%	%	%
Age—Men			
21 and under	40	67	26
22	32	57	29
23–24	29	80	24
25–29	23	90	28
30 and over	19	92	39
Age—Women			
21 and under	73	83	9
22	77	86	6
23–24	70	84	11
25–29	58	84	24
30 and over	22	92	55
Formal Training—Men			
no B.A.	25	79	31
B.A.	28	79	29
B.A. +, no M.A.	24	86	28
M.A. or higher	16	91	30
Formal Training—Women			
no B.A.	62	81	22
B.A.	70	87	12
B.A. +, no M.A.	54	90	21
M.A. or higher	58	85	24
Gross Annual Salary—Men			
$4000 or more	23	88	29
$3500–$3999	25	84	29
$3000–3499	26	79	29
$2999 or less	34	72	29
Gross Annual Salary—Women			
$4000 or more	63	90	16
$3500–$3999	69	87	12
$3000–3499	67	86	13
$2900 or less	61	81	21

Table 6.5   *(continued)*

	Five years	*Next year*	*Until retirement*
	%	%	%
Satisfaction with Salary—Men			
Very satisfactory	31	81	35
Fairly satisfactory	21	84	31
Very or fairly unsatisfactory	29	81	26
Satisfaction with Salary—Women			
Very satisfactory	70	87	14
Fairly satisfactory	65	87	16
Very or fairly unsatisfactory	63	82	16
Satisfaction with Salary Compared to Other Occupations, Same Education, Same Area—Men			
Very satisfactory	27	82	43
Fairly satisfactory	21	85	33
Very or fairly unsatisfactory	27	81	27
Satisfaction with Salary Compared to Other Occupations, Same Education, Same Area—Women			
Very satisfactory	69	86	14
Fairly satisfactory	66	87	16
Very or fairly unsatisfactory	63	86	16
Satisfaction with Superiors—Men			
Very satisfactory	23	83	31
Fairly satisfactory	29	82	25
Very or fairly unsatisfactory	46	69	27
Satisfaction with Superiors—Women			
Very satisfactory	63	87	17
Fairly satisfactory	69	82	12
Very or fairly unsatisfactory	80	76	5
Spouse's Attitude Toward Teaching—Men			
Very favorable	11	92	38
Fairly favorable	30	87	22
Very or fairly unfavorable	74	54	9
Spouse's Attitude Toward Teaching—Women			
Very favorable	57	87	25
Fairly favorable	75	77	13
Very or fairly unfavorable	95	57	2

Table 6.5 *(continued)*

	Five years	Next year	Until retirement
	%	%	%
First-year Work Experience—Men			
Contented	12	88	36
Disappointed	56	68	10
Converted	31	83	22
Unconvinced	76	58	6
First-year Work Experience—Women			
Contented	63	89	17
Disappointed	87	61	3
Converted	70	85	10
Unconvinced	86	58	4

Adapted from Mason, *The Beginning Teacher,* table 76, pp. 108–114.

*Combined percentage of those teachers planning to teach in the same school district and those planning to teach in another district; that is, those intending to remain in the classroom for the following year.

are consistent with what we know about the character of teacher training: the liberal arts tradition (particularly in the graduate schools), part-time attendance, delayed entrance into training, and the tradition of credential-gathering. None of these phenomena suggests the use of college and university experience as investments in a lifetime career.

Interestingly, the NEA's evidence on the relationship between academic preparation and commitment in its more inclusive sample of teachers (not just beginners) indicates a different pattern, as shown in Table 6.6.

Compared to Mason's findings on beginning teachers, those of the NEA show a slightly *negative* relationship between training and commitment. It is important to keep in mind, however, that the samples are vastly different as is the index of commitment; but both sets of findings say essentially the same thing: *teachers do not prepare themselves for a lifetime of work in the classroom by putting their energy into academic preparation.* It is equally plausible to argue that even when teachers do invest time, money, and energy in formal training, the training itself is not a kind that exacts long-term commitment.

It is surprising to discover that the current salary status and salary satisfaction of teachers, in both absolute and relative terms, has only a negligible impact on commitment, according to Table 6.5. Several observations are pertinent to this point. First, the annual salary range considered is small (from under $2900 to

TABLE 6.6   *The Relationship Between Academic Training and Commitment*

| | Willingness to Teach Again | |
Highest Degree Held and Years of College Completed	*Certainly would*	*Certainly or probably would not*
	%	%
No degree	63.0	5.5
Bachelor's degree and less than 5 years	49.7	9.6
Bachelor's degree and 5 or more years	45.7	13.1
Master's or higher degree	44.7	14.6

National Education Association, *The American Public-School Teacher, 1960–61*, table 43, p. 63.

$4000 and over), and may not be large enough to make a difference. Second, since 1956–1957, when Mason collected his data, teacher salaries have risen considerably. By 1961, when the NEA completed its survey, *median* salaries had climbed to $5143,[50] and that figure has undoubtedly risen in the late 1960's, with the increasing success of the unions to win salary raises through collective bargaining and striking, and of the NEA to do the same through the application of sanctions. Third, it might have been more appropriate to ask beginning teachers about *anticipated* rather than current salaries where long-term occupational commitment is concerned. Some of the teachers' organizations have grasped this point in bargaining for large salary increments for experienced teachers and for fringe benefits and pension provisions having greatest appeal to the same group of teachers, to retain those already within the teaching ranks and to make newcomers consider it worth their while economically to remain in the classroom to reap later economic rewards.

Over the moderately short run (five-year period), teachers' satisfaction with relations to their superiors (presumably principals and other members of the school hierarchy) has a greater impact on commitment than does satisfaction with salary; the quality of relations with superiors has a slightly greater effect among men than among women, a difference difficult to interpret with the available data (see Table 6.5). The long-run implications of these relationships for commitment, however, are small among both men and women. Far more important than either economic or supervisory considerations is whether the teacher's spouse holds favorable sentiments toward teaching. Among women, the effect of the husband's attitude is large; among men, the wife's attitude is massive, affecting five-year commitment by 63 percent, plans for the following year by 38 percent (a remarkable finding for a variable that otherwise tends to remain highly stable), and 29 percent for lifetime commitment (see Table 6.5). Both sets of findings (for supervision and attitude of spouse) suggest a combination of forces concerning the immediate nature of both the work situation and its implication for the household. Although the data do not specify what characteristics of the supervisory arrangement result in satisfaction or dissatisfaction (or whether the degree of work satisfaction affects the relationship with supervisors), it is plausible, particularly among beginning teachers, that satisfaction depends on helpfulness or support from superiors; and since it is fair to assume that most teachers begin work inadequately prepared for the realities of the job, supervisory relationships are likely to be crucial. Similarly, it is difficult to establish whether the attitudes of husbands and wives prevail before a teacher starts work or constitute reactions to the experiences and sentiments that teachers hold about their work and talk about at home. One can easily imagine how a teacher returning home at the end of the day with tales of woe or gratification can affect how his or her spouse feels about the work.

Finally, teachers' sentiments about the total work experience (contentment, disappointment, etc.) provide a global estimate of the work situation and perhaps of family sentiment as well. When a man or woman expresses contentment or disappointment, he or she may be judging aspects of the work situation *and* the reactions of a spouse to descriptions of and sentiments about that situation. Although the interpretive question cannot be settled with the existing data, it is not surprising to find that the assessment of work experience has a strong relationship to five-year commitment and a substantial one to both short- and long-term commitments among men (though more modest ones among women). It is also clear that these effects are not basically correlates of low remuneration. Mason does demonstrate that salary is related to general job satisfaction (with satisfaction considered both with and without salary considerations),[51] but he also shows, as I have indicated earlier, that current job satisfaction is not dramatically related to commitment.

The intention to act is one thing; to act according to intention is another. Is there evidence, then, on the extent to which teachers interrupt their working careers? In the previously cited NEA study, teachers were asked to report the number of years they were absent from teaching from the time they started. The findings, reported in Table 6.7, are aggregate and thus do not allow comparisons between the intentions of specific individuals and their subsequent actions. But the overall picture is of an occupation where substantial numbers of teachers take time away from the job and then return. Somewhat over half (55.9 percent) of all teachers sampled remained on the job without interruption; more men did than women, a fact consistent with women stopping work to raise families; more secondary than elementary teachers remained without absence, undoubtedly a reflection of the fact that most elementary school teachers are women, with the highest rate of leave-taking occurring among women. Most important for the character of the occupation is that 15.0 percent of all teachers, and larger proportions of women at both levels, leave and then return after an interval of eleven or more years. Clearly, reentry offers no serious obstacle if that large a proportion can stay away for so long a time.

Additional evidence bearing on entering and leaving the occupation comes from W. W. Charters' work on 546 graduates of the University of Illinois between 1937 and 1947. He found that approximately 40 percent of those qualified to teach never did so, half of those teaching left the occupation after two years, and only about 10 percent taught continuously for a decade.[52] The most interesting aspect of Charters' findings is that the pattern of dropping out of teaching *employment* resembles that of undergraduate defection from premedical and engineering *study* among college students (described by Davis), with the rapid loss of uncommitted and uninterested students leaving a residue of hardcore members. Although Charters' sample was limited and localized, his findings, if representative at all, suggest that teaching has "taken" the more expensive manpower alternative.

Longitudinal data on teaching careers—following a cohort of beginning teachers over time—are exceedingly scarce. In 1967, however, J. Scott Hunter drew a sample of teachers who originally participated in Mason's study of 7150 beginning teachers.[53] Table 6.8 indicates in aggregate terms what happened to a sample of the original (Mason) cohort one year later.

These figures are almost identical to those that Mason reported on the plans of beginning teachers for the following year, although they do not indicate whether those individuals planning to stay or leave are actually the ones to do so.[54] As I have indicated earlier, a one-year perspective is not long enough to estimate long-term commitment, but clearly these findings present a much more optimistic picture than that of Charters, based on his small sample of University of Illinois graduates of one or two decades earlier.

TABLE 6.7 *Years Absent from Teaching, by Sex and School Level*

Number of years absent from teaching, since beginning to teach	All teachers	Sex		School Level				
		Men	Women	Elementary	Secondary			
					Total	Men	Women	
	%	%	%	%	%	%	%	
None	55.9	76.0	46.6	48.6	65.4	75.7	51.6	
1–5 years	21.0	18.7	22.0	21.0	21.0	19.5	22.9	
6–10 years	8.1	2.5	10.7	10.6	4.9	2.4	8.2	
11 or more years	15.0	2.8	20.7	19.8	8.7	2.4	17.3	
Number	1837	583	1254	1040	797	456	341	

National Education Association, *The American Public-School Teacher, 1960–61*, Appendix A, No. 32, p. 92.

TABLE 6.8   *Activities (Fall 1957) of Those Who Began Teaching During the Academic Year 1956–1957*

Stayed in Education			86%	(n = 1709)
Teaching in public schools	96%	(n = 1641)		
Teaching in private schools working in nonteaching positions, obtaining further educational training	4%	(n = 68)		
Left Education (Permanently or Temporarily)			14%	(n = 278)
Homemaking	53%	(n = 147)		
In armed forces	24%	(n = 67)		
Training for noneducational occupation	6%	(n = 11)		
Unaccounted for	17%	(n = 53)		

Total   n = 1987

J. Scott Hunter, "The Beginning Teacher One Year Later," p. 4; adapted into tabular form from data presented in text. Hunter does not explain why 17 percent of those who left education remain unaccounted for.

If the eleven persons training for noneducational occupations are combined with the sixty-eight who were teaching in private schools, getting further educational training, or working in nonteaching educational positions, then about 4 percent of the resampled beginning teacher cohort represents a small overestimate (because the 4 percent includes a small number of private school-teachers) of teachers likely to be lost to the occupation in the short run. This contrasts sharply with Charters' figure of 40 percent loss after the first year. Of course, it is impossible to estimate from these data how many of those teaching for the second year will continue, and how many homemakers and members of the armed forces will eventually return. Most likely, more than 4 percent will. Hunter's data do indicate, however, that at least 82 percent of the beginning teachers have returned to the classroom for a second year. (It would be risky if not impossible to project for subsequent years from this figure alone.)

Among both men and women, remaining in the classroom for a second year is only slightly related to age: of those age twenty-six and younger, about 80 percent remained, and of those twenty-seven and older, 90 percent remained. Roughly the same pattern holds separately for men and women, although as expected there is a decline for women in the 23–24 age bracket. Among those *leaving education,* 12 percent were men and 15 percent were women; most of the women left for homemaking, the men for the armed forces. Very few (4 percent of the men and 3 percent of the women) left education after one year for another occupation (and therefore left teaching); and for both men and women, leaving education is inversely related to age. Leaving teaching is most frequent among men twenty-three years or younger (24 percent), newly or recently married women (23 percent), secondary school women (19 percent), and teachers from rural backgrounds (19 percent).[55] The relationship between current salary and remaining in the classroom for a second year is modest: 86 percent of those earning $4000 or more remained in teaching, and 76 percent of those earning $2500 or less remained. Differences of about the same magnitude hold for men and women separately. When sex, marital status, and salary are considered simultaneously, the better paid married men (earning $3500 or more) were most likely to remain in the classroom (92 percent), while married women (irrespective of salary) and single men earning less than $3500 were least likely to remain (75 percent ± 1 percent). Again, while these differences are greater than those related to age and sex, they are not large and indicate the overwhelming tendency of teachers to remain on the job for at least a second year.[56]

Economically, men and women manifest different patterns: both were better off financially the second year if they stayed in teaching, but men who transferred to another district got both larger raises and made more money than women, and those men who left education earned more money and got larger raises than anyone else. By contrast, women who left teaching after the first year wound up on the average with *less income than when they started* and less than their colleagues who remained in the classroom; that is, they suffered an absolute financial loss.[57] Thus, over the very short time span of one year, money and sex are each related to the chances of teachers staying in the classroom; but while money draws men out of the occupation, it holds women in even at lower salaries than men.

Academic training has only a slight positive relationship to remaining in the classroom for a second year. For both men and women, 86 percent of those with a bachelor's or higher degree remained compared to 78 percent of those without a bachelor's. Similar differences hold for men and women separately.[58] Elements of job satisfaction also have undramatic effects, with certain exceptions. Among all beginning teachers, 71 percent of those who found their relationships with superiors very or fairly unsatisfactory returned for a second year, and 85 percent of those who found these relationships very satisfactory returned. Of the dissatisfied teachers, 25 percent left education the second year.[59] Satisfaction with relationships with students has practically no effect, and general job satisfaction (with financial considerations both included and excluded) makes some difference, as shown in Table 6.9. For those beginning teachers who were very and fairly satisfied with the job as a whole, taking salary into account does not affect the likelihood of returning to the classroom a second year in judging satisfaction. But among the dissatisfied, weighing salary considerations into the assessment of satisfaction was associated with a higher rate of return to the classroom than not doing so. Since the same teachers made both assessments, it appears that weighing salary—whether it is high or low—into the calculation has the effect of counteracting other sources of dissatisfaction that might lead to leaving the occupation. There is some support for this interpretation, for when teachers *did not* include salary considerations in their calculations, 31 percent of the very and fairly dissatisfied left education; when they did include salary in their assessment, only 21 percent of the very dissatisfied and 12 percent of the fairly dissatisfied left.

Mason, as indicated earlier, classified his sample of 1956–1957 beginning teachers according to their stated likelihood of leaving classroom teaching during the next five years. Hunter, with this knowledge of five-year intentions, determined the occupational pursuits of individuals in his subsample for the fall of 1957. Of the men who as first-year teachers definitely planned to leave within five years, 51 percent reported that they had left education in 1957, 20 percent having left to enter a noneducational occupation. (Note, however, that only 140 [or 19 percent] of the men definitely planned to leave; the actual loss of these men teachers to other occupations, therefore, is only 5.8 percent.) Men with less intense desires to leave did so much less frequently. Among the women, 41 percent definitely planning to leave education actually did so; 8 percent left for another occupation. (In the case of women, 41 percent definitely planned to leave within five years —compared to 19 percent of the men—so that the numerical rate of attrition among women is higher.[60]

Among both men and women (the differences being so small between them that their attrition rates can be treated together), only the intention to leave education for another occupation starting the following year had any appreciable association with actually entering another occupation (15 percent). Planning to teach until retirement, taking a nonteaching job in education, and becoming a homemaker (either planning or not planning to return) all had negligible relationships to leaving the classroom to do anything else the following year (between 1 percent and 5 percent); returning to the classroom in one school or another was the overwhelmingly frequent outcome.[61] As expected, beginning teachers are more likely to follow anticipated plans for the next year than to follow those projected over the next five years. Accordingly, of

TABLE 6.9 *Job Satisfaction and the Likelihood of Remaining in Teaching for a Second Year*

Degree of Satisfaction	Percent Remaining in Teaching	
	For the position (except salary)	*For the position (with salary)*
Very unsatisfactory	62	76
Fairly unsatisfactory	62	81
Fairly satisfactory	82	83
Very satisfactory	86	87

Hunter, "The Beginning Teacher One Year Later," adapted from table 6, p. 24.

those planning to return to the classroom the following year, 88 percent actually did so; of those planning to enter another (non-educational) occupation, 43 percent do so.[62]

In effect, the available evidence on attrition from teaching is inadequate. There is reasonably good evidence about intentions to leave and various considerations related to those intentions, but not enough data to claim with certainty that teaching is an occupation that does not hold its members. The Hunter data do not cover a long enough period of time, and the Charters data describe only a small, localized sample. Mason and Bain provide additional but hardly conclusive evidence on teacher attrition. On the basis of a nationwide probability sample covering 1551 school districts from school opening in 1957 to school opening in 1958, they found that of 1,257,000 persons teaching in the fall of 1957, some 137,000 (or 10.9 percent) had left the occupation by the fall of 1958.[63] This figure is suggestive but represents the events of only one year and without any indication of possible later returns to the occupation. The literature on this question, moreover, is difficult to interpret because loss to an occupation is often confounded with turnover. Leaving one work setting to continue plying one's trade in another is very different from renouncing one's occupation, and the two are often confused in measures of turnover. High rates of turnover that do not entail leaving one occupation for another may actually be an index of high commitment even though they create recruitment problems in particular work settings.

What can be said about actual and potential attrition in teaching as evidence of occupational commitment? Substantial numbers of teachers want to leave the occupation in the long and moderately long run; the magnitude of actual leaving is difficult to ascertain, but it is greatest in the short run among those teachers most intent on leaving. The occupation is easy to enter in that it requires a relatively small investment of energy and time in preparation, and preparation itself can be delayed and strung out over an extended period. For men, the fact that teaching is embedded in a larger context of better paying educational occupations proves to be an economic inducement for them to leave the classroom. Whether they follow the inducement is another question, a complex one involving financial and domestic considerations as well as satisfaction with the work itself. For women, the desire to raise a family draws many, at least temporarily, out of the occupation; however, returning at a later time presents few serious obstacles. Although it is not yet possible to assess the actual rate of classroom defection, it is reasonably clear that the occupation provides no abundancy of forces militating toward work-life commitment.

THE IMPORTANCE OF COMMITMENT AND PROBLEMS OF PROFESSIONALISM

One observer has claimed that "the only common factor in definition of profession is eulogy."[64] Although the statement is at best incomplete, it contains an important element of truth: a profession is an occupation that has made a certain kind of deal with the public. To oversimplify, it trades competence for recognition. According to Goode:

> Economic supply and demand, shaped by such factors as monopoly, entrance restrictions, shifts in tastes, and the like will determine how high their incomes will be, but supply and demand operate in the markets of power and prestige as well. An occupation *can command more prestige* only if the society, applying its evaluative criteria, perceives the performance of the occupation to be better than before or higher than those of similar occupations. An occupation can enjoy more power if it can exchange some of its friendly relations, income, prestige, or political influence for legal privileges or controls.[65]

This is almost tantamount to saying that an occupation is a profession if the public thinks it is: that *prestige* is the critical consideration. Were this so, it would go some way in explaining why it is so difficult, particularly at the margins, to distinguish those occupations that are professions from those that are not. Because public opinion does not come in neat packages, no clear lines of demarcation appear; at the same time, there has been substantial public agreement about medicine, law, the clergy, and academia for a long time. In other words, to ask which occupations are professions and which are not, is to ask the wrong question.

Goode has argued that:

> In order to be accepted by society as a profession, an occupation requires special transactions in mainly the prestige markets. If these are successful, they can be used to obtain more power and money. However, merely clever transactions that yield power and money for an occupation are not sufficient to achieve acceptance as a profession.[66]

The important question, then, is what properties must an occupation have for the public to attribute prestige to it?

As I have argued earlier, it makes little or no difference for this discussion whether teaching (or any other occupation) is called a profession—is eulogized, or gains public prestige. What does matter, however, is how an occupation is organized, whether its central tasks get done, and whether it arouses public confidence. At this time in American history the questions of public confidence in teachers' capacity to teach, and of pupils' capacity to benefit from school, have come under intense public criticism; and these issues add a sense of urgency to our understanding of the occupation in addition to the desire to know as a matter of scholarly interest. Commonly recognized as professions are (1) those occupations whose practice is based on a codified body of abstract knowledge and whose clients believe in the efficacy of the practice, and (2) those occupations whose practitioners also adhere to an ideal of public service (even if circumstances do not consistently demand personal self-sacrifice), such that the practitioner, and not the client, defines the nature of the problem. But for my purposes, it is these occupational characteristics, not the public recognition, that have prime importance, and the work-life commitment of members has a crucial relationship to these characteristics.[67]

An occupation with a high degree of commitment among its members is likely to have a stable work force (i.e., low rates of defection and potential defection). It need not be characterized by a sense of personal solidarity nor need it be faction-free.[68] Commitment and stability are probably more important for what they make possible than for what they are. The core of the issue is whether the members of an occupation have mastery of a viable technology applicable to human problems, and whether they can supply the resources—through training, through channels of communication, and through mechanisms that generate new knowledge and criticize the old—which are necessary to keep that technology alive (or, in the case of teaching, to create the

knowledge in the first place). For to have confidence in an occupation, the public must not only believe in the efficacy of the technology, but it must also have sufficient trust in the occupation to
control the conduct of its members and to enforce standards of
good practice.

Enforcement, however, presents special problems for occupations that are geographically dispersed. There are at least two
alternatives. One has been adopted by the forest service, where
control over a far-flung enterprise is highly bureaucratic and consists largely of rangers submitting frequent reports to a central
office, and where there is a continuous circulation of men from
position to position.[69] Note, however, that the rangers' work is
largely routine and requires little or no esoteric expertise, a set
of conditions highly consistent with centralized control over work;
the problem of control arises mainly out of geographical dispersion.

Another alternative has been characteristically adopted by
the conventionally recognized professions and also by the skilled
craft occupations. Here, control over the work and adherence to
standards rests largely within the practitioner himself; he learns
the job and the standards governing its performance in training
institutions. The standards are largely self-enforced and are maintained by frequent association with other practitioners rather
than through policing, either by a central administrative agency
or by clients. (This is not to suggest that standards are never vio-
lated or that agencies of an occupational association never ride
some of their members out for malpractice: doctors lose their
licenses, lawyers are disbarred, priests defrocked.) The point is,
however, that these occupations rely primarily on the dedication
of the practitioner to standards of practice rather than on centralized policing.[70]

If an occupation is organized socially so that its members adhere to standards of good practice on their own and find support for the maintenance of standards in their daily work with
colleagues, this fact in itself implies a form of social organization
consistent with a number of other occupational attributes: a co-
herent set of occupational tasks that can be acquired; an intensive
and prolonged period of training that makes mastery of these
tasks possible; a sense of common identity with other practitioners;
a belief that failure to live up to occupational standards is injurious
not only to oneself but also to the occupation generally; a set of
inducements (not excluding a substantial investment of time, energy, and money in one's own training) to remain in the occupation permanently; and location in a network of communication
through which knowledge about one's work circulates.

Occupational commitment, then, is not important so much for its own sake but for what else it implies. Weak commitment as an occupational attribute, implies the existence of inductive mechanisms that do not work very well, that do not bind people in; and the existence of inducements, intrinsic to the work or extrinsic by remuneration, that make the occupation less appealing than alternatives. And without the sense of community, of identification with a common enterprise, there is not enough stability of membership to support the thoroughgoing development and maintenance of a technology. In a sense, an occupational syndrome is at issue; its parts are related to each other, but central among them is the matter of technology, not only as a core of activities around which workers can unite (whatever their other differences), but also as the basis of an adequate means of induction, of training, and of gaining public confidence.

•

CHAPTER SEVEN

Teaching,

Present and Future

•

It may appear odd, after belittling the preoccupation of teachers with professionalism and the prestige associated with it, that I return to the questions of professionalism and prestige. Goode has reminded us that professionalism involves transactions in a public market in which prestige is a negotiable—though delicate and protean—currency. Unlike commodities or money itself, prestige cannot be bought outright. The occupation that moves to increase its prestige is like the newly rich family that wants a place in the aristocracy; the place is not for sale, and the purchase of aristocratic trappings makes the speciousness of the imitation the more obvious. As the legendary Boston policeman told the tourist asking the way to Dedham: "You can't get there from here." Accordingly, and with full knowledge of the hazards of prediction, Goode tells the fortunes of several occupations.

These semi-professions will achieve professionalism over the next generation: social work, marital counseling, and perhaps city planning. . . . The following occupations will not become professional: within the medical situs, none will achieve it, with the possible exception of veterinary medicine. Osteopathy is gradually being absorbed into the ordinary status of physician. Nurses have been pressing hard toward professionalism, but will not move far. Chiropractic will remain a marginal or quack occupation, as will podiatry. Pharmacy will not change its status much. Next, schoolteaching will not achieve professionalism, nor will librarianship.[1]

The reasons are manifold and vary with the occupation, and I need not go into them here; of course, both the predictions and the reasons may be wrong. The case of teaching is an interesting one to explore; the point, however, is not to support or refute Goode's case, but to examine the considerations that may turn the outcome one way or the other.

An occupation can trade in prestige only if it has it; and the reason why prestige is such a difficult resource to obtain and to use is that the members of an occupation, or the occupation collectively, do not have complete control over it. The prestige of an occupation is a characteristic that the public attributes to it (i.e., it is not the same kind of resource, for example, as is a pension fund or an occupational journal which are its property and subject to its control). Prestige is gained to the extent that the members of an occupation gain the trust and respect of the public for the successful performance of occupational activities that serve the interests of clients—when the practitioner, not the client, defines those interests. Competence and efficacious performance, then, are the crucial considerations. To cite Goode again:

> The school teacher . . . has a . . . relationship to her knowledge base, which is not so much curriculum content—most adults believe that they could master that after a short period of study—but the *technique and principles of pedagogy*. This content is, however, relatively small in amount and shallow intellectually. More important, because the crucial matter here is the interaction of public and occupation, even in the area of teaching techniques the teacher is not thought to be a final arbiter. . . . *Nor does it seem likely that the body of pedagogic knowledge that is the teacher's area of prime responsibility will grow much over the next generation.*[2]

I would agree with Goode, then, that the development of a viable technology is the key issue for occupational change in teaching. His prediction is based on the premise that the technology will not develop sufficiently over the next generation; I would argue that the technological question should remain open, that the fate of his prediction will ride on whether the problem of competence is solved within the occupation.

If technological development is the central issue, then the programs of both the NEA and the AFT, at least in the past, have missed the boat. Although they both use the rhetoric of professionalism, they have used their resources primarily to protect the occupation, to advance its economic position, and to improve working conditions; and these strategies are tantamount to "buying" prestige—and I do not use "buying" cynically. Spokesmen for the union, and others sympathetic to its goals, have argued that it is not unprofessional to strike; and in that they are correct because striking does not have much to do with professionalism. Physicians have struck, and they are no less professional for having done so, ideological critics to the contrary; artists, particularly musicians and actors who perform collectively, are highly unionized (though soloists, poets, writers, and composers—artistic entrepreneurs—are not).[3] The NEA has said that the professionalization of teachers will depend on their becoming better trained, but under present circumstances, that can only mean better trained within the confines of the prevailing technology. Both the AFT and the NEA have argued that professional dignity depends on congenial working conditions. All these contentions are perfectly defensible; yet they implicitly accept the technological *status quo*. The goals and programs of the NEA and the AFT are certainly worthy; but even if they were achieved, teaching would be no more "professional"—even if teachers were happier—than it is now if the efficacy of its activities and the principles underlying them remain at the present level. Airline pilots, for example, make good money and work under conditions reasonably conducive to the performance of their work, yet they are not professionals; the same is true for businessmen and managers. The prestige of professionalism accrues to those occupations whose members serve the public and monopolize an esoteric expertise (and gain public respect thereby). Respect derives from competent performance, not from the perquisites and appearances of professionalism.

If the analysis in the earlier chapters is correct, the central problem of teaching as an occupation is *the state of its technology*. The critics who say that teaching methods courses in schools of education are pap are correct; the remedy, however, is not to throw them out but to find out how to do the job, by discovering what its component tasks are and instructing new recruits to the occupation in how to do them. The medical student learning to palpate, tie knots, percuss, and test for the Babinski reflex is hardly engaged in any profound intellectual enterprise; but he had better be able to do these things and know why he is doing them. The "how" is crucial because it connects a mundane task with a body of abstract scientific knowledge. Teaching will not be a profession to which people will devote their working lives until we discover what the tasks of the job are, how to do them, and understand why we do them.

Before considering some possible directions of occupational change in teaching, I treat some of the obstacles, not because they are insuperable, but because they are there. First, teaching is a large occupation employing several hundred thousand people. To effect changes in such a large body of persons is a staggering task; Flexner's reforms in medicine, early in the twentieth century, affected a much smaller number of practitioners. No logic, however, enjoins us to change every teacher; perhaps the least experienced and those planning to enter the field should be the first targets, as well as some of the old hands eager to try something new and more workable.

Second, the educational establishment—not the elite that Conant chides, but the total enterprise—is far-flung and diverse. The United States has no national ministry, but rather fifty state school systems each with its own political rules of the game and standards of licensure and accreditation. (There is, of course, comity between some of them as well as similarity.) The prevalence of such diversity makes it difficult to locate points of leverage at which change can be started and then diffused. Third, the country is now beset by intense political pressures, particularly in the central cities, and by ethnic and racial groups that have found the schools unresponsive to, if not directly frustrating of, their interests to join the mainstream of American life, pressures that have led to the massive infusion of funds into enrichment and remedial programs. Although these programs provide conspicuous evidence that something is being done to alleviate acute problems, they do little to redesign the nature of educational activities because the necessary technology is not available. Fourth, teaching, like the other people-changing occupations, rests on bodies of knowledge provided by the social sciences, disciplines that are relatively undeveloped theoretically and not well suited, at present, to provide clear guidelines for occupational practice. Although we should not dismiss technological developments that "work" for reasons we don't understand—there are many medical treatments of precisely that character—in the long run, we can expect to find a general correspondence between advances in teaching and those in the social sciences. To put the matter more bluntly, we will have to wait a long time for some important technological developments in teaching.

This list of obstacles is not exhaustive, nor is it meant to be. It does, however, indicate that the character of teaching is not likely to change overnight. More than that, knowing where the obstacles are and what they are provides strategic guidelines. We know, for example, that to make headway, we cannot simply limit ourselves to classroom experiments, however important they may be, but must consider the politics of diffusing ideas and practices; promote scientific research that has no obvious, short-term relevance to the crises of urban education; design training programs that teachers who have been doing things differently for twenty years will accept, and the like.

Whether or not the future agenda for teaching includes professionalization, I would argue that the central occupational task is the development of a viable technology; and for teachers, the task is to improve competence, not so much in the activities comprising the current and crude technology, but to master the component skills of new technological developments. Although this sounds like a single-item agenda, it indeed is not; it entails occupational strategies that move on several fronts.

Consider the case of classroom instruction. The recent work on microteaching represents one of the few attempts to identify the component skills of instruction, to analyze them into their parts, to teach each part in brief training exercises, and to tie supervisory activities integrally into the process of teacher training. One of the chief virtues of this scheme is that the brief training period devoted to a specific skill provides an opportunity for almost immediate feedback, the absence of which is one of the major difficulties that teachers now confront in trying to rectify their errors in the classroom, since they work in isolation and are subject to sporadic, out-of-context supervision at best. But the availability of rapid feedback has two other virtues. First, a microteaching training session is a collective experience, not a dyadic one between a practice teacher and a cooperating teacher. Several teachers have a stake in the proceedings because they all take their turn engaging in the same activity and confront both their own performance and the comments of their colleagues. This situation rapidly puts them all in the same boat. Second, particularly when videotape is used, visual and audible records are kept that can be reviewed repeatedly. In the conventional training situation, the record of events is forever lost save in the selective memory of the trainee who cannot possibly retain the totality of occurrences in a class period. For once, the teacher has a literal record that can be studied, restudied, and discussed, much as the doctor in training has permanent records in the form of X rays, clinical test results, and medical charts, and as the lawyer has briefs, stenographic records of court proceedings, and court reports to study. In all cases, the trainee has a *tangible* record of activities and events to study while learning his trade.

Jeanne Chall's work on reading bears on another aspect of technological development. While her book does not test or apply a particular method, she has reviewed and *codified* the available research on the teaching of reading. Lest relevant research in a particular area of practice remains a mass of discrete and disconnected studies, it is necessary that the underlying principles be formulated and stated in general terms. It is precisely this process of formulation that transforms a collection of gimmicks—however workable they are in practice—into a technology. That is, technological development consists in part of strictly intellectual efforts —no experiments, no field work, no on-the-job training—designed to reduce a mass of ostensibly unrelated ideas and practices into a much smaller number of general principles that both inform practice and suggest directions for new research.

Microteaching and reading are but two fragments of the total technological picture; I have included them simply as illustrations of two distinct points. Obviously, there is much to learn about the activities comprising classroom control, the use of sanctions, the diagnosis of learning difficulties, classroom grouping, and the like. But even the identification of teaching activities and the codification of existing research leave several areas of technological development in instruction open. Research on the efficacy of teaching activities is one example. (As I noted earlier, Allen and Ryan do not tell us what results teachers who are trained according to microteaching techniques attain with children.) We must, however, identify the character of this kind of research. It is a kind of practical research designed to discover whether things work and with what effects. For example, it is one thing to know whether a new drug contributes to the cure of an illness or to the arresting of its symptoms; it is quite another to understand its pharmacology. Different but overlapping kinds of research are involved, each of great importance. Another example is research on the scientific principles underlying practice, as distinct from the assessment research mentioned above. Convincing people in education—particularly teachers—of the importance of this second kind of research is perhaps more difficult because its connection with classroom practice is more remote, and because it proceeds at a tempo out of phase with the problems of the classroom where the need to get things done successfully—and quickly—is pressing.

To some extent, I take issue with Philip Jackson's assessment of the teacher's circumstances in the classroom. He contends:

> The personal qualities enabling teachers to withstand the demands of classroom life have never adequately been described. But among those abilities is surely the ability to tolerate the enormous amount of ambiguity, unpredictability, and occasional chaos created each hour by 25 or 30 not-so-willing learners. What is here called the conceptual simplicity evident in teachers' language may be related to that ability. If teachers sought a more thorough understanding of their world, insisted on greater rationality in their actions, were completely open-minded in their consideration of pedagogical choices, and profound in their view of the human condition, they might well receive greater applause from intellectuals, but it is doubtful that they would perform with greater efficiency in the classroom.[4]

Jackson does not take the extreme position that it is best not to ask the centipede how he walks, yet he expresses concern that a teacher's rational reflection about his work might not improve his teaching, almost as if an analysis of the pressures of the classroom, the myriad human encounters, and the unexpected contingencies will destroy the whole enterprise. There is no evidence bearing on Jackson's point either way, but it seems equally plausible that there is considerable merit in analyzing the nature of the teacher's work because it is pertinent to know how one achieves desirable outcomes (whatever one's definition of desirable), and because the schools are under attack for failing to do an adequate job for children whose social and economic circumstances are deplorable. Perhaps the schools are doing a brilliant job, perhaps an atrocious one; but we won't find out until we know something about how the teacher's activities affect what children learn. And if and when we do find out, there will still be ample room for imagination, spontaneity, and intuition, just as there is in the more technologically developed occupations.

If the history of other professions contains lessons for teaching, considerable attention must be devoted to the creation of a substratum of basic theoretical knowledge. This means basic research relevant to the social sciences; it also means a rethinking and redefinition of the relationships among school systems, schools of education, and universities. The latter question is perhaps most immediately pressing because there has been a durable tradition of three-way hostility, suspicion, and contempt—with some exceptions, to be sure. A fruitful set of relationships cannot be legislated; the problem of establishing a tradition of research linking the schools with institutions of higher learning, I believe, can be solved, though not all at once.

Academic disciplines, formalized in university departments, already possess research traditions; but the research is usually remote from the immediate problems of teachers. But if traditional academic research does not speak directly to teachers, that does not mean that all research is irrelevant. To take a page from the medical book: physicians have had an ongoing tradition of *clinical* research. Doctors, *in the course of their practice,* have often written up their experiences in the treatment and management of particular diseases. These studies are not necessarily experimental; they do not employ random samples; they do not necessarily contain the most desirable set of varying examples; but they do reflect systematic work, intensive knowledge, and direct relevance to practice. Equally important, the research is carried out by practitioners and is published so that others engaged in the treatment of similar illnesses can benefit by the experience of men with intimate knowledge about the disease. The knowledge, in other words, ceases to be private; no claim is made that it is definitive.

There is no reason that research of this kind cannot be undertaken in schools by teachers. It is necessary that they know the rudiments of doing research—the skills can be taught in the normal course of their training—and that time be made available for them to do it. For example, is there any reason why teachers, alone or in concert, cannot investigate strategies for dealing with slow learners in classes where bright students predominate, techniques for teaching reading to pupils who present particular types of reading disabilities, and methods for establishing control in classrooms where many pupils hate school? At least three benefits can result from such efforts: (1) *useful* material can be gathered and disseminated among teachers confronting similar problems; (2) a medium of communication can be established within an occupational group whose members work largely in isolation; and (3) the content of this research feeds directly into the theoretical and empirical problems studied by academicians in the social and psychological sciences.

The latter point is perhaps the most important; a form of research indigenous to schools has direct relevance to those in the universities working on general problems that subsume the specific school-related ones. Accordingly, a natural linkage based on common interest can be established, not by telling teachers and academicians to like each other and to pay attention to what the other is doing—an approach doomed to failure—but by each becoming involved in different aspects of the same line of inquiry. Under these circumstances, the generalized scientific knowledge of the academic can inform the subsequent work of the teacher doing "clinical" research in the schools; and, of course, the flow of knowledge also travels the other way. In effect, they have something to say to each other just as the physician doing clinical research on endocrine disease has something to say to the biochemist, and vice versa, even though each is engaged in a separate research enterprise. In this way I can envision a break in the traditional barrier between schools and universities, and the establishment of alliances between currently hostile parties. It is difficult, moreover, to imagine the development of teaching technology without direct contact between the two institutions and their members; and contact is not likely to be made without a universe of common discourse and actual pieces of research relevant to each. The basis of such discourse can be established by the creation of knowledge in schools deemed valuable by both. This, rather than exhortation, may lay the groundwork for Schaefer's school as a center of inquiry.

There is at least one other prerequisite for technological development in teaching: the formation of colleagueship among teachers. Although I am sure that in the past original and important ideas have come from persons working alone, there are too many cases of simultaneous invention to doubt the fact that the ideas were "in the air"; and even among those working alone, it is extremely doubtful that many original ideas came from those who were not steeped in the knowledge and literature of their fields. There are at least two kinds of colleagueship. One is based on the sense of identification among those engaged in the same enterprise even when they are geographically distant and may not know each other personally. In the academic profession, law, medicine, and architecture such colleagueship exists and is sustained largely through the medium of publication. One consumes the research, the law review articles, the building designs published in the learned and trade journals. This tradition does not prevail in teaching.

The second type of colleagueship refers to the relationships among those working at the same location; personal contact rather than a symbolic medium sustains it. This tradition is also absent in teaching primarily because the time demands and the physical isolation of teachers in separate places within the same location keep them apart. This is not to say they are unaware of each other's existence, but teachers are not known for their proclivity to discuss

the *technical* nature of their work, and their technology suffers
for it.

There is no easy solution to this problem in schools because
it has so many dimensions, so many forces militating against the
emergence of a group of colleagues. The most obvious symptom
of the problem is that teachers seldom if ever observe each other
at work. Occasional visitation might increase observability and
provide points of discussion among teachers; but this appears to
be more a palliative than a solution. Lawyers, in contrast, observe
each other frequently: as co-counsel, as adversaries in courtroom
practice, and in negotiation and in contractual matters where court
procedures are not involved. Similarly with doctors; the hospital
is a fishbowl. Interestingly, among medical practitioners, psychiatrists most frequently work alone, out of their colleagues' purview,
and it is their technology that is among the least developed in
medicine; within the medical fraternity, their status is among the
lowest in the pecking order of specialties.

To proceed from symptoms to probable causes: what law
requires that only one teacher be in charge of a classroom? Surely,
if two or more teachers were assigned to one classroom, there
would be ample opportunity for collegial observation—in fact,
sustained observation. The immediate objection to this wild idea
is that we already have a teacher shortage; where will the teachers
come from? (But I shall return to this objection; it may be illusory.)
If teaching can be analyzed into its component activities, why should
there not be a division of labor within teaching? Why assume that
if something should be taught, only one person per classroom
should teach it? One reason we assume this is that teaching has
traditionally been viewed as a unitary task; yet the work on microteaching suggests that it is not, or need not be. Moreover, if other
occupations have been able to contemplate both specialization and
delegation, why should teachers assume, in effect and *a priori*, that
no division of labor is possible? The assumption, of course, might
be correct, but without experience it is gratuitous.

A multi-teacher classroom might well contribute to the solution of two occupational problems: the absence of colleagueship
and the inappropriateness of the classroom as *both* a work and a
training setting. If, in fact, components of teaching activities can
be identified, there is no logical reason why teachers cannot be
trained at least in part as specialists. I do not refer here to "narrow"
specialists; teachers who can do one thing, and one thing only.
In medicine, internists (the modern descendents of the old general
practitioner) are an appropriate case in point. Many of them specialize in aspects of internal medicine yet also retain competence

in treating a wide range of illnesses. Several teachers in a classroom could divide up the work according to specialty; they would be colleagues in a very real sense, both as workers, observers, consultants, and critics. Moreover, some of the tasks now included in the teacher's repertoire need not be performed by teachers but could well be delegated to persons with a more limited range of skills. The analogy with nursing should be obvious.

Such a proposal clearly raises new problems. Is the classroom, as currently designed, the most appropriate setting for teaching? Perhaps not, but this raises an architectural question: what is the best design for housing diverse teaching and learning activities without foreclosing the opportunities for collegial observation? I cannot offer an answer to this question, but neither can I relegate it to the realm of impossibility.

More pressing, however, are the questions of manpower and training. As I argued earlier, teacher training is far too short and superficial. What better way is there to train teachers than in a classroom with several specialists in various teaching tasks who are sharing instructional responsibilities? On the assumption that the diverse tasks of which teaching is composed can be identified, a given classroom—or learning space—can be manned by trainees in different stages of preparation. (Hospitals, after all, are staffed predominantly by residents and interns who are really students of varying degrees of experience. Similarly, much of the work in large law firms is done by hired law-school graduates whose first job is really the "clinical" phase of their training.) The apprentice teacher, then, under this arrangement, can learn his job task by task, under the supervisory eyes of experienced specialists and of more advanced apprentices. The manpower for the multi-teacher classroom, then, consists of trainees in various stages of apprenticeship.

There have been two explanations for the shortage of teachers: one, that the occupation does not attract enough new recruits; and two, that it attracts them but cannot keep them. Whatever the merits of these explanations, at least one other is plausible: that there are too many teachers in the first place; that is, persons whose job is defined as requiring full responsibility for all activities occurring in a classroom. If we discard the latter notion, we might be able to staff our schools with a far smaller number of "full-responsibility" teachers and a larger number of "student" teachers whose apprenticeship is extended in time so that they can develop substantial competence in the component tasks of teaching on the job. These same apprentices might well participate in ongoing research relevant to the job. In effect, a learning space might contain one hundred children, divided into much smaller units—perhaps ten—according to diagnostic criteria of learning needs, and instructed by more and less experienced trainees. (One must not be misled by the term *trainee*; a fourth-year medical resident who has nine years of medical training is, in a formal sense, a trainee, yet is highly qualified to practice medicine; most hospitals, in fact, run on the backs of their interns and residents.) Moreover, each pupil is certain to fall within more than one diagnostic category; and, of course, there are still subjects each one must master. Hence, there is ample opportunity for pupils to confront many instructors in a variety of learning situations.

The work-space, whatever its architectural properties, must also provide settings for the formation of a collegial workgroup among instructors—people engaged in various phases of the same educational enterprise who see each other at work daily.

Clearly, I am not in the business of providing educational nostrums and panaceas. Yet an analysis of an occupation illuminates its weak spots, thus provoking one to think about what can be done and focusing attention on remedies to the problems. It would appear that teaching is an occupation that has some excitement to it, intellectually and socially, even though it does not appear that way in the public eye (or even in the educational eye). Its problems are manifold; their origin, I believe, lies in a technological deficiency—at least that is where my analysis points. Its inherent excitement, I believe, can emerge with an assault on the technological problems.

FOOTNOTES

CHAPTER ONE

1. George S. Counts, *Dare the Schools Build a New Social Order* (New York: John Day, Co., 1932), pp. 28–29.

2. Robert J. Schaefer, *The School as a Center of Inquiry* (New York: Harper & Row, Publishers, 1967), p. 11, copyright 1967. Reprinted by permission of Harper & Row, Publishers, Inc.

3. *Ibid.*, p. 1.

4. He recommends substantial reductions in teaching loads so that teachers at least have the opportunities for reflection about their work, the development of collegial rather than hierarchical forms of authority, the creation of conditions conducive to teachers continuing the pursuit of school-related and general intellectual activities throughout their working lives, and the establishment of mutually reinforcing connections between school systems and universities.

CHAPTER TWO

1. T. B. Bottomore and Maximilien Rubel, *Karl Marx* (London: Watts and Company, 1956), p. 146.

2. *Ibid.*, p. 136.

3. Max Weber, *The Protestant Ethic and the Spirit of Capitalism*, trans. Talcott Parsons (London: George Allen & Unwin, Ltd., 1930), p. 54.

4. Reinhard Bendix, *Max Weber: An Intellectual Portrait* (Garden City: Doubleday & Company, Inc., 1960), p. 74; my italics.

5. Talcott Parsons, "The Professions and Social Structure," in *Essays in Sociological Theory* (New York: The Free Press of Glencoe, 1954), pp. 34–49.

6. C. Wright Mills, *White Collar* (New York: Oxford University Press, 1953), p. 112.

7. For a description of large law firms that do the legal work for corporations, see Erwin O. Smigel, *The Wall Street Lawyer* (New York: The Free Press of Glencoe, 1964). The differences between large law firms and corporations are striking.

8. Everett C. Hughes, "Licence and Mandate," in *Men and Their Work* (Glencoe, Ill.: The Free Press, 1958), p. 79.

9. Morris L. Cogan, "Toward a Definition of Profession," *Harvard Educational Review*, XXIII, No. 1 (1953), 33–50.

10. William J. Goode, "The Librarian: From Occupation to Profession?" *The Library Journal*, XXXI, No. 4 (1961), 308.

11. William J. Goode, "Community Within a Community: The Professions," *American Sociological Review*, XXII, No. 2 (1957), 194.

12. Rue Bucher and Anselm Strauss, "Professions in Process," *American Journal of Sociology*, LXVI, No. 4 (1961), 325–334.

13. A. M. Carr-Saunders and P. A. Wilson, *The Professions* (London: Oxford University Press, 1933), p. 319; copyright 1933, by permission of the Clarendon Press, Oxford. My italics.

14. William J. Goode, "The Librarian: From Occupation to Profession?" p. 307.

15. Note that this does not mean that the process of professionalization is unimportant—quite the contrary; the problem of how an occupation changes its characteristics and moves up or down in the social order is a matter of great interest and importance. It is only the is-or-is-not question that is trivial.

16. For an extensive discussion of these issues, see Morton R. Godine, *The Labor Problem in the Public Service* (Cambridge, Mass.: Harvard University Press, 1951).

17. William J. Goode, "The Librarian: From Occupation to Profession?" p. 317.

18. For a discussion of this problem in the automobile industry, see Ely Chinoy, *Automobile Workers and the American Dream* (Garden City: Doubleday & Co., Inc., 1955).

19. Morris Janowitz and Roger Little, *Sociology and the Military Establishment* (New York: Russell Sage Foundation, 1965), pp. 31–32.

20. For a general discussion of the similarities and differences between professions and bureaucracies, see Peter M. Blau and W. Richard Scott, *Formal Organizations* (San Francisco: Chandler Publishing Company, 1962), pp. 60–74.

21. Theodore Caplow, *The Sociology of Work* (Minneapolis: University of Minnesota Press, 1954), p. 230; and see the chapter entitled, "Occupations of Women."

22. This list represents a summary of Lieberman's main points; Myron Lieberman, *Education As a Profession* (Englewood Cliffs: Prentice-Hall, Inc. 1956), pp. 1–6.

23. Lieberman, it should be noted, does include such considerations as the existence of a code of ethics, a self-governing organization of practitioners, and occupational autonomy, none of which refer to membership characteristics, but rather to occupational characteristics.

24. National Education Association, *A Position Paper* (Washington, D.C.: National Commission on Teacher Education and Professional Standards, 1963).

25. Robert N. Bush, "The Formative Years," in National Education Association, *The Real World of the Beginning Teacher* (Washington, D.C.: National Commission on Teacher Education and Professional Standards, 1966), p. 7.

26. National Education Association, *The Development of the Career Teacher: Professional Responsibility for Continuing Education* (Washington, D.C.: National Commission on Teacher Education and Professional Standards, 1964), p. 19.

27. National Education Association, *A Position Paper*, p. 17.

28. Charles Cogen, "The Goals of Teacher Unionism," *The United Teacher*, VIII, No. 8 (1966), 4.

29. David Selden, "Professionalism the Union Way," *ibid.*, p. 5.

30. *Ibid.*, p. 5.

31. In a later chapter I deal with the question of teacher competence and the problem of the "softness" of teaching technology.

32. Albert Shanker, "Vote No," *The United Teacher*, VI, No. 13 (1965), 2. The same sentiment is stated by Charles Cogen who contends that managerial and nonsupervisory employees should not be included in the same bargaining unit, and that school principals are managers. Charles Cogen, "The American Federation of Teachers and Collective Negotiations," in Stanley Elam, Myron Lieberman, and Michael H. Moskow, eds., *Readings on Collective Negotiations in Public Education* (Chicago: Rand McNally & Co., 1967), pp. 162–172.

33. Myron Lieberman, *Education As a Profession*, p. 485, © 1956. Reprinted by permission of Prentice-Hall, Inc., Englewood Cliffs, New Jersey.

34. *Ibid.*, p. 488.

35. *Ibid.*, p. 486.

36. Myron Lieberman, *The Future of Public Education* (Chicago: University of Chicago Press, 1960), p. 108.

37. James B. Conant, *The Education of American Teachers* (New York: McGraw-Hill Book Company, Inc., 1963), p. 113.

38. *Ibid.*, p. 140.

39. *Ibid.*, p. 199.

40. *Ibid.*, pp. 115 ff.

CHAPTER THREE

1. George Baron and Asher Tropp, "Teachers in England and America," in A. H. Halsey, Jean Floud, and C. Arnold Anderson, eds., *Education, Economy, and Society* (New York: The Free Press, 1961), p. 546.

2. I do not mean to imply that schools are populated only by teachers, administrators, and pupils. The division of labor is more complex than that, but a full description of it falls outside the scope and purposes of this discussion. From the point of view of describing the major organizational properties of schools, administrators, teachers, and pupils are the most important elements because they demarcate the major seams in what otherwise would appear to be a simply pyramidal hierarchy (which in reality it is not).

3. For a discussion of rules, their types and various functions, see Alvin W. Gouldner, *Patterns of Industrial Bureaucracy* (Glencoe, Ill.: The Free Press, 1954), and Roy G. Francis and Robert C. Stone, *Service and Procedure in Bureaucracy* (Minneapolis: University of Minnesota Press, 1956).

4. I am indebted to Robert Schaefer for his helpful interpretative comments on this point. For an analysis of the notion of "red tape," one of the charges often levelled at bureaucracies, see Alvin W. Gouldner, "Red Tape as a Social Problem," in Robert K. Merton, Ailsa P. Gray, Barbara Hockey, and Hanan C. Selvin, eds., *Reader in Bureaucracy* (Glencoe, Ill.: The Free Press, 1952), pp. 410–418.

5. It should not be forgotten, moreover, that in many of the strongest and largest American universities, the administration itself has protected the faculty's freedom of inquiry and its independence from outside attack. See, for example, Paul F. Lazarsfeld and Wagner Thielens, *The Academic Mind* (Glencoe, Ill.: The Free Press, 1958).

6. Amitai Etzioni, "Authority Structure and Organizational Effectiveness," *Administrative Science Quarterly*, IV, No. 1 (1959), 45.

7. *Ibid.*, p. 52. Although this description of two organizational forms draws the contrast in somewhat exaggerated terms and without attention to the fuzziness of the expert-administrator distinction and to the subtle and not so subtle forms of bargaining that take place among the various sectors of organizations, it still illuminates some of the basic differences between the two types of arrangements for settling the balance between the performance of central tasks and the overall management of the organization.

8. A quick perusal, if such is possible, of the Coleman Report—

Equality of Educational Opportunity (Washington, D.C.: U.S. Government Printing Office, 1966)—will indicate that this monumental study is fundamentally based on a model of schools consisting of levels, their division into classrooms, school resources, the capabilities of teachers, and the assumption that what occurs more or less effectively is a process of instruction.

9. Teachers do complain at times that pupils coming into their class from a previous hour are rowdy, blaming the rowdiness on the inability of other teachers to control their classes; but this type of situation scarcely supports the notion that teaching is an occupation that depends on the careful coordination of collective efforts.

10. This way of stating the case does injustice to the fact that in many schools a captive audience is not the same thing as an audience of captives. Many children are happy to be there and to learn what the school has to offer. I do not imply that compulsory school attendance amounts to coercion pure and simple, though undoubtedly in some cases it does.

11. It should be noted that doctors at the internship and residency stages of their *training* are affiliated with hospitals in a way that approximates hiring; their direct superiors, however, are senior physicians, not hospital administrators.

12. Both law and architecture present many more problems of affiliation that extend beyond the scope of this discussion, in large part related to the case of practitioners dependent on a single client.

13. There are, of course, other affiliative arrangements beside those mentioned here: slavery, conscription, customership, to name a few.

14. Custodians and clerical workers, actually, occupy the lowest organizational positions in schools —they take orders from the principal, not from teachers—but they are not members of the *educational* component of the administrative hierarchy.

15. With teachers, the signing of the contract provides in itself at least minimum evidence of their motivation to work.

16. Ronald G. Corwin, *A Sociology of Education* (New York: Appleton-Century-Crofts, 1965), p. 222 (my italics). He also states that it is essentially a drive for status, which, I contend, is a dubious proposition (but in any case outside the scope of this discussion).

17. Neal Gross and Robert E. Herriott, *Staff Leadership in Public Schools* (New York: John Wiley & Sons, Inc., 1965), p. 99 (my italics).

18. National Education Association, *Milestones* (Washington, D.C.: National Commission on Teacher Education and Professional Standards, 1966), p. 27.

19. According to information collected during the fall of 1960 in the National Principalship Study (Harvard University, Neal Gross, Director) based on a sample of school systems in forty-one American cities of population 50,000 and over, 98 of 189 elementary principals were men (51.9 percent), 129 of 150 junior high school principals were men (86.0 percent), and 155 of 162 senior high school principals were men (95.7 percent).

20. Theodore Caplow, *The Sociology of Work* (Minneapolis: University of Minnesota Press, 1954), p. 238.

21.   Medical schools and teaching hospitals are subject to similar problems, although their origins differ. Here the strains between men and women (nurses, medical students, and interns) develop because experienced nurses often know more medicine and more about what to do in certain situations than neophytes in the higher status occupations.

22.   Probably even more than 61.3 percent of the women are older than forty-five since men do not usually remain as elementary teachers very long.

23.   For a sensitive analysis of the problem of the principal's supervision of elementary school teachers, see Anne E. Trask, "Supervision in the School: An Exploratory Study," unpublished doctoral dissertation, Harvard Graduate School of Education (1962), pp. 157–193.

24.   National Education Association, *Evaluation of Classroom Teachers,* Research Report 1964–R14 (Washington, D.C.: Research Division, 1964), p. 26. Reprinted by permission of the National Education Association.

25.   *Ibid.,* p. 36.

26.   *Ibid.,* pp. 36–37.

27.   *Ibid.,* p. 38.

28.   *Ibid.,* pp. 64, 65.

29.   *Ibid.,* p. 64.

30.   Anne E. Trask, "Supervision in The School: An Exploratory Study," unpublished doctoral dissertation, Harvard Graduate School of Education (1962).

31.   Erwin O. Smigel, *The Wall Street Lawyer* (New York: The Free Press, 1964), p. 260.

32.   National Education Association, *What Teachers Think,* Research Report 1965–R13 (Washington, D.C.: Research Division, 1965), p. 41. This poll was taken in 1963 and unfortunately does not differentiate between experienced and inexperienced teachers.

33.   Data gathered as part of the National Principalship Study indicate the primary importance that both principals and teachers assign to helping new recruits. Whether the help is forthcoming, of course, is another story.

34.   Dan C. Lortie, "The Balance of Control and Autonomy in Elementary School Teaching," in Amitai Etzioni, ed., *The Semi-Professions and Their Organization* (New York: The Free Press, 1969), p. 10.

35.   Robert K. Merton, "The Role of the Intellectual in Public Bureaucracy," in *Social Theory and Social Structure,* rev. ed. (Glencoe, Ill.: The Free Press, 1957), pp. 207–224.

36.   *Ibid.,* p. 214. Merton originally published his paper in 1945, and the formulation expressed in it may not represent his current thinking. For a sharply dissenting view, see Harold L. Wilensky, *Intellectuals in Labor Unions* (Glencoe, Ill.: The Free Press, 1956).

37.   *Ibid.,* Chaps. 4–7. Wilensky distinguishes between "facts and figure men," "contact men," and "internal communications specialists," and considers whether they approach their jobs as "missionaries," "professional experts," "careerists," or "politicos."

38.   *Ibid.,* p. 160 (my italics).

39.   Mary E. W. Goss, "Influence and Authority Among Physicians in an Outpatient Clinic," *American Sociological Review,* XXVI, No. 1 (1961), 49.

40.   Donald C. Pelz, "Some Social

Factors Related to Performance in a Research Organization," *Administrative Science Quarterly*, I, No. 3 (1956), 321 (my italics).

41. See footnote 17. Note, however, that their formulation of the autonomy question was appropriate to the particular argument of their book.

42. See Gross and Herriott, *Staff Leadership in Public Schools*, pp. 14–21.

43. It should be noted that the phrase "written lesson plans" is not defined in the question, and there can be considerable variation in what these plans actually represent ranging all the way from weekly reports written in considerable detail to perfunctory outlines covering large blocks of time. Some systems presuppose that teachers leave written lesson plans in their desks in the event of their absence from school and where a substitute teacher must take over for a day or more. Such arrangements do not necessarily involve the principal's (or other administrator's) direct surveillance but simply the fact that a written document must be there.

44. National Education Association, *The American Public-School Teacher, 1960–61*, Research Monograph 1963 M-2(Washington, D.C.: Research Division, 1963), p. 91.

45. The consideration of percentages favorable and unfavorable to principal supervision yields results largely consistent with those obtained by considering mean scores.

46. See, for example, August B. Hollingshead, *Elmtown's Youth* (New York: John Wiley & Sons, Inc., 1949).

47. Edwin H. Sauer, *Contract Correcting: The Use of Lay Readers in the High School Composition Program* (Cambridge, Mass.: School and University Program for Research and Development, Harvard Graduate School of Education, 1962), p. 3.

48. Everett C. Hughes, "Mistakes at Work," in *Men and Their Work* (Glencoe, Ill.: The Free Press, 1958), pp. 88–101.

49. I intentionally exclude the custodial and secretarial staffs of schools as falling beyond the scope of this discussion. Their place is best described as part of the line organization of the school, directly subordinate to the principal though not subordinate to teachers even though teachers occupy a higher position in the hierarchy. That is to say, there are two line hierarchies within schools, one with teachers at the bottom, the other with clerical and custodial staff members at the bottom—at least in formal terms. The distribution of power and influence is quite another matter and does not necessarily follow the formally defined lines of organizational charts.

50. See, for example, Max Weber, *The Theory of Social and Economic Organization*, trans. A. M. Henderson and Talcott Parsons (New York: Oxford University Press, 1947), Part III; Chester I. Barnard, *The Functions of the Executive* (Cambridge, Mass.: Harvard University Press, 1956); Peter M. Blau, *The Dynamics of Bureaucracy*, rev. ed. (Chicago: University of Chicago Press, 1963); Alvin W. Gouldner, *Patterns of Industrial Bureaucracy* (Glencoe, Ill.: The Free Press, 1954); Carl J. Friedrich, ed., *Authority* (Cambridge, Mass.: Harvard University Press, 1958).

CHAPTER FOUR

1. Bryan R. Wilson, "The Teacher's Role—A Sociological Analysis," *British Journal of Sociology*, XIII, No. 1 (1962), 25.
2. *Ibid.*, p. 27.
3. Dan C. Lortie, "The Balance of Control and Autonomy in Elementary School Teaching," in Etzioni, ed., *The Semi-Professions and Their Organization* (New York: The Free Press, 1969), p. 9.
4. Richard L. Simpson and Ida Harper Simpson, "Women and Bureaucracy in the Semi-Professions," in Etzioni, ed., *The Semi-Professions and Their Organization* (New York: The Free Press, 1969), p. 203.
5. For general discussions of the importance of rules in bureaucracies, see Max Weber, *The Theory of Social and Economic Organization* (New York: The Free Press, 1964); and Alvin W. Gouldner, *Patterns of Industrial Bureaucracy* (Glencoe, Ill.: The Free Press, 1954).
6. Louis M. Smith and William Geoffrey, *The Complexities of an Urban Classroom* (New York: Holt, Rinehart and Winston, Inc., 1968), p. 68 (my italics).
7. Blanche Geer *et al.*, "Learning the Ropes: Situational Learning in Four Occupational Training Programs," in Irwin Deutscher and Elizabeth J. Thompson, eds., *Among the People: Encounters with the Poor* (New York: Basic Books, Inc., 1968), pp. 209–233.
8. Jerome S. Bruner, *The Process of Education* (Cambridge, Mass.: Harvard University Press, 1960), p. 7.
9. *Ibid.*, p. 9. Also, "Research on the instructional process . . . has not been carried out in connection with the building of curricula." Jerome S. Bruner, *Toward a Theory of Instruction* (Cambridge, Mass.: Harvard University Press, 1966), p. 54.
10. In speaking about learning episodes appropriate for children at different stages of development, Bruner draws heavily on the work of Piaget and his distinctions between enactive, iconic, and symbolic stages.
11. Harry Levin, Thomas L. Hilton, and Gloria F. Leiderman, "Studies of Teacher Behavior," *Journal of Experimental Education*, XXVI (September 1957), 82.
12. *Ibid.*, pp. 84–85.
13. *Ibid.*, p. 90.
14. Wilson, "The Teacher's Role —A Sociological Analysis," p. 20.
15. Robert Rosenthal and Leonore Jacobson, "Self-Fulfilling Prophecies in the Classroom: Teachers' Expectations as Unintended Determinants of Pupils' Intellectual Competence," in Martin Deutsch, Irwin Katz, and Arthur R. Jensen, eds., *Social Class, Race, and Psychological Development* (New York: Holt, Rinehart and Winston, Inc., 1968), pp. 230–234.
16. *Ibid.*, pp. 230–231. Note that the study included more dependent variables than just I.Q., as indicated in the preceding quotation.
17. *Ibid.*, p. 234.
18. *Ibid.*, p. 32. The Rosenthal-Jacobson study design did allow them to eliminate the expenditure of additional time with members of the experimental group as the explanatory mechanism.
19. Harold W. Massey and Edwin E. Vineyard, *The Profession of Teaching* (New York: Odyssey Press, Inc., 1961), p. 111. I have made no attempt here to survey and summarize the whole litera-

ture on how teachers motivate pupils but rather have chosen one treatment of the problem that is broadly illustrative of what many people have said even though the selection of this particular text was not made rigorously.

20. *Ibid.,* p. 113.

21. Philip W. Jackson, *Life in Classrooms* (New York: Holt, Rinehart and Winston, Inc., 1968), pp. 106–107.

22. Massey and Vineyard, *The Profession of Teaching,* pp. 149–154.

23. *Ibid.,* p. 158.

24. National Education Association, *What Teachers Think: A Summary of Teacher Opinion Poll Findings, 1960–1965,* Research Report 1965–R13 (Washington, D.C.: Research Division, 1965), p. 19.

25. *Ibid.,* p. 19.

26. *Ibid.,* p. 18. Symptomatically, a substantial proportion ("nearly half") of teachers in 1964 favor "the judicious use of corporal punishment as a disciplinary measure in *secondary* schools." This finding is perhaps more an index of teacher despair over a problem they can cope with only with difficulty than a sign that an effective remedy has been removed from their hands (by law), if in fact corporal punishment was ever effective.

27. Dwight Allen and Kevin Ryan, *Microteaching* (Reading, Mass.: Addison-Wesley Publishing Co., Inc., 1969), p. 61; copyright 1969. Reprinted by permission of Addison-Wesley Publishing Company, Inc.

28. In the early 1960's Judson Shaplin conservatively estimates that approximately 45,000 pupils were engaged in team teaching programs; even if the number had been ten times as large, only

a small proportion of all American pupils would have been involved. Judson T. Shaplin, "Description and Definition of Team Teaching," in Judson T. Shaplin and Henry F. Olds, eds., *Team Teaching* (New York: Harper & Row, Publishers, 1964), p. 2.

29. *Ibid.,* p. 3. This is not the only definition extant, but it is stated in broad enough terms to cover a substantial number of them.

30. I make no invidious comparisons here between organizational and instructional benefits (if benefits they are); there is no reason to impute greater importance either to instructional or organizational changes.

31. Shaplin, "Description and Definition of Team Teaching," pp. 12, 15, and 16.

32. For a more complete statement about the autonomy-equality pattern, see Dan C. Lortie, "The Teacher and Team Teaching: Suggestions for Long-Range Research," in Shaplin and Olds, eds., *Team Teaching,* pp. 270–305, especially pp. 272–280.

33. Note that the first alternative appears more consistent with Shaplin's concern with establishing a hierarchy among teachers to develop a career line within teaching itself to counteract the flight of teachers from the classroom into administration.

34. Lortie, "The Teacher and Team Teaching: Suggestions for Long-Range Research," p. 282.

35. For a detailed discussion of the problems involved in implementation, see Joseph C. Grannis, "Team Teaching and the Curriculum," in Shaplin and Olds, eds., *Team Teaching,* pp. 123–169.

36. My statements here draw

almost completely from Glen Heathers, "Research on Team Teaching," in Shaplin and Olds, eds., *Team Teaching*, pp. 306–344.

37. John I. Goodlad and Robert H. Anderson, *The Nongraded Elementary School*, rev. ed. (New York: Harcourt, Brace & World, Inc., 1963), p. 21. The writers justify their program on academic grounds (in terms of its inherent importance and of its tactical importance in gaining public acceptance), and in terms of intended gains in the mental health of children.

38. *Ibid.*, p. 83.

39. *Ibid.*, p. 73.

40. Only about six pages of the book deal with measurement and assessment in any quantitative way.

41. "A major thesis of this volume is that the traditional graded organization is one of the most inhibiting forces in children's lives." Goodlad and Anderson, *The Nongraded Elementary School*, p. 137. There is no evidence presented supporting this claim. See also p. 167 for claims about the harmful effects of graded schooling on teachers.

42. Fred M. Newmann and Donald W. Oliver, "Education and Community," *Harvard Educational Review*, XXXVII, No. 1 (1967), 61–106. Note that Newmann and Oliver use the concept "community" in a special sense of their own, while in the sentence above I have used it in a commonplace and residual way to denote a general social reality outside the school.

43. *Ibid.*, p. 88.

44. *Ibid.*, p. 96.

45. See, for example, James S. Coleman *et al, Equality of Educational Opportunity* (Washington, D.C.: U.S. Government Printing Office, 1966); and U.S. Commission on Civil Rights, *Racial Isolation in The Public Schools*, Vols. I and II (Washington, D.C.: U.S. Government Printing Office, 1967).

46. For one of the few systematic studies of the correlates of the racial composition of schools and the segregation experiences of pupils, see Nancy Hoyt St. John, "De Facto Segregation and Interracial Association in a High School," *Sociology of Education*, XXXVII, No. 4 (1964), 326–344.

47. Jeanne S. Chall, *Learning to Read: The Great Debate* (New York: McGraw-Hill Book Co., 1967), p. 5.

48. *Ibid.*, p. 79.

49. Louis M. Smith and William Geoffrey, *The Complexities of an Urban Classroom* (New York: Holt, Rinehart and Winston, Inc., 1968).

50. *Ibid.*, pp. 97–98; my italics.

51. Dan C. Lortie, "Teacher Socialization: The Robinson Crusoe Model," in National Education Association, *The Real World of the Beginning Teacher* (Washington, D.C.: National Commission on Teacher Education and Professional Standards, 1967), p. 59 (my italics).

52. Jackson, *Life in Classrooms*, p. 145. Lortie, in "Teacher Socialization: . . . ," makes a similar point about teachers' language. "Teachers," he notes, "possess very little in the way of a set of shared terms or concepts about the subtleties of teaching as an interpersonal transaction" (p. 58).

53. Allen and Ryan, *Microteaching*, p. 7 (my italics).

54. *Ibid.,* p. 23.

55. Jackson, *Life in Classrooms,* p. 149.

CHAPTER FIVE

1. James B. Conant, *The Education of American Teachers* (New York: McGraw-Hill Book Company, Inc., 1963), p. 113.

2. The proposed standard appears absurdly low especially when compared with apprenticeship training in other professionalized occupations: for elementary teachers, Conant recommends at least eight weeks of practice teaching with a minimum of three hours spent in the classroom daily and three weeks of complete responsibility for running a class, directed by a cooperating teacher ⁄and supervised by a clinical professor.

3. James D. Koerner, *The Miseducation of American Teachers* (Boston: Houghton Mifflin Co., 1963).

4. *Ibid.,* p. 8.

5. *Ibid.,* p. 17.

6. *Ibid.,* p. 31.

7. How either of these indications of competence shall be obtained without doing research remains unexplained. Koerner appears unaware of the difficulty involved in attributing what children learn to the conduct of the teacher.

8. See, for example, Martin Mayer, *The Schools* (New York: Harper and Bros., 1961); Seymour B. Sarason, Kenneth S. Davidson, and Burton Blatt, *The Preparation of Teachers* (New York: John Wiley & Sons, Inc., 1962); Jean D. Grambs, *Schools, Scholars, and Society* (Englewood Cliffs, N.J.: Prentice-Hall, Inc.,

1965); Robert J. Schaefer, *The School As a Center of Inquiry* (New York: Harper & Row, Publishers, 1967); among others.

9. I reserve the discussion of teaching careers for the following chapter.

10. Harold L. Wilensky, "The Professionalization of Everyone?" *American Journal of Sociology,* LXX, No. 2 (1964), 138 (my italics). He goes on to state: "While this traditional model of professionalism, based mainly on the 'free' professions of medicine and law, misses some aspects of the mixed forms of control now emerging among salaried professionals, it still captures a distinction important for the organization of work and for public policy."

11. For a well-aimed critique of stage approaches in general and of Wilensky's in particular, see William J. Goode, "The Theoretical Limits of Professionalization," in Amitai Etzioni, ed., *The Semi-Professions and Their Organization* (New York: The Free Press, 1969), pp. 274–276. "[T]hese formal steps miss the essential elements of professionalization. They do not keep separate the core, *generating* traits from the derivative ones." *Ibid.,* pp. 275–276.

12. Wilensky, "The Professionalization of Everyone?" p. 157.

13. *Ibid.,* p. 149.

14. Ward S. Mason, *The Beginning Teacher* (Washington, D.C.: U.S. Government Printing Office, 1961), table 30, p. 39; table 34, p. 44; and table 76, p. 110.

15. R. Gordon McIntosh, "Teacher Education and Professional Socialization," unpublished manuscript, Harvard Graduate School of Education (1967), p. 10.

16. *Ibid.,* pp. 54–55.

17. James A. Davis, *Undergraduate Career Decisions* (Chicago: Aldine Publishing Company, 1965). Davis describes his study as follows: "Data for this report are based on self-administered questionnaires . . . completed in the spring of 1961 by 33,982 June graduates from 135 colleges and universities." *Ibid.,* p. 1. The technical questions involved in doing the study are reported in the first chapter and in the appendices of the volume. There are two points of special relevance here: first, Davis studies a random sample of seniors (not institutions), and hence this is not a longitudinal study of a cohort; and second, the data on freshmen were obtained by the retrospective questioning of seniors.

Davis' data include a category of "Other Professions" from which I obtained information about the following additional occupations: nursing; religion and theology; architecture; journalism, radio, and communications; librarianship; and social work. I am indebted to the National Opinion Research Center for supplying the additional data, and especially to Patrick Bova and James A. Davis who helped me with the tabulation and analysis.

18. Note that among medical students, Thielens finds more early deciders and greater satisfaction with career choice than among law students. Wagner Thielens, "Some Comparisons of Entrants to Medical and Law School," in Robert K. Merton, George G. Reader, and Patricia L. Kendall, eds., *The Student Physician* (Cambridge, Mass.: Harvard University Press, 1957), pp. 131–152.

19. Davis, *Undergraduate Career Decisions,* p. 17.

20. Becker and Carper observe that students taking advanced degrees in physiology are often dropouts or failures from medical schools. When someone has pursued medical studies for an extended time, there are relatively few other occupations in which he can put those skills to work. Howard S. Becker and James W. Carper, "The Development of Identification with an Occupation," *American Journal of Sociology,* LXI, No. 4 (1955), 289–298.

21. In this discussion I have drawn heavily on the work of Blanche Geer in her paper, "Occupational Commitment and the Teaching Profession," *School Review,* LXXIV, No. 1 (1966), 31–47.

22. Laurence Iannaccone and H. Warren Button, "Functions of Student Teaching" (St. Louis: Washington University; U.S. Office of Education, Cooperative Research Project No. 1026, 1964).

23. *Ibid.,* p. 60. Note that these writers deal only with elementary teachers.

24. How far the Iannaccone and Button findings can be generalized, we don't know.

25. For a more completely and carefully drawn description of law schools, see Dan C. Lortie, "Laymen to Lawmen: Law School, Careers, and Professional Socialization," *Harvard Educational Review,* XXIX, No. 4 (1959), 352–369.

26. *Ibid.,* p. 364.

27. Erwin O. Smigel, *The Wall Street Lawyer* (New York: The Free Press, 1964), p. 74.

28. Paul A. Freund, "The Legal Profession," *Daedalus,* XCII, No. 4 (1963), 693.

29. Harold L. Wilensky and

Charles N. Lebeaux, *Industrial Society and Social Welfare* (New York: Russell Sage Foundation, 1958).

30. *Ibid.*, p. 289.

31. For a more detailed and comprehensive discussion of supervision in social casework agencies, see W. Richard Scott, "Professional Employees in a Bureaucratic Structure: Social Work," in A. Etzioni, ed., *The Semi-Professions and Their Organization*, pp. 97–110. Scott makes the interesting point that social work supervisors frequently use "therapeutic" methods of supervision—using psychiatric case work techniques with psychiatric case workers—possibly as a means of attributing strains in the agency itself (perhaps most effectively remedied by organizational solutions) to their subordinates as persons (i.e., viewing complaints and nonconformity as personally irrational in origin).

32. Howard S. Becker, Blanche Geer, Everett C. Hughes, and Anselm L. Strauss, *Boys in White* (Chicago: University of Chicago Press, 1961).

33. There is no reason to believe that in time these students would not have been able to decipher faculty expectations without the help of fraternity members; however, the presence of fraternity members undoubtedly speeds the process up.

34. Becker *et al; Boys in White*, p. 163 (my italics).

35. To account in part for the *origin* of occupational unity is not to account for its maintenance, although its establishment early in training at least lays the groundwork for its continuation. One should not, however, underestimate the cleavages that develop within occupations based on specialization, different types of practice, and social composition—related to religion, ethnicity, sex, age, and the like—of different segments of the total body of practitioners. Moreover, problems arise in practice, long after the conclusion of formal training, that encourage the formation of unity within the occupation: common political interests, threats to jurisdictional boundaries, the policing of ethical codes, and the like.

36. For discussion of the development and maintenance of occupational communities, see Seymour M. Lipset, "The Political Process in Trade Unions," in Theodore Abel and Charles H. Page, eds., *Freedom and Control in Modern Society* (Princeton: D. Van Nostrand Co., Inc., 1954), pp. 82–124; and Clark Kerr and Abraham Siegel, "The Inter-Industry Propensity to Strike—An International Comparison," in Arthur Kornhauser, Robert Dubin, and Arthur M. Ross, eds., *Industrial Conflict* (New York: McGraw-Hill Book Co., Inc., 1954), pp. 189–212.

37. If this contention is correct, it is apt to be so only when students spend a considerable amount of time earning money to remain in school. Few, if any, occupational training programs demand a complete commitment of time. Of course, one could also argue the opposing case: a student's willingness to pay his own way may be a good indication of his already-formed occupational commitment. In any case the relationship between financial support and the development of occupational allegiance is likely to be complex. But when students must spend a great deal of time supporting themselves, to that extent they cut themselves off from some of the influences of the training institution whatever the intensity of their occupational motivation.

38. Note that when I speak of "advantages," I implicitly adopt the perspective of the conventional standard-bearers of an occupation. This is obviously not the only legitimate perspective.

39. Peter M. Blau, *The Dynamics of Bureaucracy*, rev. ed. (Chicago: University of Chicago Press, 1963), p. 228.

40. Jerome E. Carlin, *Lawyer's Ethics* (New York: Russell Sage Foundation, 1966), p. 152. Disciplined lawyers are those who have been disbarred, suspended, or censured by the court. Violators are lawyers who fail to follow a set of ethical precepts defined by Carlin. The two concepts are practically the same. It is important to note that there are many other reasons for unethical conduct among lawyers besides attending a "lower-quality law school," and Carlin discusses them at considerable length.

41. Dan C. Lortie, "Shared Ordeal and Induction to Work," in Howard S. Becker, Blanche Geer, David Riesman, and Robert S. Weiss, eds., *Institutions and the Person* (Chicago: Aldine Publishing Co., 1968), pp. 252–264.

42. *Ibid.*, p. 255 (my italics). See also Douglas T. Hall, "Identity Changes During the Transition from Student to Professor," *School Review*, LXXVI, No. 4 (1968), 445–469.

43. *Ibid.*, p. 258 (my italics).

44. It does not follow that all occupations in which members achieve a substantial sense of mastery and to which they devote their whole working lives must experience a form of training punctuated by the intense crises found in academia. Some have argued that medical students' first introduction to a cadaver produces a similar cohesive effect; but perhaps the problem of managing the work load is the more important condition. The latter is not a crisis, but is certainly a long-term confrontation with strain. Similarly, law students' first examinations, especially when they cover a whole year's work, may constitute a crisis; but cohesiveness among law students may emerge more out of the unrelenting grind over three years of class preparation. Training for an academic career does not involve a sustained grind but rather alternating periods of intense and more relaxed efforts.

45. Lortie, "Shared Ordeal and Induction to Work," p. 261.

46. Ida H. Simpson, "Patterns of Socialization into Professions: The Case of Student Nurses," *Sociological Inquiry*, XXXVII, No. 1 (1967), 49.

47. JoAnne D. Medalie and Daniel J. Levinson, "Professional Development and Organizational Role: A Study of Student Nurses in a Psychiatric Hospital," unpublished ms., Center for Sociopsychological Research, Massachusetts Mental Health Center, n.d., p. II-6.

48. *Ibid.*, p. III-2.

49. It is important, however, to be aware of variations within nursing practice.

50. Stanton Wheeler, "The Structure of Formally Organized Socialization Settings," in Orville G. Brim and Stanton Wheeler,

Socialization After Childhood (New York: John Wiley & Sons, Inc., 1966), p. 61. Wheeler illustrates his four types of socialization settings as follows: (1) individual-disjunctive, oldest child in a family; (2) collective-disjunctive, summer training institute; (3) individual-serial, new occupant of a job previously held by another; and (4) collective-serial, schools and professional training centers.

51. Note, for example, that Becker and his colleagues, in their study of the Kansas Medical School, discussed medical students in terms of the individual-collective dimension but not the serial-disjunctive dimension. We discover how members of a given class work out adaptive solutions to the work load problem *among themselves*, but not whether they learn anything from upper classmen.

52. Paul S. Russell, "Surgery in a Time of Change," in John H. Knowles, ed., *The Teaching Hospital* (Cambridge, Mass.: Harvard University Press, 1966), p. 58; copyright 1966. Reprinted by permission of Harvard University Press. My italics. An operating room, moreover, has many of the same properties as a ward for teaching and learning.

53. Renee C. Fox, "Training for Uncertainty," in Robert K. Merton, George G. Reader, and Patricia L. Kendall, eds., *The Student Physician* (Cambridge, Mass.: Harvard University Press, 1957), p. 222.

54. It should not be assumed that the effects of this treatment-training arrangement are always salutary. Although students may benefit, patients may suffer from being used as a tool of instruction. Lying in bed and being subject to a variety of indignities by a team of cruising physicians and students can be a deeply upsetting experience.

55. Israel Scheffler, "University Scholarship and The Education of Teachers," *Teachers College Record,* LXX, No. 1 (1968), 1.

56. Some schools of education have developed more extensive apprenticeships in summer programs that involve extensive observation and criticism by the trainees themselves as well as by supervisors.

57. Allen and Ryan, *Microteaching* (Reading, Mass.: Addison-Wesley Publishing Co., Inc., 1969), p. 5 (my italics).

58. See, for example, Schaefer, *The School As a Center of Inquiry; The Graduate Study of Education,* Report of the Harvard Committee, (Cambridge, Mass.: Harvard University Press, 1966); Smith and Geoffrey, *The Complexities of an Urban Classroom* (New York: Holt, Rinehart and Winston, Inc., 1958); Allen and Ryan, *Microteaching;* Anthony Oettinger and Sema Marks, *Run, Computer, Run* (Cambridge, Mass.: Harvard University Press, 1969); Bruce R. Joyce, *The Teacher-Innovator* (Washington, D.C.: U.S. Office of Education, Project No. 8–9019, 1968); Peter H. Rossi and Bruce J. Biddle, eds., *The New Media and Education* (Chicago: Aldine Publishing Co., 1966); Robert Gordon McIntosh, "A Comparative Study of Clinical Training," unpublished Ed. D. dissertation (Cambridge, Mass.: Harvard Graduate School of Education, 1969); and Arthur S. Bolster, review of John H. Knowles, *The Teaching Hospital,* in *Harvard Educational Review,* XXXVII, No. 2 (1967), 273–281.

CHAPTER SIX
1. For more detailed discussions of the nature of careers, see Seymour M. Lipset and Reinhard Bendix, *Social Mobility in Industrial Society* (Berkeley, Calif.: University of California Press, 1959); Ely Chinoy, *Automobile Workers and the American Dream* (Garden City, N.Y.: Doubleday & Co., Inc., 1955); and Harold L. Wilensky, "Work, Careers, and Social Integration," *International Social Science Journal*, XII, No. 4 (1960), 3–20.
2. These generalizations about the aggregate characteristics of college freshmen opting for one occupation or another are based on data reported in James A. Davis, *Undergraduate Career Decisions* (Chicago: Aldine Publishing Co., 1965), table 2.3, p. 11, and on data collected by NORC for the same study but not reported in this volume. "Being female, not wanting to make a lot of money, and wanting to work with people are the strongest correlates of education. Sex and the two value items are not only the best discriminators for senior choice, but are also related to freshman choice, retention, and recruitment." *Ibid.*, p. 79.
3. Ward S. Mason, *The Beginning Teacher* (Washington, D.C.: U.S. Government Printing Office, 1961), pp. 12–20. The Davis and Mason figures are not directly comparable, Davis' being correlational, Mason's being tabular; the trends, however, are consistent; and, of course, they deal with different samples.
4. National Education Association, *The American Public-School Teacher, 1960–61* (Washington, D.C.: Research Division, 1965–66), table 9, p. 15.

5. National Education Association, *Milestones* (Washington, D.C.: National Commission on Teacher Education and Professional Standards, 1966), pp. 9, 18, and 21.
6. Robert W. Hodge, Paul M. Siegel, and Peter H. Rossi, "Occupational Prestige in the United States: 1925–1963," in Reinhard Bendix and Seymour M. Lipset, eds., *Class Status, and Power*, 2nd ed. (New York: The Free Press, 1966), p. 324. The 1963 replication ranked instructors in the public schools at 27.5 and public school teachers at 29.5, a small move upward in occupational prestige.
7. Beardsley Ruml and Sidney G. Tickton, *Teaching Salaries Then and Now* (New York: Fund for the Advancement of Education, 1956), pp. 36–38. Between 1947 and 1953, they find people employed in education obtained salary increases comparable to those working in industry, with teachers in small urban areas gaining the most. (The transformation of income into purchasing power figures involved subtracting taxes from wages and salaries and adjusting the remainder according to changes in the cost of living.)
Sidney G. Tickton, *Teaching Salaries Then and Now: A Second Look* (New York: Fund for the Advancement of Education, 1961), pp. 14–15. Ruml and Tickton, in the earlier report, also indicate that railroad workers (engineers, conductors, firemen, and switchtenders) earn higher salaries than all but the best paid large-city teachers (and the salaries of these teachers exceed only those of switchtenders); and that automobile workers, bituminous coal miners, electric machinery workers, and workers in stone, clay,

and glass all earn wages roughly the same as teachers (as of 1953). Ruml and Tickton, *Teaching Salaries Then and Now*, p. 44.

9. National Education Association, *Economic Status of Teachers in 1965–66*, Research Report 1966–R7 (Washington, D.C.: Research Division, 1966), table 25–A, p. 33.
10. *Ibid.*, table 15, p. 25.
11. National Education Association, *The American Public-School Teacher*, 1960–61, table 18, p. 18. These figures, of course, make the picture blacker than it is by minimizing salary differences over time. Teachers with twenty or more years of experience undoubtedly *started* with salaries lower than $4300, and those now starting at that figure will earn far more than $5700 in twenty years what with the increasing strength of the American Federation of Teachers, especially in the large cities, and with the increased militancy of the NEA in economic matters. Moreover, these salary figures do not include fringe benefits, particularly medical benefits, which amount to substantial gains in economic status.
12. National Education Association, *Economic Status of Teachers in 1965–66*, table 12, p. 21.
13. National Education Association, *The American Public-School Teacher*, 1960–61, table 14, p. 21.
14. Harold L. Wilensky, "The Moonlighter: A Product of Relative Deprivation," *Industrial Relations*, III, No. 1 (1963), 111. By way of exception, teachers do not characteristically have disorderly worklives; neither are their work schedules deviant in the usual sense of that word, but their work leaves them with substantial blocks of time beginning in mid-afternoon.

15. Cited in Myron Lieberman, *Education As a Profession*, (Englewood Cliffs, N.J.: Prentice-Hall, Inc., 1956), pp. 229–230. Note that the figures pertain to students, not to teachers.
16. Mason, *The Beginning Teacher*, adapted from table 1, p. 5.
17. National Education Association, *The American Public-School Teacher*, 1960–61, table 8, p. 13. The remainder are separated, divorced, or widowed.
18. *Ibid.*, adapted from table 7, p. 13.
19. U.S. Department of Health, Education, and Welfare, *Digest of Educational Statistics* (Washington, D.C.: U.S. Government Printing Office, 1966), adapted from table 7, p. 5. These proportions are approximated very closely in the sample studied by the National Education Association, *The American Public-School Teacher, 1960–61*, Appendix A, p. 84.
20. National Education Association, *The American Public-School Teacher, 1960–61*, table 6, p. 11.
21. For descriptions of the recruitment procedures in New York, Chicago, Philadelphia, and Detroit, their similarities and differences, and of the sources of prospects from which they draw, see Daniel E. Griffiths, John S. Benben, Samuel I. Goldman, Laurence Iannaccone, and Wayne J. McFarland, *Teacher Mobility in New York City* (New York: Center for School Services and Off-Campus Courses, School of Education, New York University, 1963), pp. 88–97.
22. *Ibid.*, table III–12, p. 81. There were similar proportions of substitute and licensed teachers over the years 1958 to 1961.
23. Adapted from the discussion by Griffiths *et al.*, *Ibid.*, pp. 138–141.

24. *Ibid.,* table III–13, p. 85. Note that the number of cases actually studied was substantially smaller than the number originally drawn into the sample; 194 cases were lost from the total of 607 identified by names that appeared on approved requests in 1950 for certification for those with substitute licenses. *Ibid.,* p. 13. Only 413 cases from the original cohort met all criteria for inclusion. *Ibid.,* p. 23. Although it is difficult to determine how this sample loss affects the proportion never having done practice teaching, it is unlikely to have changed the extraordinarily high proportion of teachers without such experience in any radical way.

25. Mason, *The Beginning Teacher,* adapted from table 24, p. 35. Note that he also shows that 90 percent of those with substandard qualifications were preparing to obtain regular certification. *Ibid.,* table 20, p. 32.

26. NEA data indicate that 72.8 percent of the teachers in its sample either strongly oppose or tend to oppose merit pay systems. National Education Association, *What Teachers Think: A Summary of Teacher Opinion Poll Findings, 1960–1965* (Washington, D.C.: Research Report 1965–R13, Research Division, 1965), p. 31.

27. Fred H. Goldner and R. R. Ritti, "Professionalism as Career Immobility," *American Journal of Sociology,* LXXII, No. 5 (1967), 490 (my italics).

28. There are other educational alternatives, primarily guidance and college teaching. But like administration, both of these, though undeniably educational, represent vastly different occupations than classroom teaching. More teachers, however, take the administrative road to advancement, and guidance may not represent advancement in any sense, but simply a lateral change in occupation.

29. Oswald Hall, "The Stages of a Medical Career," *American Journal of Sociology,* LIII, No. 5 (1948), 336.

30. Patricia L. Kendall and Hanan C. Selvin, "Tendencies Toward Specialization in Medical Training," in Robert K. Merton, George G. Reader, and Patricia L. Kendall, eds., *The Student Physician,* (Cambridge, Mass.: Harvard University Press, 1957), p. 173.

31. Griffiths *et al., Teacher Mobility in New York City,* p. 137. Although this phenomenon is found in New York, there is no reason to believe it is peculiar to that city, nor that it is always as benign as Griffiths describes it, either in New York or elsewhere.

32. William H. Whyte, *The Organization Man* (New York: Simon & Schuster, Inc., 1956). For a discussion of recruitment in the academic profession, particularly its informal aspects, see Theodore Caplow and Reece J. McGee, *The Academic Marketplace* (New York: Basic Books, Inc., 1958), especially chapter 6, "The Procedures of Recruitment"; and for the law, see Smigel, *The Wall Street Lawyer* (New York: The Free Press, 1964), chapters 3 and 4.

33. *Ibid.,* p. 159.

34. David Rogers, *110 Livingston Street* (New York: Random House, Inc., 1968), p. 289.

35. *Ibid.,* p. 289.

36. Goode, "The Theoretical Limits of Professionalization," in Etzioni, ed., *The Semi-Professions and Their Organization* (New York: The Free Press, 1969), p. 267.

37. The median rank of some twenty-five such occupational fields included in Davis' list is 58 percent; physical sciences predominate among those ranking high, ranging from 86 percent to 73 percent, and the social sciences and humanities rank mainly in the middle. James A. Davis, *Great Aspirations* (Chicago: Aldine Publishing Co., 1966), table 2.3, pp. 50–51.

38. Mason, *The Beginning Teacher*, table 76, p. 110.

39. Davis treats educational administration separately.

40. The "later" category is perhaps the least clearcut of the three since it undoubtedly includes those who really plan to start their training later, with perhaps military training and raising a family following directly after college graduation—and both experiences may have the effect of keeping job selection an open matter—and those who have not yet made up their minds. In each case, postponement may indicate a decrease in commitment to the occupational field listed and portend a subsequent choice of another occupation.

41. Indirect evidence of the importance of starting graduate study immediately following college graduation, as opposed to making a tentative or delayed decision, is shown in a study of seniors choosing careers in the law and actual law school entrants. Of the seniors definitely planning to begin law school in the fall following college graduation, 91 percent actually entered law school; of those with tentative plans, 64 percent entered law school; and of those with plans to start law school in the future, 9 percent entered. We don't know, of course, what proportion of the last group eventually attended law school; neither do we know whether what is true for lawyers is also true for teachers. These findings do indicate, however, that seniors intending to become lawyers act according to their plans to an overwhelming extent. Seymour Warkov, *Lawyers in the Making* (Chicago: Aldine Publishing Co., 1965), p. 29. Warkov's study was based on the lawyer contingent of the Davis-NORC study of college seniors and included a follow-up of those actually attending law school the following fall.

42. Mason, *The Beginning Teacher*, pp. 98–99.

43. *Ibid.*, adapted from table 70, p. 100.

44. *Ibid.*, adapted from table 70, p. 100.

45. *Ibid.*, p. 102. Among those planning definitely or probably to leave within five years, 65 percent are women and 26 percent men; the marital status of both men and women has a negligible effect. *Ibid.*, adapted from table 72, p. 102.

46. *Ibid.*, adapted from table 73, p. 103.

47. Most likely the bulk of these teachers intend to go into administration, but the figure undoubtedly includes some who plan to work in guidance, some who wish to enter the academic profession, and others who contemplate working in government educational agencies.

48. It should be noted that intentions to teach next year are least susceptible to variation for probably obvious reasons; by the spring of the previous academic year, most people have made up their minds about their occupational plans; and there is something of a tacit tradition that one stays in teaching at least two years rather than one to give it a try (unless the first year is a disaster), since the first year can be so difficult and unpredictable.

49. Mason, *The Beginning Teacher*, table 76, p. 110. Among women, advanced training affects nonteaching educational plans in the same way, but the figures run from 6 percent to 18 percent.

50. National Education Association, *The American Public-School Teacher, 1960–61*, p. 17.

51. Mason, *The Beginning Teacher*, table 62, p. 80.

52. W. W. Charters, "Survival in the Profession: A Criterion for Selecting Teacher Trainees," *Journal of Teacher Education*, VII, No. 3 (1956), 253.

53. J. Scott Hunter, "The Beginning Teacher One Year Later" (Washington, D.C.: U.S. Department of Health, Education, and Welfare, n.d.), pp. 1–50. Hunter's sample of 1987 cases represented an 88 percent usable return of 2240 questionnaires mailed out.

54. Mason, *The Beginning Teacher*, table 70, p. 100.

55. Hunter, "The Beginning Teacher One Year Later," table 1, pp. 6–7.

56. *Ibid.*, table 3, p. 16. Hunter does not indicate whether the salaries of teachers in his follow-up sample are for 1956–57 or for 1957–58.

57. *Ibid.*, table 4, p. 18.

58. *Ibid.*, table 2, p. 11.

59. *Ibid.*, table 6, p. 24.

60. *Ibid.*, table 9, p. 32.

61. *Ibid.*, table 10, p. 33.

62. *Ibid.*, table 12, p. 42. The differences between men and women are negligible; hence, combined figures for all teachers can be used without distortion.

63. Ward S. Mason and Robert K. Bain, "Teacher Turnover in the Public Schools 1957–58" (Washington, D.C.: U.S. Department of Health, Education, and Welfare, Circular No. 608, n.d.), pp. 2–7.

64. Cited in Cogan, "Toward a Definition of Profession," *Harvard Educational Review*, XXIII, No. 1, 48.

65. William J. Goode, "The Theoretical Limits of Professionalization," in Etzioni, ed., *The Semi-Professions and Their Organization*, p. 269; copyright 1969 (my italics). Reprinted by permission of The Macmillan Company. These exchanges, according to Hughes, are the bases of an occupation's license.

66. *Ibid.*, p. 269.

67. I have drawn heavily on Goode's work in this discussion. *Ibid*, pp. 266–313. Concerning the question of service, he states: "The professional community sets up a system of rewards and punishments such that 'virtue pays': i.e., in general, the practitioner who lives by the service ideal must be more successful than the practitioner who does not." *Ibid.*, p. 279. In teaching, at least for men, the problem is not that virtue doesn't pay, but that it often leads to administration. In a sense it pays (or pays off), too well.

68. For a discussion of faction and conflict, much of which runs deep, in medicine, see David R. Hyde and Payson Wolff, "The American Medical Association: Power, Purpose, and Politics in Organized Medicine," *Yale Law Journal*, LXIII, No. 7 (1954), 938–1022.

69. See Herbert Kaufman, *The

Forest Ranger (Baltimore: Johns Hopkins Press, 1960).

70. For a discussion of work standards in craft occupations, see Arthur L. Stinchcombe, "Bureaucratic and Craft Administration of Production: A Comparative Study," *Administrative Science Quarterly*, IV, No. 2 (1959), 168–187.

CHAPTER SEVEN

1. William J. Goode, "The Theoretical Limits of Professionalization," in Etzioni, ed., *The Semi-Professions and Their Organization* (New York: The Free Press, 1969), pp. 280–281; copyright 1969. Reprinted by permission of The Macmillan Company.

2. *Ibid.,* p. 286 (my italics). Given the assumption that members of an occupation dedicate themselves to the service of clients, the technology of a profession is based on a body of abstract principles, while that of a skilled craft is not (or is not to nearly the same extent).

3. Ballet dancers are not themselves unionized, but are represented by other unions depending on the nature of the performance in which they participate. I am indebted to my colleague, Ian Westbury, for his observations on the unionization of artists.

4. Philip W. Jackson, *Life in Classrooms* (New York: Holt, Rinehart and Winston, Inc., 1968), p. 149.